GROUP IDENTITIES ON FRENCH AND BRITISH TELEVISION

GROUP IDENTITIES ON FRENCH AND BRITISH TELEVISION

EDITED BY
MICHAEL SCRIVEN AND EMILY ROBERTS

Berghahn Books
New York • Oxford

Published in 2003 by **Berghahn Books**
www.BerghahnBooks.com

Reprinted in 2004

Library of Congress Cataloging-in-Publication Data
Group identities on French and British television / edited by Michael Scriven and
Emily Roberts.
          p. cm.
     Includes biliographical references and index.
     Contents: Fragmentation of the nation / Michael Scriven and Emily Roberts –
Adjusting to Diversity : the case of England and France / Jean-Claude Sergeant –
Constructing the national : Television and Welsh Identity / Kevin Williams –
Changing expectations : Holyrood, television and Scottish national identity / Adri-
enne Scullion – Storm clouds of the millennium : regional television news in
Aquitaine and the west of England / Michael Scriven and Emily Roberts – The rep-
resentation of Maghrebis on French television / Joanne Helcke – From comic
Asians to Asian comics / Marie Gillespie – Curiosity, fear and control : the ambiguous representation of hip-hop on French television / Chris Warne – Green activist
identities on British television / Derek Wall – Going out to the straight community: television and heteronormative logics in representations of homosexuality /
Murray Pratt – Constructing the postmodern group / Michael Scriven and Emily
Roverts – Annex I, Taking the initiative : fictional representations of the Maghrebi
population on French television : interview with Akli Tadjer – Annex II, Making
things sweeter : interview with Nina Wadia.
     ISBN 1–57181–793–X (cloth : alk. paper) – ISBN 1–57181–580–5 (pbk. : alk.
paper)
          1. Television broadcasting–France.   2. Television broadcasting–Great
Britain.   3. Minorities on television.   I. Scriven, Michael, 1947–   II. Roberts,
Emily.

PN1992.3.F7 G76 2002
791.45'0944–dc21   2002018268

British Library Cataloguing in Publication Data
A catalogue record for this book is available
from the British Library.

Printed in the United States on acid-free paper.

ISBN 1–57181–793–X (hardback)
ISBN 1–57181–580–5 (paperback)

Contents

ACKNOWLEDGEMENTS

The Editors wish to thank all colleagues from Britain and France who have contributed to the successful completion of this multidisciplinary research project. In particular, we are grateful to the University of the West of England Bristol, the Arts and Humanities Research Board and the British Council for the financial support that underpinned the project. Thanks are also due to the Ambassade de France and the Institut Français in London for their support for the project, to the Association Bordeaux-Bristol and the Pôle Universitaire Européen de Bordeaux for their generous help and advice, and to BBC West, FR3 Aquitaine and M6 Bordeaux who accorded us interviews and access to promotional material and programme recordings.

PREFACE

Group Identities on French and British Television is the product of an on-going interest in the role of television broadcasting in contemporary social, political and cultural transformation. An initial project undertaken in the mid-to-late 1990s led to a Berghahn publication entitled *Television Broadcasting in Contemporary France and Britain*. Edited by Michael Scriven and Monia Lecomte, this book explored a series of interrelated issues on audiovisual broadcasting in two representative European nation states, focusing specifically on national regulatory and political structures, the new media, programming and Europeanisation. The overriding aim was to offer a comparative analysis of the manner in which television broadcasting was organised and financed within France and Britain, whilst providing at the same time insights into programming structures, the impact of new media technologies, and responses to the emerging European audiovisual agenda in the two countries. An implicit and ever-present theme in this initial work was the role of television in shaping and influencing public opinion, whether it be directly through programme content and/or ideological bias, or more surreptitiously through the formal framing devices of the audiovisual medium itself, framing devices accentuated as a consequence of the exponential development of new audiovisual technologies. This generalised problematic of televisual influence, either as a force for social change, or as a force for the consolidation of hegemonic cultural values, crystallised over time into an interest in television and identity construction. In the post-modern societies of twenty-first century France and Britain, the all-pervasive presence of television cannot be separated from the manner in which social groups perceive themselves and are perceived by others. Television is both a weapon in the armoury of state devices aimed at perpetuating certain assumptions about national identity and cohesiveness, and a potentially subversive political device (particularly in the wake of audiovisual liberalisation and developments in new interactive technologies) that can be used to serve the ends of groups wishing in some way or another to differentiate themselves from hegemonic social, political and cultural images/ideas. This second book is accordingly a contribution to the debate on the function and importance of television in constructing, perpetuating and occluding the identity of social groups in contemporary Western society.

The Editors

CHAPTER 1

FRAGMENTATION OF THE NATION

NATIONAL IDENTITY AND TELEVISION IN FRANCE AND BRITAIN AT THE TURN OF THE TWENTIETH CENTURY

Michael Scriven and Emily Roberts

The fourth and final part of *Television Broadcasting in Contemporary France and Britain*[1] was devoted to an analysis of Europeanisation. The challenge of the emerging European audiovisual landscape to existing broadcasting structures, attitudes and ideas within France and Britain was seen to be considerable and to be progressively gathering momentum. In particular, supranational audiovisual legislation and cross-national televisual production initiatives were slowly transforming fundamental assumptions and premises, albeit to varying degrees, in both France and Britain. Given the close link that can be drawn between expressions of national identity and popular culture, it is a legitimate and logical question to enquire how such European audiovisual developments might impact on expressions of national identity and unity. *Group Identities on French and British Television* proposes to explore this question in detail through a selective assessment of the televisual representation of clusters of peer identification in France and Britain.

The growing influence of the European Union upon constructs of national identity in Britain and France has been accompanied by other highly significant factors, originating both internally within nations and on a more global scale. Internally, minority groups, defined according to their political beliefs, ethnicity, sexual predilections, geographical locality or socially marginalised status, have become increasingly more vocal in their demands for greater representation. This demand for a forum for their views, goals and grievances – not least on the relatively monochrome medium of television, with its normative depictions of heterosexual, white, urban, politically mainstream individuals – inevitably necessitates a reconsideration of national identity that moves beyond definitions predicated upon shared ethnic values or a common cultural heritage. The future of national identity would paradoxically appear to reside in a more federal structure that acknowledges and embraces the reality of internal differences, in all their diversity. In a similar vein, and in line with the growing influence of Europeanisation, the economic and cultural effects of globalisation have also led to fears for the future of the nation-state as the most powerful locus of shared aspirations, views and values, the bedrock of group identity. As Hutchinson and Smith have demonstrated, some even predict that 'we are moving into a "post-national" era as a result of the impact of globalisation.' (Hutchinson and Smith, 1994: 11).

This book explores the hypothesis that national identity in Britain and France is ceding its position as the most symbolically powerful locus of group identification, and is in the process of fragmenting into smaller units of group identity. It examines the manner in which the central problematic of diversity within the nation is negotiated on national television in Britain and France, through an examination of representations of both state endorsed geopolitical identities, and minority or 'othered' identities within the nation. Although focused primarily on both privately and publicly funded terrestrial television, the book also includes an assessment of the impact of nationally broadcast cable and satellite television, and the potential for the appropriation of the televisual medium by minority groups.

Television undoubtedly has a major impact upon the formation and formulation of group identities, and appears to be 'destined to continue to have a role of significance' (Patterson, 1993: 1). It is a potent form of popular culture that has replaced the hearth as the focal point of the household living space. It can serve as a cohesive element that helps to define the 'imaginary community of the nation' (Anderson, 1990). Its significance in terms of the provision of information and the formation of popular views has long been recognised by the nation-states in Britain and France. The history of state intervention in the televisual domain has in the past engendered a fierce debate concerning the independence of the public television channels, in France in particular (see Kuhn, 1995). Terrestrial television in France and Britain, be it independently or state funded, is dominated by the paradigm of the national network, which prioritises its brief to represent the nation as whole. Although regions, 'national regions' and nations within the nation (Scotland and Wales) have been receiving a greater degree of televisual autonomy and air time, and despite the inroads into the televisual representation of minority groups, terrestrial television in France and Britain stubbornly continues to respect the primacy of national identity.

The pre-eminence of the prescriptive representations of white, apolitical, heterosexual, solvent individuals as the norm is, however, undercut by the occasional representations of those designated as belonging to a minority. Although these figures are often used to bolster the normative values of the diegetic televisual world, as will be demonstrated in the course of this book, they can be subjected to reinterpretation by the viewer. They are effectively re-read to reflect the life experiences, views, goals and even grievances of the viewer. This subversive reworking of the televisual depiction of 'minority' or 'Othered' groups allows for a reaffirmation of their specific identity.

The Impact of Audiovisual Advances

The immense influence of television, both as an industry and as a source of representation, is a result of audiovisual technological advances, as well as politico-economic factors (Urry, 1990). These advances in cable, satellite and now digital technology have allowed television to reach beyond the national scope, leading to the establishment of global and pan-European television channels. Taken at face value, the development of telecommunications and audiovisual technology appears primarily to be to the advantage of the forces of globalisation.

An alternative reading of the effects of these advances, however, would emphasise the profusion of choice, as the consumer can access a plethora of stations representing a breadth of interests and social or cultural allegiances. Digital technology in particular allows for cheaper televisual production, and the possibilities of internet television are still in the process of being explored. The subversive reading of minority representations on national terrestrial television could therefore be supplemented by the opportunity for submediated self-representation. In this light, another, *complementary* process can be identified: the band of group allegiances is tightening, with group identity becoming 'localised' in terms of place or interests. The process of localisation appears to constitute a necessary aspect of the process of globalisation. They enjoy a symbiotic relationship. The new audiovisual communication technologies present new opportunities for the expression of the drives for specificity and collectivity. The question of whether the possibilities for the expression of a globally shared identity, or for a 'federation' of group identities, constitutes a serious threat to the nation-state will underpin the chapters in this book.

Now, in 'this period of global balkanisation' (Friedman, 1996: vi), with the re-assertion of ancient territorial identities and the burgeoning demand for the representation of minority groups within the nation, it is salient to evaluate the formulation of group identities on French and

British television. As the debate concerning the culturally globalising/localising effects of new telecommunications and audiovisual technology continues to rage, this book proposes to provide an appraisal of the depiction of a select number of group identities, ranging from umbrella geopolitical identities to special interest groups, on television in France and Britain. Given the plethora of group identities in France and Britain, the selective approach adopted in relation to group identity studies reflects the logistical impossibility of providing a comprehensive study of the multitude of group identities in France and Britain. The ensuing chapters will retain the broad framework of a national context for consideration of the subject as a whole, but will place the analysis of national group identity on an equal footing with other forms of collective self-understanding and objectification. The aim is consequently to examine the hypothesis that collective allegiances are moving away from the national paradigm towards a more localised model within a global or pan-national context, reflecting the specificities of internal groups. To keep pace with this change and to retain its relevance, the nation will have to learn to see itself as a federation of different groups with a common interest and shared locality, rather than as an entity rooted in a shared cultural or ethnic past. It is confronted with the need to cease propagating televisual images that prescribe a normative mould that fits only the few. National television will need to adjust its portrayal of the members of the nation-state, if it is to reflect contemporary French and British society in all its diversity.

The book is divided into two sections. Firstly, it addresses the representation of state-endorsed geopolitical identity, and the underpinning audiovisual policy of the national television channels, at a national, 'national regional' and regional level in Britain and France. The first section of the book aims to reflect the national composition of Britain and France, engaging with the issues of regionalisation and devolution. The second section considers the depiction of a selection of minority or 'Othered' collective identities on national television in the two nations. Through this approach, the book aims to illustrate an overall thesis on group identity construction and conceptualisation, putting forward the idea that the dominant paradigm of national identity is giving way to a more 'federal' structure of group identity in a national context. Both sections explore whether the expressions of group identity on television are more openly localised, in terms of territoriality and/or collective interests and allegiances. The examination of different types of group identity will show the ways in which plurality is negotiated within larger constructs of group identity, and how the smaller units of collective identity read and react to the mediated images of their fellow group members on the national screen.

The Prioritisation of the National:
National, 'National Regional' and Regional Television

The first section focuses on the televisual portrayal of geopolitical/terri-
torial group identities that are determined by the physically bounded
space that they occupy. The term 'geopolitical' is applied to group identities that primarily correspond to a recognisable, delineated geographical
area. They are reflected in a political and economic infrastructure. These
group identities are externally recognised and recognisable, beyond their
own social or geographical boundaries. All of these group identities are
territorially rooted. In the context of this section, British, French, Welsh,
Scottish, and regional group identities are explored. The inclusion of
chapters devoted to Wales and Scotland reflects the fact that Great
Britain comprises three distinct nations; England, Scotland and Wales.
With the exception of England, the former 'national regions' have been
granted political autonomy and self-representation. In France, May 2001
saw the granting of limited autonomy to Corsica, although the issue of its
impact on the 'unified and indivisible republic' is fiercely debated. The
electoral successes of Basque nationalists in Spanish Basque country,
again in May 2001, led to soul-searching on the part of elected representatives in French Pays Basque, who fear that radical acts of violence could
spill into French territory. Devolution is now a reality in Great Britain,
which has effectively become a federation of national identities. In contrast, France is still moving along the rocky road of regionalisation, trying
to reconcile the need for 'national regional' self-expression with the
Jacobin principle of a monolithic French nation.

This first section is centred on the ways in which regional and 'national
regional' television coexist, albeit in a subordinate position, with the
national television of Britain and France. Regional and 'national regional'
television is systematically confined to an opt-out slot, placed firmly
within a national programme schedule. The rather hierarchical relationship between London-based British television and Welsh and Scottish
television is also indicated by the fact that the latter are referred to as
'national regions', rather than nations in their own right. In France,
'national regions' only merit six-minute news broadcasts. The prototype of
British and French national news is used to provide the format of regional
news programmes, an indication of their relative status. These approaches
indicate a desire to retain the pre-eminence of the national over the
regional, both in British and in French national television networks. The
concept of national television consequently still dominates the audiovisual
landscape, despite limited devolution in the regions and 'national
regions'. It looms large as the programming framework, constantly
emphasising the status of the regional programme as an anomaly, rather
than the norm. It provides a reference source for the composition of
regional programmes which rarely choose to implement innovative struc-

tures reflecting their specifically regional status. Furthermore, national television remains the site of policy decision-making and implementation.

The chapters in this first section illustrate the complexity of the issue of devolved representation, indicating the diversity within smaller units of geopolitically defined group identity within the British and French nations. Jean-Claude Sergeant provides the background to the subject, examining the increasing importance of regional representation in national televisual policy. This development is more notable in Britain than in France, as a result of the impact of devolution. In the following chapter, Kevin Williams examines the representation of Welsh identity on Welsh television, commenting upon the marginalisation of Welsh affairs on British television. Adrienne Scullion observes the same phenomenon in her appraisal of Scottish identity on Scottish and British television. Both chapters demonstrate that the process of creating a Scottish or Welsh identity is a self-conscious exercise, drawing on largely outdated conceptions of national identity, although devolution provides an indispensable opportunity for a new conception of national identity, and an opportunity for a more representative devolved television service to accompany it.

In their chapter on regional television, Michael Scriven and Emily Roberts appraise the coverage of the millennium celebrations in Aquitaine and the West of England. They posit that the coverage reveals the ambivalent role of national television and its regional offshoots, as both an institution designed to represent the nation, and an instrument of democracy representative of grass-root regional views and interest. This chapter complements Sergeant's contribution, developing the contention that regionalisation and devolution are the way of the future, although France is at a different stage in terms of its institutional and televisual attitude to its 'national regions'.

Challenging the Hegemonic Norm: Minorities and the 'Othered' on National Television

The second section deals with the portrayal of a broad range of minority and 'Othered' identities on French and British television. The consideration of group identities that are not primarily defined through the geographic locality of its members provides an interesting counterpoint to the previous section, while simultaneously deconstructing any 'monolithic' understanding of national identity. These groups lack the close institutional links of the geopolitical groups examined in the previous section. They may be represented by pressure groups and collectives, rather than politicians on the inside of the state political structures. They may be actively disavowed or marginalised, deemed to be 'deviant' from the prescribed national 'norm'. They constitute the stranger within. The groups can also have come together through a shared sense of social, political, or economic persecution. In many cases, these groups have a strong sense of their own collective identity and difference, and can appropriate the medium of television to serve their own ends.

The first two chapters of the section address the portrayal of ethnic minorities on French and British television. Joanna Helcké and Marie Gillespie address the representation of Maghrebis and British Asians on French and British television respectively. A complementary industry perspective is available in the annex to the book, in the shape of interviews with Maghrebi scriptwriter Akli Tadjer, and *Goodness Gracious Me* actress Nina Wadia. These groups are defined according to their ethnic and cultural specificities. The term 'ethnic' applies to groups that are linked culturally and/or linguistically. They have a common familiarity with a homeland, or ancestral homeland and shared kinship structures. They share a sense of a community of interests and goals. They may have a common awareness of a shared persecution, and operate within the establishment of a network, designed to help the community as a whole. There is also often a problematic relationship or tension between the hegemonic group identities and these identities, but they are nonetheless recognised as integral parts of the 'social mosaic'.

Although advances have been made in the representation of ethnic minorities on French and British television, and much rhetoric concerning 'social mosaics' and 'rainbow nations' has been bandied about in the political spheres of both countries, there is still some way to go and the future development of this enterprise is by no means assured.

The study of ethnic minorities on French and British television is followed by three studies of 'Othered' group identities to be found in France and Great Britain. These 'Othered' groups form a socio-cultural grouping in their own right. The 'Otherness' attributed to these groups is evidence of their status as a source of fear or hatred, within both geopolitical and socio-cultural groupings. The 'stranger within' may be rejected as a result of their sexual orientation, socio-economic status, political beliefs or ethnicity. Chris Warne detects an approach to the portrayal of hip-hop *banlieue* culture – a specifically French phenomenon, which nonetheless drew some of its inspiration from American hip hop – on French television that is characterised by a mixture of good intentions, curiosity and fear. This posits the socially and economically marginalised inner city group as either 'exotic' victims of circumstance, or as dangerous and vengeful 'Others'.

The Green movement has received an increasing amount of consideration in Britain over the past few decades. Although Green activism is receiving more attention in France, it does not parallel the amount of coverage in Britain. Derek Wall explores the exploitation of Green activist identity – a politically determined, consensual group identity based on direct action and opposition to industrial and road developments – as fodder for British television drama. The Green activist figure on British television is either used for propagandist purposes to introduce the principles behind direct action, or as a bogeyman who threatens the *status quo*, underlining again the 'stranger within' designation.

Another 'Othered' group that has acted as a locus of popular fears is the homosexual community. In his chapter on the representation of homosexual group identity on French and British television, Murray Pratt highlights a combination of prurient curiosity focusing on the more sensational aspects of personal homosexual experience, patronising attempts at representation by shoehorning the gay figure into codes of behaviour that pose no threat to the doxa of the heterosexual 'norm', and the spectre of the AIDS epidemic, posited as the 'gay' epidemic, that is reminiscent of the good intentions, curiosity and fear outlined by Chris Warne in relation to *banlieue* identity.

The timing of this study, at the advent of the new, 'digital' millennium, raises a number of interesting issues as far as the characterisation of our era is concerned. At a time when satellite, cable and now digital television are held responsible for the perceived spread of a globalised culture, the examination of identities on television within the two nations provides an instructive insight on the future of national televisual culture. Whether the audiovisual media promote a rigid dominant perception of national identity, or whether they reflect a 'federation' of group identities in a national context, will consequently be an issue at the forefront of what follows.

Note

1. Scriven, M. and Lecomte, M., eds, *Television Broadcasting in Contemporary France and Britain*. Oxford, 1999, pp. 139–221.

SECTION I

GEOPOLITICAL GROUP IDENTITIES

GEOPOLITICAL GROUP IDENTITIES

Michael Scriven and Emily Roberts

'Geopolitical' refers to a sense of identification based upon an affiliation with a circumscribed geographical area. This section focuses on the national, 'national regional' and regional television of Britain and France, at a time of devolution and an increasingly insistent call for more regional autonomy. Although devolution has not occurred in France, despite the agitations of such national groups as the Basques and Corsicans, the devolution of Scotland and to a lesser extent Wales has provoked a crisis in the understanding of the nature of English and, by extension, British identity. Whereas Great Britain, a traditional union of disparate national groups with varying degrees of self-rule and self-expression, has taken definitive steps towards the devolution of power away from London, the French government is still wrestling with the issue of relinquishing the stronghold of Paris-based centralised control.

The aim of this section of the book is therefore to address the following issues: How resilient is the umbrella construct of national identity on French and British television? Is it ceding to a federation of regional or 'national regional' identities? What is the relationship between national institutions and the regions? And how does televisual policy affect the relationship between television and the promotion of national unity?

The opening chapter by Jean-Claude Sergeant provides an initial con-textualisation for all subsequent contributions to the book. Sergeant examines in detail how a national terrestrial channel, especially a state channel with a public service brief to uphold the principle of national unity, should grasp the nettle of internal geopolitical diversity. He does so with reference to the televisual policies adopted towards regional representation by state-funded and independent television stations in France and Britain, as well as digital satellite local channels. A cautious attitude towards the regions appears to prevail in French television. This reflects a distrust of the implications of increased regionalism, dictated by the primacy of the concept of the 'one and indivisible' Republic. This is contrasted with the impact of devolution upon attitudes towards the regions in Britain, which have enjoyed a renaissance of interest. Sergeant assesses how internal plurality is negotiated within a larger national paradigm, and how the representation of a 'federation' of identities is framed within the scope of national television.

The extent to which this renaissance of interest in regional televisual representation has translated into a new, confident and independent television service in Wales and Scotland is called into question by Kevin Williams and Adrienne Scullion respectively. Kevin Williams elaborates upon the relationship between the London-based terrestrial television channels, and their Welsh subsidiaries. Not only has London-based terrestrial television continued to marginalise Welsh television and affairs, but Welsh television has, he believes, failed to represent adequately the diversity of its people. An outdated conception of Welshness prevails, which glosses over the linguistic and cultural divisions within Wales in its representation of Welsh national identity.

Adrienne Scullion also perceives a need for Scottish television to reassess its portrayal of 'Scottishness' following devolution. Although expressions of Scottishness have, in some contexts, become increasingly European and international, devolution presents a valuable opportunity to redefine Scottishness away from its dominant male-centred, rural or depressed urban modes. This would in her view facilitate the creation of an identity that embraces the values embodied in the newly devolved Scottish political system – namely openness, egalitarianism, and pacifism. Scottish television also suffers from the endurance of televisual paradigms borrowed from British national television, perhaps an indication of its existing lack of confidence. The need for more representative Scottish television has been in part the result of the neglect and marginalisation of Scottish affairs on British national television. She contends that this neglect of Scottish news, regarded as being of almost provincial interest in the English capital, will lead to a more powerful and high-profile role for Scottish-based production companies. Scullion expresses the hope that the impact of devolution upon representations of Scottish identity will be positive, posing a challenge to existing unrepresentative stereotypes.

As Sergeant establishes in his chapter, the majority of regional television in Britain and France is devoted to news and current affairs. In the final chapter of this section, Michael Scriven and Emily Roberts expand upon this theme, examining regional television in the West of England and Aquitaine. In the French instance, they demonstrate the neglect of Basque country affairs, and the relegation of the representation of this 'national region' to a six-minute broadcast, placed on a similar footing to the local broadcasts representing Bordeaux alone. This is illustrative of Sergeant's contention that 'French regional diversity has not yet come of age'. The subsequent analysis of the representation of the regional millennium celebrations on the regional news of Aquitaine and the West of England uncovers the enduring subordinate positioning of the region in relation to the nation.

The same artificiality and self-consciousness that can be detected in the televisual representations of Welshness and Scottishness underscore the use of regional millennium celebrations as a focal point for national and regional identification. Significantly, they fail to inspire the regional populace in either country. Geopolitical identities are still a powerful force to be reckoned with, in terms of structures of identification and institutional endorsement, but they now appear to be undergoing a crisis of confidence. Smaller units are struggling to redefine themselves following devolution, or still striving to achieve some semblance of official and televisual recognition, in the case of the 'national regions' in France. Overall, what emerges is a fundamentally ambivalent attitude towards the regions.[1] On the one hand, they are a form of geopolitical identity, and as such are endorsed by the national institutions. On the other hand, regionalisation necessarily implies a decentralisation of power that poses a threat to the national power base. Although regional television attempts to foster a sense of regional identity and pride, paradoxically the fear of fragmentation looms large behind the institutional representation of regional diversity in the televisual arena. The notion of a more federal schema of geopolitical identities, replacing the overarching national identity, is still regarded with suspicion in France.

Note

1. See Scriven, M. and Roberts, E., 'Local Specificity and regional unit under siege: territorial identity and the television news of Aquitaine', *Media, Culture and Society*, Vol. 23, No. 5, September 2001: 587–605.

CHAPTER 2

ADJUSTING TO DIVERSITY

THE CASE OF ENGLAND AND FRANCE

Jean-Claude Sergeant

Britishness was shaped by the Protestant religion and successive wars with France. This, at least, is the central thesis of Linda Colley's important book *Britons: Forging the Nation*, published in 1992. With the weakening of religion and the extinction of open conflicts with their hereditary enemies, the British people, Colley suggests, may well lose their national identity. By the turn of the second millennium, Britishness has become an even more opaque concept in which subnational components have assumed an increased prominence, with the exception of the English one. If there is an identity crisis in the United Kingdom, it is nowhere more palpable than in England where few voices, except perhaps in the north, are demanding that their regional/national specificity be acknowledged either economically or politically.

It is certainly more baffling to attempt a definition of Englishness as opposed to Britishness, to the extent that the English people are themselves a less than homogeneous group of individuals with strong local attachments. In a way, regional diversity is the essence of Englishness, as each region – no matter how vague the term is – tries to promote its own identity. This trend has been encouraged by audiovisual policy makers responsible for broadcasting, who have always criticised the London-centred culture of the BBC and have deliberately imposed on ITV a strong regional constraint.

With the retreat of the state from most economic fields and the growing acknowledgement of minority cultures and values, it was inevitable
that the broadcasting authorities should accede to the demands of local
groups for getting their share of the spectrum to air their views and treat
themselves to their kind of music. Hence the proliferation of independent
local radios and restricted TV services, forty of which had been authorised
by the end of 1999. Yet even on national terrestrial television channels
there was no dearth of popular programmes with a strong regional flavour,
Emmerdale, Brookside, The Cops among others, as if some kind of genuine
local rooting was the necessary ingredient of success.

Not so in France, where admittedly fewer long-running television series
are produced. The most popular are usually set in a not-too-remote past,
sometimes located in one of the former French colonies *(Les Gens de
Mogador)* and usually relate the story of a family extending over several
generations (e.g. *Le Plaisir de Dieu*, based on a book by Jean d'Ormeson).
The local reality, however, only provides an exotic background to an all too
predictable scenario. French regional diversity has not yet come of age, at
least in fiction programmes.

This is, however, going to change as a result of the increased recognition of the regional dimension both in politics and broadcasting. The
historic Matignon agreement of 28 July 2000, providing for the possible
adaptation of French laws to the local Corsican situation, is likely to sound
the retreat for traditional French *Jacobin* culture. A number of regions are
now demanding to be granted extended powers and to be allowed to experiment with increased local autonomy. This, along with the minimal
recognition in 1998 by the French government of the status of minority
languages as legitimate components of national identity, is likely to upset
the traditional distribution of power between the state and the peripheral
territories. Such a trend will be reflected in the growing number of
local/regional broadcasting outlets, of which the nascent *TV Breizh* is the
most remarkable. France is poised to rediscover its regional diversity at a
time when England is at pains to define its identity.

National Identity: England

The way in which diversity is reflected in broadcasting, or the extent to
which it is promoted by radio and television, is shaped by the structural
organisation of broadcasting systems, which are themselves largely
defined by political decision-makers. The early recognition of the discrete
identity of historic nations with special needs by British broadcasting officials is the natural offshoot of the formation of the United Kingdom as
much as the result of the inevitable accession to the assumed desire of the
general public to be increasingly heard and seen, in accordance with the
accepted role of broadcasting systems as agents of political empower-

ment. In this respect, the setting up in 1999 of a Scottish Parliament and a Welsh Assembly together with the return of Northern Ireland to its former self-governed status can be seen as the logical outcome of a historical process which has aggregated different peoples into a single nation. In other words devolution, if this is the proper term to describe a process which in the case of Scotland at least rather underrates the amount of powers transferred to the new Parliament, was included from the start in the making of Britain. Reflecting on Gladstone's conception of British national identity, Vernon Bogdanor summed up his approach to the issue in the following words:

> Unity was to be achieved not by absorbing the identity of these nations into one undifferentiated whole but by explicitly recognising that Britain was a multinational state, and devising institutions which allowed the various identities of her component nations to be expressed. (Bogdanor, 1999: 18)

If the case for allowing Scotland and Wales extended control over their own government appeared indisputable, while the solution to the crisis in Northern Ireland was increasingly sought within a pan-Irish context, England was in comparison very much bypassed by the recent devolution process. As Simon Heffer remarks in a somewhat bitter mood:

> Throughout this whole current process of devolution – and it was as true in the 1970s as it has been in the 1990s – the English have not been accorded the same rights as those granted to the Scots and Welsh [...]. It is as if the very fact of being in a majority somehow removes any obligation on a government to treat those in the majority with any constitutional respect. (Heffer, 1999: 102)

One reason for this obvious dissimilarity has to do with the commonplace identification of England with Britain. Foreigners – and not just foreigners – could easily be forgiven for confusing the dominant component of the United Kingdom with the whole national entity. After all, England accounts for 85 percent of the population of the UK and sends 529 of the 659 MPs to Westminster besides contributing by far the largest share to the national wealth.

Was there a case for providing England with some mechanism to express its own identity, while it was so visibly proclaimed in everything British? Besides, if calls for proper recognition could be heard beyond the border and on a lower key in Wales, the concept of an English Parliament or of devolved Assemblies in the English regions did not seem to be a burning issue for English people. If for some time the Tory leader considered making political capital out of the idea of an English Parliament, he quickly gave up the project after realising that such a parliament would be locked in competition with Westminster and would undermine the legitimacy of the national parliament.

The current Labour government is fully aware of the fact that by grant-ing devolution to Scotland and Wales they have set in motion a process which may well be unstoppable. Its side-effects are likely to affect some English regions more than others. Tony Blair keeps an open mind on the issue and has postponed any commitment to devolve government powers to the regions until after the next General Election. In the mean time, they will have to make do with regional development agencies and the pro-jected election of mayors in England's larger cities on the lines of the mayoral election in London in May 2000.

Blair's government's cautious approach to English assemblies may stem from the realisation of the upheaval the creation of such assemblies would entail in terms of the organisation of local government. Currently largely based on a two-tier structure, it would have to be completely over-hauled. The apportioning of functions and responsibilities between the local authorities and the assemblies would prove a formidable task. How-ever, perhaps the single most important explanation for the government's wary attitude to the issue probably lies in the perceived lack of appetite for such constitutional developments at grass-root level. In a MORI poll for *The Economist* published in March 1999,[1] just 50 percent of the 1,810 English respondents supported the idea of 'giving greater powers of gov-ernment to regions in England'. While 67 percent of them agreed that 'a regional assembly would look after the interests of the area better than central government', not more than 45 percent could favour the setting up of an elected assembly in their regions. Paradoxically those regions with the strongest identification rate did not come out as the most dedi-cated supporters of devolution for the regions. For example, if 97 percent of the respondents in the north-west correctly identified the regions they lived in, only 42 percent of them felt like having an elected assembly of their own. Even in the north-east, Yorkshire or the south-west where the cause of regionalism stirred a stronger response, rates of support did not exceed 51 percent. The suspicion that such assemblies would probably not be able to raise taxes or pass primary legislation has certainly dampened whatever enthusiasm the concept might elicit.

If the level of regional consciousness remains as yet rather low from a political point of view, devolution has at least prompted broadcasting offi-cials to reorganise their operations in order to reflect the new distribution of forces between London and the national regions. This process had already been set in train by the end of the 1990s when the government's plans for devolution had been confirmed. As early as July 1997, Channel Four, whose remit does not include regional commitments, announced its intention to beef-up its output from the nations. A head of programmes for Scotland, Wales and Northern Ireland was appointed and plans were made for the opening of an office in Glasgow. Additionally, Channel Four officials promised to spend 30 percent of the programme budget (about £30 mil-lion) outside London. Until then Channel Four spent about £50 million a year on only four programmes produced by regional companies among which *Brookside* and *Hollyoaks*, the two popular series from Mersey TV.

Devolution also meant more efforts by the BBC to match the increased political autonomy of the nations with increased resources particularly in the field of news and current affairs. BBC Wales received £6 million extra funding to cover the cost of a newsroom in the Welsh Assembly while BBC Scotland had to recruit fifty new staff to cover Scottish politics. The next step will be to encourage regional output in all kinds of programmes, including drama and entertainment. Five years ago, a quarter of all BBC TV and radio network schedules originated from the regions and nations. In 1999 that proportion accounted for one third of the total programmes broadcast by the BBC in keeping with the recommendations of the Hatch report[2] released in 1994 which suggested that the share of regional productions in programme schedules be brought up to 33 percent within three years. On the basis of the renewed interest for the regions, the new Director-General of the BBC, Greg Dyke, was not unduly optimistic when he forecast a brilliant regional future for his organisation: 'It is within the BBC's reach to become unchallenged as the local and regional broadcaster in England.'[3] With £160 million to spend for 1999–2000, the new controller of English regions Andy Griffee could reasonably commit himself to speed up the drive to 'localness' which includes the extension of the on-line sites from the present two located in Bristol and Manchester as well as the preservation of the current edge of BBC regional news at 18.30 over similar ITV news programmes broadcast thirty minutes earlier.

This is clearly a new development in the policy which had traditionally considered the regions as contributors to the national network rather than as specific areas with special tastes and needs to be catered for from local resource bases. Not that the regional dimension in broadcasting has been ignored by the BBC, far from it. As Asa Briggs, the official historian of the BBC, puts it: '"regionalism" was an old issue which has always played an important part in the history of British Broadcasting' (Briggs, 1995: 365). He recalls that as early as 1936 a specially commissioned report drafted by a senior official of the BBC recommended the promulgation of a 'Charter of regional rights' which did not get much support. The BBC was soon enlisted to extol national virtues and to arouse the fighting spirit of the British, which left little scope to cultivate local particularities. The wartime BBC was in direct contrast to what it had been at its origin when a thriving regional programme drawing on local talents and resources for a large part of its output complemented the national programme which Reith was to transform into the mainstay of British Broadcasting. The word 'region' lost its traditional meaning in the process. A region was no longer an area where people shared a common sense of belonging shaped by physical features and historical tradition; it had become the catchment area covered by a transmitter, that is, a mere technical unit which ignored human realities.

The 'signified' element of the word was indeed to prove permanently baffling to BBC officials. In 1965 a Working Party on English Regions remarked that the English geographical regions were arbitrary unlike the so-called 'areas' that were normally subdivisions of regions which the members of the working group found to be more meaningful in terms of identity and 'intrinsic cohesiveness', their conclusion being that the titles should be interchanged (Briggs, 1995: 666).

Even if Robert Foot, the Director-General of the time, reflected in 1943 on the feasibility of extending the role of regional centres, aware as he was of the excessive weight of London in the output of the Corporation, his efforts were constrained by the shortage of frequencies. The organisational pattern which emerged at the end of the war provided for the existence of three English regions alongside the traditional national regions as they were then called. Some BBC officials advocated a more dynamic course of action to bring the BBC closer to the people. Frank Gillard in particular was the most vocal advocate of 'localness'. Drawing on his experience as a popular war reporter, he wanted to 'take the microphone to the people', a stance he was later to develop as Head of Programmes for the West Region. In his eight-page paper entitled 'An Extension of Regional Broadcasting' (February 1955) he discussed the contribution local broadcasting and particularly radio could make to the overall operation of the BBC. Starting from the premise that 'culture draws its vitality from the culture of its components', Gillard insisted that the regions could operate as providers of news for local audiences. He was in fact outlining the local radios that Hugh Greene, the then Director-General, was to require in his submission to the Pilkington Committee.

If the BBC has fairly early considered the provision of local radio services very much as a response to the increasing popularity of pirate radios in the mid-1960s, regional TV did not seem to be such a burning issue. The Beveridge Report (1951) included a chapter devoted to 'Devolution' which largely ignored the problem of England. The setting-up of national broadcasting Councils for Scotland, Wales and later for Northern Ireland together with the appointment of three national governors – one for each nation – was largely the outcome of the recommendation of the Beveridge Commission. However, regional opt-outs were introduced. By 1959 all three English regions (North, West and Midlands) had all added to the regular programme schedules ten-minute daily bulletins and fortnightly magazine programmes.

Lord Pilkington, who was appointed to chair the next Committee on Broadcasting (1960–62), was even less sympathetic to the plea of the regions for increased recognition: 'We cannot say that there is a strong and widespread demand for more programmes addressed to their (the regions') special needs.'[4] This dismissive view was in stark contrast to the belief of the Director-General of the BBC, Hugh Greene, who was confident that the government expected the BBC to give the regions a higher profile in the general output of the Corporation. It was not until the end of the decade, however, that the BBC actually acknowledged the legitimacy of an increased regional presence in BBC television schedules. The seminal document entitled *Broadcasting in the Seventies* outlined a new organisational structure in which the former three oversize regions were to be replaced by eight new regions more easily identifiable in sociological and geographical terms. Additionally, the post of 'Controller English Regions' was to be created with the view to giving this long-neglected component of the national fabric a proper spokesman in the management hierarchy. The current holder of the post, Andy Griffee, appointed in 1999, has a budget of £160 million to spend on local BBC radios and regional BBC Television. This is more than half the budget earmarked for BBC devolved operations in Scotland. Far from being a marginal element in the development plans of the BBC, regional broadcasting, including radio, constitutes a high priority sector which perhaps suffers from the higher visibility achieved by the BBC in its effort to ensure proper broadcasting support to the newly devolved nations.

The case for the English regions has always benefited from the indirect support of two distinct groups of BBC critics or well-wishers. There were those who felt that the BBC was excessively dominated by London and the south-east and that a more geographically balanced output could only serve the fulfilment by the BBC of its institutional commitments. On the other hand, some perceptive analysts had argued from the start of commercial television that the best way to stave off the competition of the regionally based ITV companies was to promote the regional component in the BBC TV schedules.

Indeed, while the voice of the regions was gradually, and somehow reluctantly, allowed to be heard on the BBC, which was originally conceived as a national broadcasting organisation, the ITV system was organised from the start – although not at the initiative of the government – as a pattern of regional TV companies serving under the terms of their licenses the needs of a specific area. Quite logically, the Independent Television Authority – the commercial television regulator created by the Television Act of 1954 – decided to award its first franchises for the three most densely populated areas in the country, that is London, the midlands and the north. In each of these three areas franchises were split between weekdays and weekends to ensure some competition between the franchise-holders. The smaller regional franchises which were awarded later to single operators completed the mapping of the country. Subsequent territorial adjustments were made in 1967, particularly in the north where Yorkshire Television was awarded a franchise covering a larger area than the county properly speaking while the catchment area of the franchise allocated to Granada was confined to a smaller territory west of the Pennines. The regional pattern worked out by the ITA remained virtually intact when the Independent Broadcasting Authority, as the regulator was then officially called, released its verdict on the renewal of the franchises for the fourteen regions, the only change affecting the former Yorkshire area which was then split into two different franchises.

This ritual exercise took place in 1980, three years after the Annan Committee which was to report on the status and remit of the projected fourth television channel had recommended that the IBA be renamed the Regional Television Authority, a suggestion that the new Conservative government chose to ignore.

The 1990 Broadcasting Act did not alter the structural pattern of commercial television even if it brought about a radical change in the way franchises were attributed. This bidding process replaced the more esoteric exercise by which the IBA decided behind closed doors which company was to enjoy a ten-year exclusive right to provide advertising-funded programmes to millions of households over a given region. A number of observers felt that the ITC (Independent Television Commission) set up by the 1990 Act to replace the IBA might have seized the opportunity to redraw the map of the regional franchises with a view to creating fewer but stronger champions able to compete on the international market with continental, if not American, companies. This was not to be. The ITC maintained the original boundaries inherited from the IBA and merely changed a limited number of franchise-holders. This missed opportunity was to be corrected later through the pressure of the ITV Association, which campaigned successfully for a relaxation of the rules prohibiting the holding of two large franchises by the same operator.

Yet the 1990 Act as well as the subsequent Broadcasting Act of 1996 confirmed the necessary regional component in the programme output of all fifteen licensees. Additionally, the ITC set up a network of national and regional offices to liaise with the licensees as well as with local viewers. Eight such regional and sub-regional offices were operating in England by 1996. One of their most important tasks was to monitor the performance of each franchise-holder in relation to the ITC programme code and by reference to the commitments of each licensee for each category of regional programming, that is news, factual, entertainment, education, religion, sport and children's programmes. Not all those categories are included in the licence requirements agreed by the licensee. For instance the licence requirement for Yorkshire Television does not include a set proportion of children's programmes but specifies that 4 hours 35 minutes of the weekly output should be devoted to jobfinding programmes. On the whole over 162 hours of regional programmes were to be broadcast in 1997 by the fifteen licensees, the proportions varying from 3 hours 33 minutes by London Weekend Television to 15 hours 47 minutes for Meridian, the highest required output for an English regional franchise-holder. The actual performance of all licensees exceeded the prescribed proportions sometimes by a comfortable margin as in the case of Central Television which broadcast three hours more than the 15 hours 21 minutes prescribed amount of regional programming.

The main category of programmes in which the regional component can be most easily expressed is news and current affairs programmes. This category, which represents at least two thirds of the regional output, invariably includes two daily news bulletins which usually follow the national ITN news programmes as well as a weekly news magazine. Moreover, seven of the licensees whose franchises cover extended areas have to operate subregional news services. For instance, HTV which broadcasts over Wales and a part of the west of England provides two simultaneous daily news programmes, *Wales Tonight* and *The West Tonight*. Regional diversity also involves the reflection of the multi-ethnic and multicultural facets of the community served by each licensee. This is particularly true of the Midlands where Asian viewers are targeted with a daily programme of Indian news called *Asian Eye*. Central Television also broadcasts *Eastern Mix,* a factual series intended for the same category of audience. On a more limited scale, Channel TV offers Sunday programmes in French and Portuguese and even experimented with the broadcasting of programmes in old French which used to be spoken in the Channel Islands.

Regional television companies are also very active in promoting local sports and cultural events such as the Celtic Film and Television Festival sponsored in 1997 by Westcountry. Regional identity, however, is not confined to local constituencies. Through the ITV Network organised between the fifteen regional companies, the 23 million television households which have access to Channel 3 can watch series or drama programmes that convey to the whole of the UK their original regional flavour. After many decades of service *Coronation Street*, produced by Granada, still managed to attract an audience of 14.5 million viewers on Monday, 29 May 2000 – forty thousand fewer than the popular Euro 2000 football match in which England played Portugal. *Coronation Street* has invariably topped the ratings tables and displaced only by special events such as the Olympics or football championship matches. The three weekly episodes of *Emmerdale* produced by Yorkshire Television also has a guaranteed following verging on the ten million mark. This rural series which has been on air for the past twenty-five years has now become a tourists' attraction following the building of a comprehensive location site near Leeds. All major English regional companies have attached their names to major ITV series rooted in regional realities, *Inspector Morse* (Central Television), and *Ruth Rendell Mysteries* (Meridian) being among the longest lasting and most popular such programmes.

The requirement concerning not only the broadcasting of regional news and fiction programmes but also of producing a prescribed proportion of programmes locally is something that the ITC monitors very closely, particularly when franchises are acquired by new holders as a result of take-over transactions. This process has accelerated since the relaxation of anticoncentration rules allowed by the Secretary of State for National Heritage who was then responsible for the media. When the control of Westcountry, HTV and Yorkshire/Tyne Tees TV was transferred to Carlton, United News & Media and Granada respectively, the ITC obtained confirmation from the latter that the former agreements regarding quality and range of regional programmes were to be maintained. However, in view of the increased consolidation currently gathering pace in the ITV, the regulator seems prepared to trim ITV quotas from the present thirteen categories of programmes to just three – news, current affairs and 'other'. The ITC even suggests that the overall amount of regional programming might be cut down in exchange for a commitment by franchise-holders to schedule fewer repeats and to improve the quality of their productions.

The White Paper on Broadcasting under consideration at the Department for Culture, Media and Sport is likely to remove all obstacles to the increased consolidation of independent television which would eventually be dominated by two, perhaps three, major operators. At the same time regional programmes are to remain key components in a more highly concentrated ITV structure. This is at least the belief of Peter Rogers, the ITC's chief executive who introduced in June 2000 the publication of a consultation paper on the protection of regional news and current affairs with the following comments: 'The ITC believes that regional and national identities across the UK are stronger than ever and that viewers identify with, and wish to be informed on aspects of local life, particularly with the introduction of devolved assemblies and government policies to strengthen regionalism.'[5]

Reconciling an increased commercial autonomy for the ITV licensees with the preservation of substantial regional programming commitments will probably be one of the most serious challenges facing the government experts in charge of drafting the next Broadcasting Bill due to be introduced in Parliament in 2001.

National Identity: France

France has long been a country of repressed diversity. In his masterly analysis of France's diversity, Fernand Braudel insists that 'no structuring force has ever succeeded in standardising a uniformity endowed with some kind of vegetable-like resilience. It will crop up again in spite of all the efforts to eradicate it' (Braudel, 1986: 68). French unity will only emerge after the birth of France as a nation, a relatively recent development according to Braudel. Just as British national cohesion was cemented by the successive wars waged on the French, the rallying cry of the leaders of the Revolution movement in 1792 – *La patrie est en danger* (The nation is in peril) – epitomised the feeling of togetherness which brought thousands of untrained and ill-equipped volunteers to the battlefields of eastern France where national ideals were being put to the test. The victory of Valmy, against considerable odds, did probably as much to prop up the credibility of the new state arising out of the *Ancien Régime* as the purely administrative reforms which were to be introduced by the *Convention*. Military victories legitimised the government of the leaders of the Revolution who then felt strong enough to reorganise the traditional pattern of local powers that the previous regime had been unable to modify. The creation of the *départements,* the basic local administrative units, was meant to dismantle the previous cluster of *provinces* inherited from the past considered to be the strongholds of outdated, if not reactionary, feelings of loyalty and identity. The *département* was a logical construction which ignored the traditional demarcations delineated by haphazard historical developments. With the introduction of the metric system, the *Convention* proclaimed the necessity of standardising a motley array of weights and measurements which sometimes differed from one valley to another. In a nutshell, regional diversity was the enemy of the ideals and values on which the Revolution rested. The disposal of the Girondins, who supported a federal state, by the Montagnards put paid to the efforts of those who argued against an increasingly centralised state with little patience for local idiosyncrasies.

Yet dissent and opposition never really disappeared even during the fanatical years of the *Terreur.* The Republican troops – *Les Bleus* – never really managed to quell the rebellion of the *Chouans* in the Vendée area. This bloody episode of French history can be seen as another aspect of the long chain of divisions and rifts which has shaped the course of French nationhood starting with the feud between *Armagnacs* and *Bourguignons*, down to its more recent avatar during the troubled years of the German occupation. Ironically the German rulers confirmed the traditional partition between the northern and southern parts of France, the former being subject to full occupation while the latter was temporarily left as a free zone. Recalling that Racine during his trip to Uzès in the South of France could hardly believe that he could not understand the local people, Braudel posits that 'there has always been, there is today and there always will be towards the South another France' (Braudel, 1986: 68). In addition to the obvious local phonological specificities, family patterns, the more rural aspects of the economy, the wider popular support for the Reformed Church, not to mention the markedly different weather conditions, have traditionally contributed to forging a distinct identity for the *langue d'oc* country as opposed to the northern part of France identified with the *langue d'oïl* area.

This broad partition could be further refined into a finer pattern of provincial identities, themselves fragmented into subprovincial groups living in distinct areas dominated by a major city sometimes referred to as *pays*. The phrase *'de pays'* typically suggests an unadulterated link with some sort of genuine, pre-industrial local reality that wine-growers and cheese-makers often claim as a mark of quality. Some local radio stations born in the wake of the 1982 broadcasting law by which the state gave up its monopoly as a producer of broadcasting services also chose to emphasise their 'localness' by describing themselves as *'radios de pays'*. [6] In her book entitled *Les Territoires de la Communication*, Isabelle Pailliart suggests that the word 'territory' is perhaps more convenient because of its flexibility to encompass the various shades of localness that the available labels of regions, provinces and areas fail to convey (Paillart, 1983).

Despite the strenuous efforts made by successive regimes from the Revolution onwards to keep the country united and to erase its disparities, local specificities have persisted nonetheless. However, it is only in 1982 with the law on decentralisation which established the regional councils later to be elected by universal suffrage that the state started to divest itself of some of its administrative powers, in direct contrast to the Gaullist national ethos which concentrated all decision-making processes in central government. Decentralisation, however, did not entail more than the transfer of powers in the field of the provision of services and infrastructures. The more political claims to autonomy voiced in some peripheral regions – Brittany, Alsace, Corsica in particular – were too radical at the time to get a proper hearing in Paris. France, however, could not keep the lid too long on those regional demands for increased recognition if only because of the examples set by its EU neighbours with a long tradition of devolved governments but more importantly because regional identities have been enhanced by the increased transfer of national powers to the institutions of the European Union. France appeared to be the odd man out in Europe clinging to its centralising Jacobin tradition and reluctant to admit that the country's national heritage could be enriched by allowing cultural diversity free expression.

Signs that the situation is evolving have, however, been noted recently. In May 1999 the French government eventually signed the 1992 charter of the Council of Europe on regional and minority languages. This official recognition of the fact that the six regional languages spoken in France by about nine million people (seven of whom speak Occitan) needed a proper status and realistic support was long overdue. The adamant refusal by French officials to acknowledge the linguistic diversity of the country was justified by the fear of dissolving the very fabric of the Republic which fined its quintessential expression in the first two articles of the Constitution. The second article in particular provides that 'French is the language of the Republic', a principle which does not sit easily with the insistence of the European Charter that an individual's right to use a regional language in his/her private and public life be considered as an inalienable right. Anticipating this constitutional difficulty, President Chirac, who in 1996 had privately expressed his support for the Charter, decided to refer the matter to the *Conseil constitutionnel*, the French Supreme Court, which not unexpectedly pointed out the unconstitutional character of some aspects of the Charter (June 1999). The solution would be to modify the first two articles of the Constitution, a cumbersome and dramatic procedure that Lionel Jospin's government would rather dispense with if only because this would require the approval of Jacques Chirac, which cannot be taken for granted in spite of his proclaimed sympathy for the objectives of the Charter. Jacques Chirac believes that French regional languages can be given full recognition of their role in society without amending the Constitution to that effect. Another course would be for the *députés* themselves to take the initiative of the amendment, a move which would however require the support of the government.

The situation cannot be left however on the back burner particularly after the agreement to a new future status for Corsica which provides for the compulsory teaching of Corsican in pre-elementary and primary schools, unless parents ask for the exemption of their children. This important concession is part of the general accord negotiated between the government and the representatives of Corsican political forces, including the nationalists, which the Corsican Assembly set up in 1990 adopted at the end of July 2000. Widely hailed as an innovative accommodation of Corsicans' demands for increased autonomy, the new plan transfers large chunks of responsibilities to the local Assembly, particularly in the areas of land and urban planning, economic development, training and education. It is certain to spark similar demands from other regions. Leaders of the Basque nationalist party (PNB) have lost no time in denouncing the double standards applied by the government, and were wondering if they too were to resort to bomb attacks to catch the ear of the government officials. One of their priorities – the creation of a Basque *département* – was constantly denied by the former Home Minister, Jean-Pierre Chevènement, who warned that 'the spreading of the phenomenon of regional nationalism … feeds exclusion'.[7] Among the Breton autonomists, notably in the ranks of the Breton Democratic Union (UDB), there is no doubt that the demand for regional autonomy will rank high among the issues debated during the next regional elections. The supporters of a devolved Savoie region as well as those whose argue in favour of a more autonomous Alsace feel that the time is now ripe to handle the problem of devolution on a grand scale.

The gradual emergence of devolved regions will necessarily heighten the differences from one region to another. The growing awareness of specific regional identities will be fed by supportive broadcasting media which will increasingly complement the traditional local media, the press and more recently local radio stations. It is the regional press which has for a long time maintained the feeling of togetherness based on the celebration of a common past and the reporting of collective achievements (in the sports pages for instance) or the local events affecting the community. Local radio stations among which can be numbered the 39 local stations of Radio France, the national public-funded radio organisation, have also added a more concrete dimension to the representation of communal identities.

The spawning of hundreds of local commercial radios in the wake of the 1982 broadcasting law had however been preceded by the launching in 1974 of FR3, the third channel of the public television system, described by its promoters as 'a privileged instrument for the knowledge of local life, an outlet for regional languages as well as a means for promoting regional cultures'. The choice of the name of the station was also meaningful. FR3 stood for 'France Régions 3', a reference to its regional commitment which was soon to be forgotten by the average viewer except that FR3, now called France 3, since the setting up of the France Television holding in 1995, was the channel where regional and local issues were given the largest airing. Originally local news was reported in regional bulletins broadcast by the three public channels which then made up the public system of television. This was due to the fact that the FR3 programmes were only gradually made available to viewers as more transmitters and relays were being built to ensure nation-wide reception. TF1 and Antenne 2 discontinued the broadcasting of regional news in 1985 and 1988 respectively, whereas the local and regional mission of FR3 (France 3) was firmly enshrined in its remit. The brief of the channel is to give priority to decentralised news and to regional events, in particular cultural and sports events. This channel, 75 percent of whose staff are working in the regions, is required to respond to the expectations of a diversified public by providing a coverage of local, regional, national and international news. By the mid-1990s, France 3 had unquestionably become identified as the regional channel of the public system of television, which had been reduced to two channels following the privatisation of TF1 in 1987. In 1999, the channel offered over 10,576 hours of regional programmes (news programmes included) against 7,000 hours of national programmes, showing an increase of over 50 percent by comparison with the output of 1990. The volume of news programmes for the same year was slightly under 5,000 hours. It consisted mainly of the twenty-four regional editions of new programmes, broadcast daily from 12.20 to 12.35 and from 19.10 to 19.30 completed by a five-minute summary from 19.55 to 20.00. Since 1990 France 3 has also provided local opt-outs of six minutes before the opening of the evening regional news programme in some regions. Twenty such local news 'nutshells' were on air in 1996, some of which were in regional languages, in Basque for the *Euskal Herri* bulletin produced by the Bayonne studio, in Breton for the six-minute programme broadcast from Brest and partly in Alsatian for *Rund Um* for the benefit of viewers in the Strasbourg area. This local output is typically the fruit of the cooperation between the local crews of France 3 with the local authorities and/or regional newspaper publishers. New developments have concerned the production in partnership with foreign television organisations of six-minute bulletins for populations straddling over a frontier. The first such experiment was launched in 1995 with Télévision Suisse Romande with the view to bringing to the people living in the *Canton* of Geneva and those in upper Savoie a round-up of the day's news in pictures. Besides, France 3 has entered into agreements with a number of cable systems to allow the pick-up of its regional and local programmes on the local cable channel of the networks, thus paving the way for what could be a fruitful cooperation between terrestrial television and cable distribution.

There is no limitation to the number of regional and local opt-outs that France 3 can operate; nor are there any guidelines in the channel's remit as to the length and content of such news programmes. In view of the high audience ratings scored by those programmes which are watched by a wider public than the national news programme broadcast on the same channel,[8] the management has decided to increase the share of regional output in the channel's programme schedules. In November 1999, they launched a live news magazine programme drawing on the 130 daily TV reports shot by the thousand journalists of the channel who work across the country. Every day a major news story is presented through various local approaches while in a second part called 'citizens and their environment' original communal initiatives get some in-depth treatment. This new programme, launched under the ambitious title of *Régions.Com*, has been strategically placed at 13.20 as an introduction to the afternoon slot. It is still too early to gauge its popular appeal but it testifies to the efforts made by the public channel to vindicate its reputation as the leading regional/local channel.

France 3 is not the only terrestrial channel to have catered for the appetite of the public for local stories. As early as 1989, M6 (Métropole Télévision), a commercial channel which went on air in 1987, started its first local opt-out over the Bordeaux area in cooperation with the regional newspaper publisher Sud-Ouest. Unlike France 3 which as a public TV channel is not answerable to the broadcasting regulator as regards its objectives and policies, M6 had to seek permission from the *Conseil Supérieur de l'Audiovisuel* (CSA) set up in 1989. Being a terrestrial channel with a national coverage (in fact 16 percent of the population still cannot access M6 programmes), M6 can run local opt-outs only under the following conditions: these opt-out programmes, which must be very brief (six to seven minutes), can only serve audiences of a few hundred thousand people. These programmes, for which M6 retains full editorial responsibility, cannot benefit from funding by local advertisers nor can they be sponsored in the case of news programmes. By 1996, M6 operated ten local opt-outs in major French cities with a combined population of twelve million. Each opt-out consisted of a six-minute news bulletin broadcast daily except during the week-end at 20.35. Some of these local news bulletins are picked up by the cable networks in Tours, Nantes and Marseilles in particular. Besides, M6 has produced a number of short factual programmes of local interest in partnership with regional press groups. One of the long term objectives of M6 would be the launching of a local opt-out over the Paris area, a request that the CSA has so far turned down arguing that the size of the population and the length of the projected opt-out would not be compatible with the key principles in the convention passed between the commercial broadcaster and the regulating agency. The CSA will probably have to prove more flexible taking into account the considerable interest that established or potential broadcasters are showing for the capital city. Recently Amaury, the newspaper group which publishes *Le Parisien* and *L'Equipe* has applied for a terrestrial TV licence to run a channel dedicated to Paris. For its part, France 3 is currently considering the feasibility of a new channel for the Ile-de-France region. So far, the CSA's response has been rather guarded as the agency must take into consideration the implications of the forthcoming launching of digital terrestrial channels.

The fact that M6 – only a marginal news provider – should give such prominence to local news illustrates the importance of 'localness' or 'proximity', to use the preferred French term, in the strategic planning of major broadcasters with the exception perhaps of TF1, the most popular terrestrial TV channel. Yet, a distinctive regional flavour can be felt in the midday news programme of TF1, which Jean-Pierre Pernaut has presented since 1988. 'Ten years ago' said Pernaut 'proximity and regional languages were felt to be old hat, now they have become popular topics; I was ahead of the trend' (*Télérama*, 9 December 1998). Deliberately ignoring the institutional and cultural items imposed by the Paris agenda, Pernaut and his team bring their audience of old-age pensioners, housewives and farmers a grass-roots reflection of their daily problems among which weather conditions get a high priority.

Local television cannot however be equated only with the provision of regional opt-outs by national broadcasters or with the emphasis on regional stories in national news programmes. As early as 1987, five local terrestrial channels were licensed by the broadcasting regulator, three of them, TLM in Lyons, TLT in Toulouse and Télé Bleue in Nîmes covering urban areas, the other two described as 'country TV channels' (*télévisions de pays*) serving larger geographical areas: one in the Savoie region and one in the Dordogne department. One of the three urban channels – Télé Bleue – went off air in 1996 as a result of its inability to broadcast its required volume of programmes. A total of nearly three million people were covered by the remaining four channels which operate under a convention agreed with the regulator for a renewable period of five years (four years only for Aqui TV available in the Dordogne area). Even if the constraints are theoretically the same as those that a national television service has to respect, local television channels have no obligations as regards production requirements of French audiovisual works or concerning their contribution to the production of films. Besides, these local television channels are allowed a larger volume of commercials than the average six minutes per hour imposed on national channels. The main constraints concerned the amount of original locally produced programmes broadcast daily – two hours – and the 10 percent minimum proportion of programmes devoted to the arts and cultural events.

The original programmes were complemented by acquired programmes (documentaries, children's and fiction programmes) which in the case of TLM and TLT accounted for 13 percent and 8 percent of the total schedule respectively in 1996.[9] The four local channels even tried to beef-up their programme supply in the early 1990s by relaying substantial amounts of programming bought from MCM, the European music channel. This rather costly arrangement which the *Conseil d'Etat*, a consultative assembly which acts as the supreme administrative tribunal, found incompatible with the provisions of the conventions agreed by the regulator was discontinued in 1992. This episode shows the difficulty for local TV channels which the law forbids like the other commercial TV channels, to take commercials from retailers to provide enough programmes to fill their schedules, hence the constant interrogation of the CSA about the economic viability of such channels.

Nevertheless the CSA advertised six new franchises in November 1998 and February 1999 for local television channels, three of them concerning the urban areas of Clermont-Ferrand, Bordeaux and Tours. Not all of them have been awarded yet. The decision by the CSA to award the franchise concerning Clermont-Ferrand to an operator in which the local newspaper publisher, La Montagne, holds 48 percent of the capital shows the determination of local press groups to diversify their presence on the local media scene. This significant development is likely to allay the fears of the CSA that local television channels might erode the sustainability of local media (radio but above all local newspapers) by competing for a limited amount of local advertising resources.

Regional press groups are currently putting pressure on the CSA to advertise new local television franchises. They believe that twenty to thirty such franchises could be allocated immediately without waiting for the introduction of digital technology. They feel that because of their intimate knowledge of the needs and aspirations of local populations they should be the privileged operators of whatever licences the CSA would choose to award. They insist that local opt-outs from national channels are no substitute for genuine local television services. They further argue that the future implementation of the digital terrestrial television plan included in the 2000 broadcasting law should not be used an excuse to deprive the French public of local channels which could be immediately operated. In April 1999, seventeen regional and local publishers joined together to found a consortium called Télévision Presse Région (TPR) acting as a pressure group to look after the collective interests of regional press groups in the field of local television. In October of the same year, five members of the consortium introduced a request for the creation of local television channels in Lille, Metz, Nantes and Rheims which has not yet been met by the CSA.

The broadcasting regulator will probably take its time before reacting to the request of the regional publishers. The CSA is aware that the local press is losing ground; between 1993 and 1997 regional titles have lost 13 percent of their readers. At the same time the regional press can justifiably claim that it constitutes a well-tested and probably indispensable channel of local democracy. Furthermore the considerable efforts made by regional publishers to digitalise their production in order to feed their web sites could constitute an asset when digital terrestrial channels were available. DTT is precisely the problem. The CSA is reluctant to commit itself to opening up new analogue frequencies before the attribution of the six digital multiplexes is sorted out. In the meantime, the CSA is likely to award a limited number of local franchises while considering favourably applications with regional press groups as leading partners. This piecemeal policy is unlikely to meet the expectations of the consortium, which reckons that the only way to ensure the economic viability of local television channels is to create a network of about twenty such channels offering a large enough market to national advertisers whose commercials could be aired on a syndicated basis. Shrewdly enough, the members of TPR do not require the removal of the rule which forbids access to commercials for retailers' chains. Understandably, regional publishers would rather keep to themselves the resources from that category of advertising which provides 27 percent of their own funding.

Meanwhile a true regional channel is about to go on air for the benefit of the four million people living in Brittany and the two million Bretons outside the region. Called TV Breizh, this new channel, with its headquarters in Lorient, will be available on cable or directly via the two digital satellite bouquets CanalSatellite and TPS. This channel is the brain-child of Patrick Lelay, the Director-General of TF1, a staunch supporter of the Breton cause who has managed to find the FF 100 million necessary to launch the channel. Not surprisingly TF1 has 21 percent of the capital, nearly as much François Pinault's company Artemis (22 percent). Local industrialist and banking groups have also been enlisted along with Rupert Murdoch's News Corp. and Berlusconi's Fininvest which will hold 13 percent of the capital each. The alliance forged by TF1 with the two media moguls in their European strategy may not be alien to the feeling of friendship for Brittany that the two magnates have expressed as their reason to join the new venture.

TV Breizh intends to broadcast seventeen hours of programmes daily, five to six hours of which will be original programmes shown between 17.30 and 22.30; because of the cost no news programmes will be shown. Instead the emphasis will be on sports, music – plans for sixty-minute programmes of Celtic music daily are being finalised – as well as the regional heritage and the sea. Programmes will be broadcast simultaneously on two frequencies, one for French, the other for the Breton version of the programmes. TV Breizh managers have also announced weekly films dubbed in Breton. Patrick Lelay does not expect the channel to break even before five years; he also expects to enlarge the audience of the channel through a digital terrestrial channel by 2002. TV Breizh went on air at the beginning of September 2000. Its programmes should dramatically enrich the supply of Breton TV products which hitherto has been confined to the daily five-minute news bulletin and the two weekly current affairs magazines broadcast by the regional studio of France 3.

Equally available on CanalSatellite as well as on the cable network operated by NC Numéricable (a subsidiary of Canal +), i télévision is the latest all-news channel launched by Canal + in November 1999. With sixty journalists across the country, i télévision intends to give extended coverage to local news. In this field the new channel will have to compete with the Régions channel, a satellite and a cable channel launched by France Télévision in 1998 which two years after its creation has still to find its audience.

If localness seems to have become a major incentive in the development of new TV services, the concept does not comprehend all the various aspects of diversity. Localness implies a closer attention to the reality of life in the regions which tended to be ignored by Paris-based news-rooms. Other groups of citizens, however, claim access to television: members of action groups, militants of radical associations or more simply groups of local people who want to air their concerns on television have for a number of years put pressure on the CSA to be granted television terrestrial frequencies. The regulator's response had been so far to authorise temporary licences up to six months for the coverage of special local events; but the CSA had constantly pointed out that under the terms of the 1986 broadcasting law associations or citizens' groups could not apply for a television licence. Only companies who can demonstrate their economic sustainability are allowed to do so. Moreover the shortage of available frequencies has often been held as an additional argument to turn down the requests of this new category of applicants. Various pirate operations organised by members of the *Coordination permanente des médias libres* (Permanent group for free media) have demonstrated the irrelevance of this technical excuse. Invited to take part in a colloquium staged in January 2000 by the Green Party and the *Coordination*, Hervé Bourges, the chairman of the CSA, suggested that the only way to award citizens' associations a permanent local TV channel was to change the law.[10] Catherine Trautmann, the previous Communication Minister who introduced the current broadcasting Bill, favoured the recognition of citizens' associations as *bona fide* applicants for the operation of the forthcoming digital terrestrial channels. During the debate on the Bill the supporters of public access television have been partly satisfied. An amendment to the draft has allowed associations to apply for local terrestrial franchises, but they are still barred from applying for national terrestrial franchises even if a non-commercial citizens' channel can now under the new law promulgated in June 2000 be carried by cable networks and included in satellite bouquets.

Digital terrestrial television will undoubtedly facilitate a more truthful representation of the diverse aspects of the national community. So will the statutory dedication of one channel in every cable network to local programmes often produced with the support of local and regional authorities. Although the risk of seeing the local channels being used for institutional propaganda purposes cannot be ruled out, the multiplication of local outlets can but allow the new media to fulfil their role as agents of change in a situation where the concept of the state and the nature of identity are increasingly challenged.

Conclusion

The chances are that France will evolve towards a looser national structure in which regional components will assume greater autonomy. This will be paralleled by the growth in local broadcasting outlets with limited audiences. The recent decision by the legislator, in the broadcasting law passed in June 2000, to forbid local associations from applying for national terrestrial analogous TV licences, is bound to limit the scope of these new broadcasters, who might find themselves suffering from ventriloquy. Accommodating regional diversity has always entailed the danger of fragmentation and an inward-looking propensity, detrimental to the notion of national togetherness.

Paradoxically, England, which has not until now claimed the recognition of any special position in the kingdom with which it has identified, has never really had problems expressing its diversity through broadcasting channels. Regionalism sells. The BBC boasts of having more popular regional news programmes than ITV. For all the recent upheavals that a highly concentrated independent TV sector has experienced, it remains highly dependent for ratings and advertising revenues on the loyal support of audiences who in turn can watch their own identities reflected along the weekly programme schedules. This is, however, a transitory situation that opportunities provided by digital terrestrial television are likely to alter within the present decade.

Notes

1. British Public Opinion (MORI newsletter), Vol. XXII, no. 3, April 1999.
2. David Hatch, former director of BBC Network radio was a special adviser to John Birt.
3. *Broadcast*, 7 July 2000: 16.
4. *Report of the Committee on Broadcasting 1960*, Cmnd. 1753, para. 108: 136.
5. Reported in *Press Gazette*, 9 June 2000: 1.
6. Radio Pays is, in particular, the name of a true independent radio station set up as early as 1981 in Paris to provide a forum for speakers of regional languages. Occitans, Basques, Corsicans, Catalans and Bretons share the station which provides local communities living in the Paris areas with news, cultural magazines and local music programmes. Run by an association (the French equivalent of a charity) the station which claims about 350 members has always refused advertising funding and relies on a team of non-paid members for the making of its programmes.

7. Quoted in *Le Monde*, 12–13 March 2000.
8. On Monday, 3 July 2000 for example, 9.3 million people watched the regional early evening news bulletin, that is 300,000 more than those who watched the national news which followed at 19.30. The regional news programme attracted the second largest audience in this access prime time slot after the French version of *Who Wants to be a Millionaire?* shown on TF1 and watched by 10.7 million viewers.
9. Data provided by the CSA report *Les Télévisions de proximité* published in May 1996.
10. 'Le tiers secteur audiovisuel : un accès citoyen à la télévision', a colloquium held on 31 January 2000 at the *Assemblée nationale* in Paris at the initiative of the Green Party, *la Coordination des médias libres et la Fédération nationale des vidéos de pays et de quartiers*.

CHAPTER 3

CONSTRUCTING THE NATIONAL

TELEVISION AND WELSH IDENTITY

Kevin Williams

It has been said that 'contemporary Wales could be defined as an artefact produced by broadcasting' (Davies, 1994). Whether this sweeping statement is accepted or not, debate about Welsh identity has remained intimately tied to the development of broadcasting. In its early days, radio was seen by the Welsh Board of Education as 'one of the most serious menaces to the life of the Welsh language' (quoted in Howell, 1992: 221). Saunders Lewis, the father of modern Welsh nationalism, believed that the BBC was threatening 'the complete anglicisation of the intellectual life of the nation' (quoted in Davies, 1994: 48). Lewis described the BBC as *Bradwr Budr Cymru*, the 'dirty betrayer of Wales', and he launched a campaign for access to the airwaves for the Welsh language and culture. The outcome was a separate Welsh Home Service in 1937, the first of a series of concessions from the centre which allowed the Welsh language its place in the ether. The struggle for the recognition of language and identity in Welsh broadcasting is seen as being finally won with the establishment of Sianel Pedwar Cymru (S4C) in 1982. Described as the 'prize of a tooth and claw struggle all the way' (Blanchard and Morley, 1982: 37), S4C is almost unique in Western Europe in that it is a television channel born out of the political struggles of its audience and committed to the preservation of a language and culture.

This chapter examines the debate about broadcasting and identity in Wales. It begins with an overview of the problematic nature of this identity and then outlines the development of broadcasting following the birth of S4C. This entails describing the broadcasting structures that have emerged as well as the debate around representation that has underpinned them. At the heart of this debate is the continual struggle between Wales and London over how to represent Welshness. It can be argued, however, that this debate reveals obscured issues within Welsh television over how to represent Wales in a rapidly changing economic, social and political environment.

What is Wales?

What is Wales is continually being redrawn and redefined in accordance with pressures from inside as well as outside Wales. Some attribute the survival of Wales as a collective entity to the power and ability of the Welsh to continually reinvent themselves as a people (Humphreys, 1989). While myth and history have always mingled side by side in the discussion of national identity it is the more concrete social, economic and political factors that explain the contemporary nature of group identity. Unlike Scotland, Wales has not experienced the strong development of previous structures or institutions of control to form a historical political base for its national identity (Constitution Unit, 1996: 48). Prior to conquest, Wales never really existed as a separate territorial entity. Only briefly had the different 'houses' of Wales been united under one ruler. However, the sense of Welsh nationhood has stubbornly persisted without the exercise of military or political power nor any indigenous control of the economic base.

Pressure for greater institutional expression for Welsh identity came in the nineteenth century and initially took the form of protest to defend the Welsh language. Through protest, Welsh consciousness began to emerge. However, efforts to establish separate political institutions failed. It was not until the post-war period that Wales received any political acknowledgement of its distinctiveness. The Welsh Office was established in 1964 and a *Welsh* civil society has slowly emerged since this time. This society is weak and many of those professional organisations identified as central to a strong civil society are lacking, with the Welshness of what has developed remaining a matter of doubt (Paterson and Wyn Jones, 1999: 173).

The one feature of Welsh life which makes Wales clearly distinctive from any other country is the Welsh language. Most of Wales was Welsh speaking in 1800. By 1991 the Welsh speaking population had fallen to 18.6 percent (Aitchison and Carter, 1999). Decline has been accompanied by the territorial shrinkage of Welsh-speaking regions with corresponding concerns about the ethnolinguistic vitality of the language. Measures – both official and unofficial – have been taken to preserve and protect the language in these shrinking zones. The Welsh Language Acts, the Dyfed education policy of Welsh only primary schools, the activities of Meibion

Glyndwr (better known outside Wales as the 'cottage burners') and the non-violent Welsh Language Society have all been in response to the perceived threat to the language. The special treatment for the language is seen by some non-Welsh speakers as a threat. The tension between Welsh and non-Welsh speakers is 'not merely linguistic. It was also a fracture in the economy and society which led to a difference in collective psychology' (Smith, 1984: 8). There are two separate communities in Wales. These are not simply language communities. Their culture, histories and roots are distinct. These different histories, traditions and experiences were for many years reinforced by an educational system which taught very little Welsh-speaking history.

The sense of Welsh national identity has been undermined by inward migration which began in earnest in the nineteenth century as the rapid industrial development of parts of Wales proved a magnet for drawing in people from elsewhere in Britain and beyond. This pattern of migration has skewed the structure of society. While 90 percent of the people who live in Scotland and England today were born in those countries, in Wales only 79 percent of the population are indigenous (Talfan Davies, 1996). Incomers into Wales have located themselves in particular areas, which has given Wales a distinct political and cultural geography captured by political scientist Denis Balsom (1985) in his 'Three Wales Model'. He makes a distinction between Y Fro Gymraeg, Welsh Wales and British Wales. The former is the Welsh-speaking heartland of the nation, taking in north and west Wales with the exception of Pembrokeshire, where the language is most commonly spoken on a daily basis and agriculture and rural life dominate. It is in this area that Plaid Cymru, the nationalist party, enjoys its greatest political support and the highest vote in favour of the National Assembly for Wales was recorded in the 1997 Referendum. Welsh Wales – or the Valleys – is the industrial belt across South Wales which has served as Labour's electoral heartland for its dominance of Welsh political life. Economic decline and deprivation are features of this area as the coal and steel industries disappear and people leave in growing numbers. British Wales is the rest; the coastal belts of north and south-east Wales and the border areas. This area has received the bulk of inward investment coming into Wales and has the highest rates of economic growth. Modernisation has taken place most rapidly in British Wales and it is where the issue of identity is most contested. Welsh identity and nationhood is negotiated differently in each of these 'areas', an indication of Welsh internal diversity.

The Welsh Television Nation

Television in Wales reflects the general disunity of Wales. Until 1955 it was the sole responsibility of the BBC when it was joined by the regional ITV contractor for Wales and the West. The BBC in Wales has always been firmly part of the Corporation, a 'national region' in an organisation that has throughout most of its career vigorously pursued a policy of making the people of the United Kingdom part of one *British* happy family (see Scannell and Cardiff, 1991). At times BBC Wales has proved a difficult child to manage because its output has been in two languages; but for much of its history BBC Wales has had limited autonomy from London to develop its own policies and programmes (see Davies, 1994). Commercial television was introduced partly to act as an antidote to the centralised nature of the BBC. It had a mandate to reflect life in the 'regions'.

The birth of ITV in Wales was a shambles. Wales West and North (WWN), which began broadcasting in September 1962, was the only ITV company to collapse. A number of technical, cultural and financial reasons have been cited for this débâcle but the main reason was that the audience was already receiving ITV programmes from Cardiff and Manchester. The first Welsh-language programmes were produced by Granada. Television West and Wales (TWW) produced programmes from Cardiff for audiences in the west of England, south Wales and Welsh-speakers in Wales. The size, poverty and low purchasing power of Wales has prevented the establishment of an independent TV channel serving Wales alone. In commercial broadcasting terms, Wales has never been treated as a national entity.

S4C changed broadcasting in Wales. The main purpose of the channel is to enable Welsh speakers, as S4C's chief executive puts it, 'to communicate and entertain each other in our own language' (Jones, 1995). By broadcasting in the Welsh language the channel also provides the affirmation of a separate Welsh identity. Research shows that the 'broadcast media in the Welsh language appear to have a relatively clear identity, linked to a perception of Wales as a spatially defined political, social and cultural entity' (Hume, 1986: 331). S4C provides Welsh-speakers with a Welsh perspective on international affairs through news and current affairs and dramas which represent popular culture and life in Wales. The main evening news bulletin *Newyddion* presents a Welsh perspective on international, British and national affairs in the Welsh language. *Newyddion* is produced by BBC Wales, which, as part of the original agreement to establish the channel, provides ten hours of programmes free for S4C. The arrangement is an acknowledgement by the BBC that people in Wales have a right to express themselves in their own voice on the main issues of the day – as long as that voice is Welsh.

The aspirations of making more programmes for a Welsh audience have had to be realised in a less conducive environment in the 1990s. The commercialisation and de-regulation of broadcasting in the United Kingdom has made it more difficult to produce programmes of quality to cater for the diversity of Welshness. S4C has become a commercial player in its own right and some see tension between the channel's commercial role and its cultural remit. These changes have exacerbated tensions between language and nation in S4C's operation. Early efforts to represent the bilingual and multicultural nature of Welsh society in drama programmes such as *Bowen a'i Bartner* were criticised by 'linguistic purists' for slipping from the remit to serve the Welsh language. Matters came to a head over the launch of an early-evening magazine programme, *Heno*, broadcast not from the traditional base of Welsh-language television production, Gwynedd and Cardiff, but from Swansea. *Heno* was established to appeal to the working-class Welsh-speakers of industrial south Wales - not the traditional speakers of the north – by using 'street Welsh' and a mixture of Welsh and English. The move was criticised by traditionalists who condemned the channel for 'lowering standards'. Behind this difference of opinion over the language is a conflict over the concept of Welsh national identity. Traditionalists see the 'Welsh way of life' as focused on the chapel, the language, the 'oldest literary tradition in Europe'; Wales is represented as an 'essentially rural society' whose cohesion and stability and completeness has been undermined by the forces of urbanisation and 'anglicisation' (Bevan, 1984). This is Balsom's Y Fro Gymraeg and traditionalists see the role of S4C as defending this 'heartland'. However, the recent revival of the language has been in urban areas in the south; most Welsh learners are located in this part of Wales. These realities are drawing S4C to where the largest slice of the Welsh speaking audience is now located, South East Wales. It is possible to see different kinds of engagement with Welshness on S4C. In her research of S4C's highest-rated programme, the daily soap *Pobol Y Cwm*, Griffiths has documented how its representation of Welshness has changed since its inception on BBC Wales in 1974 (Griffiths, 1995). In recent years S4C has also made efforts to breach the linguistic divide in Wales: over 50 percent of the channel's output is now subtitled in English and a subtitling service has been designed for Welsh-learners. The problems of serving two language communities, representing Welsh life in all its diversity, and balancing commercial and cultural requirements has posed and will continue to pose a dilemma for the channel.

While the success of S4C has improved the service to Welsh-speakers, provision for English-speakers in Wales remains limited. Overall Welsh television broadcasts around fifty-eight hours of programmes each week but only just under half are in the English language. There is only around twenty-two hours of television every week for English-speakers in Wales, who make up four fifths of the people living in Wales. This has led to calls for a dedicated English-language channel for Wales. English-speakers in Wales have become used to tuning into television from English regions. This is partly a result of the geography of the country. It is estimated that 35 percent of Welsh people live in areas which overlap with English transmitters – compared with only 2.5 percent of Scots who live in areas which can receive news and information from England – while nearly 400,000 people in Wales do not receive Welsh television (Welsh Affairs Committee, 1999). Others make a conscious decision to reject Welsh television (see

Osmond, 1990). Over the years little effort was made by either BBC Wales or HTV Wales to mount a campaign to persuade viewers to tune into Wales. That segments of the Welsh audience watch programmes from the midlands, Manchester and the west of England is sometimes explained by the poor quality of Welsh-made programmes. However, performance indicators in the industry present a more complicated picture (see K. Williams, 1997). Welsh broadcasters say many people are too lazy to get around to changing their aerials or are unwilling to meet the cost involved; but it is clear that many English-speaking viewers believe the range of programmes on Welsh television is limited.

Representing Wales

The growth of Welsh television has to be seen in the context of London's resistance to and prejudice against things Welsh. The lack of attention paid to Wales on British television was recently illustrated by the fact that in the year August 1995 to 1996, only 0.2 percent of Channel Four's output was commissioned from Welsh independent companies. One *Sunday Times* article (12 May 1996) highlighted the 'anti-Welsh' bias of British broadcasting. It is, however, not only a matter of omission; what has been commissioned has been criticised for its narrow representation of Welshness. Criticism is levelled at the stereotypical images of rugby, choirs, drink and the lads. Whether it is the *twp* (stupid), sex-mad P.E. teacher in the BBC comedy *May to September* or the gloomy, monosyllabic DC in ITV's *Minder*, the representation of what it is to be Welsh on the English-dominated national television has often been seen as narrowly drawn and derogatory.

In recent years Welsh broadcasters have reiterated that the role of television is not only to provide information and entertainment, but also to play a significant role in the development of Welsh identity. The BBC Controller made the commitment in 1992 that 'BBC Wales's programme agenda should be dominated by that which is significant to the lives of the people of Wales'. Two years earlier, HTV's Director of Television emphasised that the *raison d'être* of the company was 'the reinforcement of our identity; to present the Welsh to the Welsh and to be proud, in so far as it is justifiable, of who we are'. There is, however, a problem over the best ways to represent Welshness. London's prejudices are sometimes used to cover up shortcomings closer to home. Questions have been raised over the ability of BBC Wales and HTV to 'sell' and present themselves to the network; but, more importantly, confusion exists over how to provide people in Wales with a sense of themselves, which is particularly acute in English language television.

Welsh television can be criticised for its failure to represent the contradictions of Welsh identity, riven as all national identities are by the experience of racial, social, linguistic, gender and age divisions. Images of choirs, heavy industry and singing the praises of the rugby team at the Millennium Stadium are out of touch with modern Welsh society which has far more women on low wages in service industries than men in traditional employment. People in north Wales complain of the southern bias in the Welsh media – 'Radio Rhondda' as some of them call BBC Radio Wales – while critical voices have been raised about the portrayal of North Walians in S4C's *Pobol y Cwm* (Griffiths, 1995). Ethnic groups have been virtually absent from Welsh television. In response to the difficulties of representing 'many Welsh voices' the easy option is to fall back on traditional stereotypes; and television practitioners in Wales can be as capable of reproducing these stereotypes as their colleagues in London.

Representing the multilingual nature and cultural diversity of Wales is an anathema to some programme-makers. Reference has been made to television drama being 'saddled with a representational burden' (Blandford and Upton, 1996). To describe programme-makers as struggling with the 'burden' of representation illustrates a lack of confidence in Welsh culture. Writers and artists should feel able to speak unself-consciously from and about their culture. The intervention of a mission to represent Wales directly can get in the way of making good television; but the makers of television in Wales have over the years been handicapped by the shortage of cash. For example, Welsh television drama has had to be realised at a cost well below the average cost for television drama. The result is an end-product that can look 'cheap and half-realised, especially to an audience raised on sophisticated production values' (Blandford and Upton, 1996). The process of devolution has resulted in more money flowing into Welsh television, particularly into the BBC, but the representational imbalance in the Welsh TV nation as a whole will continue, above all, to be determined by the economic circumstances of contemporary broadcasting and film-making.

CHAPTER 4

CHANGING EXPECTATIONS

HOLYROOD, TELEVISION AND SCOTTISH NATIONAL IDENTITY

Adrienne Scullion

This is about more than our politics and our laws. This is about who we are, how we carry ourselves. There is a new voice in the land, the voice of a democratic Parliament. A voice to shape Scotland as surely as the echoes from our past: the shout of the welder in the din of the great Clyde ship-yards; the speak of the Mearns, with its soul in the land; the discourse of the Enlightenment, when Edinburgh and Glasgow were a light held to the intellectual life of Europe; the wild cry of the great pipes; and back to the distant cries of the battles of Bruce and Wallace.

From the speech of the First Minister Donald Dewar MP, MSP, at the opening of the Scottish Parliament, 1 July 1999.[1]

The election for the first Scottish Parliament for 292 years took place on 6 May 1999; on the same day elections for the new Welsh Assembly took place. These elections marked a radical reorganisation and recreation of British political structures, shifting completely the role and the idea of Westminster, and creating two new variously autonomous legislatures.

For us living in Scotland the creation and implementation of the new, devolved Scottish Parliament (elected through a voting system that included an element of proportional representation [PR]) will alter our whole understanding of and relationship with government, bringing deci-sion-making closer and encouraging a more immediate sense of responsibility and empowerment. In a country with a population of a little over 5.1 million, a Parliament at Holyrood will see government as a more tangible and personal affair than ever before, ensuring that politicians are more accountable and encouraging the electorate to be more involved in the processes of government.

As a further consequence of these constitutional changes within the nation, it seems inevitable that the 'imagined' nature of Scotland will also necessarily change. Scottish culture, and within that issues around representation and identity, has been much preoccupied with ideas of colonialism, marginalism and parochialism but, in a context where a significant degree of political independence has been achieved, the dynamic must shift from aspiration and desire to definition and responsibility. It seems clear that the fact of the Holyrood Parliament will change how we as Scots understand and participate in the dynamic processes of Scottish national identity.

This chapter aims to consider ideas of national identity in Scottish television against this backdrop of political and legislative devolution. It responds to the rhetorics of Scottish devolution and identity politics through its structure and organisation. The chapter begins with a brief overview of ideas of and engagements with national identity in modern critical literature and, in particular, in Scottish critical literature. It then splits into two main phases: the first part considering the experience of devolution in its factual television coverage, both before the election and after; and the second addressing the portrayal of Scottish identity on television, in particular in television drama, again both before devolution and after. In this way the chapter aims to give an overview of both institutional and representational practices in contemporary Scottish broadcasting. I argue that neither factual nor fictional television has yet responded to the radical revisioning of Scotland that devolution allows – and, indeed, that neither has been as bold in their resetting of the rhetorics of Scotland as was Donald Dewar in his speech at the opening of the Parliament on 1 July 1999. This speech – a section of which is quoted at the beginning of this essay – was a surprising, daring and, indeed, moving piece of oratory that was, quite simply, about Scottish national identity. Dewar boldly paralleled contemporary parliamentary structures with the images and the iconography of mythic and historical Scotland, seeing 'imaginary' Scotland as just as significant, just as potent and just as 'authentic' a national symbol as legislative and civic Scotland.

Ideas of National Identity in Scotland

I want to begin with the words that I have always wanted either to say or to
hear someone else say: the Scottish Parliament, which adjourned on 25
March 1707, is hereby reconvened.

> From the speech of the 'oldest qualified member',
> Dr Winifred Ewing, MEP, MSP, at the swearing-in of the
> members of the Scottish Parliament, 12 May 1999.

The dynamics of identity and representation are key themes across the
whole of Scottish culture. In arguing for the efficacy of the imaginary and
of the nation as 'an imagined political community' Benedict Anderson
influentially outlines a version of belonging which is eclectic, multifarious
and resists closure (Anderson, 1990: 15). He allows for a version of the
nation, an identity, which is open, egalitarian and peace-loving – this
being very much in line with the sets of identity that Scottishness prefers.

In opposition and in practice, however, the application of the idea of
the nation, the actual functioning of the state, may be less tolerant; for
nations also define themselves as exclusive and sovereign, building barriers (literal and metaphoric) to limit access and to regulate membership,
determinedly separating the elect from the ostracised. The point in the
establishment of society at which one group, one identity, is legitimised
and the other disenfranchised, marginalised, cast, however crudely, as
'other', is a result of the socio-cultural development of the community. It
is a conjunction of historical, economic, social and political factors, that
is defined in the nation's traditions, myths and collective imagination, and
is replayed in its cultural texts.

Like any peripheral culture Scotland expends inordinate amounts of
energy defending and defining a sense of national identity to bolster the
pervasive economic attraction of the various cultural cores. Both politically and economically Scotland has seemed tied to a series of ideologies
and discourses which artists have increasingly found to be restrictive in
depicting their own experiences and their own fantasies, and which critics
too have increasingly found to be reductive and limiting. Problems based
on economic realities shape representations of Scotland – and the images
of 'tartanry', 'kailyard' and 'Clydeside' have proved sound propositions,
creating highly marketable, if regressive, and perhaps repressive, representations of Scots and Scotland.[2] (See the chapter by Kevin Williams for
a description of a similar aspect of the televisual representation of Welsh
nation.) It has been argued that Scottish identity focuses on these key
tropes with each eliciting a predictable series of representations and narratives, and each being played out against its preferred topographies of
cityscape and rural landscape. However, within an expanding arts and
broadcasting industry – where we must, and with mounting confidence
can, talk about an artistically varied and economically vibrant and diverse

Scottish culture – writers and producers are, perhaps, able reuse the traditions, the emblems and the motifs of kailyard and tartanry, of the country and the city, of myth and history, of Enlightenment, war and democracy in a questioning and active way. One might even argue that the potential for rereading and resetting the preferred identities of Scottish culture allows for unexpected engagements with satire, irony, critical and reflexive deconstruction. But this resetting goes further. If Scottish culture has been seen to be obsessively attracted to a set of easily transferable character stereotypes, ubiquitous images and predictable politics, it has been argued by David McCrone, Craig Beveridge and Ronald Turnbull and others that Scottish criticism has merely added to the myopia by validating and perpetuating debilitating and constraining versions of national and gender identities.[3] Such easy assumptions, predicated upon patriarchal and colonial models of experience and criticism, cannot go unopposed in the new context of devolution.

McCrone argues that cultural theory in Scotland reaches a political and cultural impasse because it sets out to find a Scottish 'national culture' when this is an 'illegitimate' project (McCrone, 1989: 172). A more useful agenda, it is suggested, is one willing to acknowledge that modern societies do not experience 'a national culture which will speak to people in their own terms, an integrated discourse which will connect with political and social realities in Scotland' but are essentially 'pluralistic' and paradoxical (McCrone, 1989: 168). While this wider vision is certainly one to be encouraged and sought out, it is nevertheless important to acknowledge that a 'national' view is one which practitioners and critics in Scotland have long held up as the ideal of indigenous culture. One might speculate that in the pragmatic economy of broadcast television and the *realpolitik* of high-stakes parliamentary elections this tendency towards traditional and more or less fixed identities becomes ever more significant, caught as it is between a colonial model of cultural understanding and a potentially new, post-devolution contextualisation of Scots and Scotland.

The range and scale of cultural activity in Scotland in the last two decades has been arguably greater and more apparent to a wider audience than at any other point in recent history and this has raised awareness of and influenced (both subtly and significantly) issues of identity within Scottish culture. The cultural life of late twentieth-century Scotland has been significantly eclectic. The 1960s and 1970s saw the impact of the folk revival, the 'rediscovery' of Scottish history, the opening up of the Highland touring circuit to theatre and music-makers, and the flourishing of an extraordinarily diverse range of urban theatres. After the failure of the devolution movement of the 1970s and the election of the Conservative government in 1979 the culture of Scotland seemed at its most confident when it was oppositional. This encouraged an energy that was productive but also resulted in a social context in which artists felt under-valued and, at times, disenfranchised. Frustrated and alienated by the political and cultural and social and financial ideologies of London, the period saw Scottish artists working in two contrasting but oddly complementary ways: on the one hand Scottish artists refocused their attentions on work for and in Scotland, looking to the past with new application, creating texts of linguistic and visual specificity, reassessing the cultural influences that make Scotland; on the other there was an increased internationalism of outlook in terms of influence, process and market. Both dynamics were about bypassing London, or at least finding ways of working beyond the 'them and us' identities that the Thatcher government engendered in Scotland.

But, of course, this dynamic presented particular problems for broadcasters who worked in an industry that was economically centred on London. Despite the arrival of Channel 4 and its remit to find and support new models of commissioning and programme-making, despite the growth of the decentralised independent producing sector during this time most programming decisions were still being filtered through London-based management.

Nevertheless, this system sought a new model for balancing the demands of the 'national' British network (and indeed the demands of the international broadcasting market-place) and the needs of the regions. It facilitated the production of high-quality programming of extraordinary regional and national distinctiveness (programmes such as *Tutti Frutti* [BBC, 1987] to which this chapter will return) that achieved significant broadcast success in the whole UK market. However, it also encouraged investment in independent and semi-autonomous producers in the regions and it led to the development of expertise in making programmes for just the local or regional audience. (The strength of current affairs broadcasting in Scotland and the evolution of the Comedy Unit based at BBC Scotland in Glasgow might be seen as two examples of the type of developments possible within this infrastructure.)

The huge changes in the political life of Scotland that build on history and the independent civil society but also create new institutions and policies make this an important time for us to reflect on both the legislative and imaginary issues of representation and identity across the whole of Scottish society and, of course, on issues raised by devolution politics in relation to broadcasting, be it factual or fictional. This despite, or because of, the fact that while the Holyrood government has significant authority in terms of arts and cultural policy but the devolution settlement does not extend to broadcast legislation, with Westminster retaining authority in this area.

The culture of the 1990s and of contemporary Scotland is as multifarious as in earlier decades but also has the potential to be more sustainable because of the energy released by the devolution process. Making work in and for Scotland has been redefined as anything but parochial. The potential for internationalism is still significant, still inspiring, still evolving. London has been recovered as a potential market-place and a potential partner; although for many Scottish artists success is still found abroad, in a more international context, than it is in London.

In Scotland culture has been celebrated as one of the key factors that made devolution possible. The economic success and the popular appeal of our artists bolstered a positive and outward looking version of our culture. But, a significant part of Scottish culture in the 1980s and even in the 1990s was content to be 'not English': for example, 'Scottish collective identity defines itself, to a significant degree, by differences in attitudes, values and behaviour between the Scots and the English' (Meech and Kilborn, 1992: 246). Jane Sillars is right to describe 'a trend to explore differences *from* Scotland; while differences *within* Scotland have been put to one side' (Sillars, 1999: 252). Part of the project of culture – and of cultural criticism – in the post-devolution world is to recognise and analyse the variety and diversity of 'differences *within* Scotland', to reinvent identity as more that reactive, and much more than 'not English'.

Devolution and its Television Coverage

There shall be a Scottish Parliament.
> *Scotland Act*, 1998, Part I, clause I, subsection I.[4]

Broadcast news coverage in Scotland from the BBC and the two independent stations, Scottish Television and Grampian Television, is generally respected and 'qualitatively different to that found in the English regions' (MacInnes, 1993: 93). Unlike the broadcasters of the English regions and indeed in Wales, news producers in Scotland have always had a distinctive and independent set of institutions to report. Even prior to devolution the Scottish Office offered a political focus, there is an autonomous legal system and judiciary, a unique infrastructure for and system of education, distinctive religious institutions, as well as specifically Scottish sports leagues and national teams. All these elements contribute to a civil society that creates and implements the policy that shapes Scotland: in these ways Scotland was framed in ways that the English regions lacked completely and that Wales lacked in some degree. Over time, then, and in response to these differences, Scottish current affairs broadcasters have developed a rhetoric that marks their work as 'nationally' (and thereby not merely 'regionally') significant.

However, it remained the fact that Scottish television's locally produced news output has been, as John Macinnes puts it, 'additional to rather than a substitute for the British national news'. This has had the advantage of allowing Scottish broadcasters to develop expertise not just in understanding and interpreting current affairs in Scotland but also in interpreting and 'explor[ing] in much greater depth… [the] Scottish angles on British national themes' (MacInnes, 1993: 93). But, it has also allowed the British national news something of a get-out clause in their coverage of Scotland: a story can very easily be flagged as exclusively of interest in Scotland and shifted from the 'national' news when there is a safety net that will see it broadcast for that specific audience. This may have contributed to the expertise of the Scottish broadcasters but it also led the London producers to indulge in colonial and centralising strategies, to label events and stories along an axis of British/Scottish interest, and to marginalise the stories of Scotland into 'opt-out' slots.

Within this model, and despite the (British) 'national' significance of devolution, the casting of that story as merely of 'Scottish' or indeed 'Welsh' interest by the London broadcasters was, perhaps, inevitable. One might judge that the tension, excitement and, indeed, emotion of Scottish and Welsh devolution – as well as a sustained interrogation of the issues and the policies of the parties involved – proved an odd absence in television coverage of the campaign and election. It has been suggested, by politicians and commentators alike, that the marginalisation of the devolution campaigns within the London-produced news – wherein the elections were invariably presented as provincial and inconsequential – was a contributory factor in the relatively low turn-out in each nation's poll, and the parallel lack of knowledge about the new election systems and the lack of knowledge about the role of PR and the status of the so-called 'list' MSPs. The electoral system and constitution of the Scottish Parliament is certainly rather different from other models of government that exist within Britain at local, national and even at European level. The 'list' vote, for example, is relatively straightforward but it was a new procedure. Furthermore, its PR-component made it unfamiliar. Although the mathematics applied to the list candidates can appear complicated and not a little unwieldy, the process is at least logical and systematic.[5] Instead of facilitating and supporting the explanation of the poll the broadcast media did nothing other than declare that the system was complicated.[6]

In addition to the distinctive nature of the poll there are aspects of the new Scottish parliamentary structure and process that are quite different from the Westminster model and which, perhaps, need to be reported, described and analysed in different ways. For example, the electoral system for the Scottish Parliament all but guarantees to deliver government by coalition; the Scottish Parliament is unicameral and works to a fixed calendar (with elections falling on the first Thursday of May every fourth year); the constitution of the Executive results in the model of 'ministers without ministries' (and the information-gathering potential of ministries), although the committees are potentially very powerful; and, the Scottish Parliament can debate a 'draft budget'. All of these aspects are unfamiliar from the Westminster model and in just the same way that they offer a new model of parliamentary procedure, one might suggest that they also demand a new rhetoric, or at least a new calendar, of reporting.

In addition, it seems clear that those same aspects of the new Parliament – equitable representation, clarity of responsibility, and access to decision-makers – are very deliberately construed as embodying the preferred identities of Scotland as fair and inclusive and democratic and true. They are presented as offering a distinct model of democracy that balances the weight of tradition and history with a modern and fair voting system, the authority of Enlightenment ideology with strategies of open government, and the established infrastructure of the Scottish civil society with the principle of social inclusion and access. All are histories and values that contemporary political culture is keen to appropriate and endorse as part of Scottish national identity.

So broadcasting Holyrood is not just a matter of the networks picking up and scheduling Scottish-produced work that debates and informs the Scottish electorate and the wider British population – although that is itself a significant task. Broadcasting Holyrood implies a reappraisal of the national and cultural assumptions normalised in our existing broadcasting infrastructures.

Issues of huge public interest within Scotland – the first private member's bill on warrant sales and poinding, the bill on ethics and standards in public life that framed the debate around homosexuality, education, local authorities and the privately funded campaign to resist the repeal of Section 28/Clause 2a, the debate about the design and construction of a new parliament building, and the chaos around the release of the 2000 Scottish Qualifications Authority examination results – were all but marginalised within British (London-produced) news coverage but dominated press and television within Scotland itself. Indeed, the all-too-obvious lacunae in London's coverage of these issues exposed, or at least questioned, the authority of the London media's engagement with and understanding of Scotland. Even before the Scottish Parliament sat, Murray Pittock argued that the broadcasters were responding to the new political infrastructure in a negative, inferiorising and colonial manner. He argued that:

> The BBC in particular can clearly be seen to continue its allegiance to Reithite *de haut en bas* educative centralism in significant areas of underlying policy. Even in news and current affairs programmes, it can be strongly monologic in its portrayal of Britain and Britishness. ... politics cannot be different in different parts of Britain, because then it would not be British politics, seems to be the assumption. (Pittock, 1999: 143)

Against such a static and conservative a model of 'Britain', the truly radical nature of devolution and, in particular, of devolution as experienced in Scotland begins to emerge, and the crucial point in Pittock's argument is strengthened: that broadcasting in a devolved Scotland demands a reimaging of existing conventions of news and current affairs in order that broadcasters might respond to and even challenge what the new Parliament might mean across the whole of Britain.

The immediate reaction of the broadcasting institutions to referendum and devolution was to invest additional funds in political and current affairs broadcasting for Scotland. The BBC's anticipated investment of some £10 million aimed to produce daily programmes on BBC Radio Scotland (including a weekly review in Gaelic on BBC Radio Nan Gaidheal), the much debated *Newsnight Scotland* (the Scottish opt-out at the end of BBC television's late-night news programme *Newsnight*), live broadcasts of key debates from Holyrood, and to establish a Parliamentary Programmes Unit based adjacent to the new parliament building in Edinburgh. However, all these programming choices – all produced in Scotland – were only broadcast to Scotland. In addition, their programmes matched almost exactly existing models and conventions: even the BBC's two flagship programmes – *Holyrood*, its weekly review of Parliament, and *Holyrood Live*, broadcasting key debates from the Scottish Parliament – merely mirror the existing high-profile and well-respected current affairs programme *Scottish Lobby*, which focused on Scottish issues and Scottish MPs in Westminster, and *Westminster Live* with its live television coverage of proceedings from Westminster. Neither of these programmes, nor any of the other initiatives offered by the BBC, Scottish or Grampian Television offered the radical or bold news broadcasting that Pittock's analysis suggests would be appropriate. None of the broadcast solutions in place at present truly test the Parliament's aim to be accessible or inclusive. Nor do they set about reimagining Scotland.

However, it is early days in the life of the Scottish Parliament, the Welsh Assembly and, indeed, the Northern Irish Assembly, and it is certainly the case that the provision of factual programming after devolution remains under review, at least within the BBC, as the result of the formation of a devolution programme review group. Still, one might suggest that the London media's failure to represent devolved Scotland adequately will result in longer-term policy changes in broadcasting: with the idea of a 'national' news under scrutiny; with Scottish-based production companies being ever more high-profile and powerful within the media market-place; and with the legislative authority of the Holyrood Parliament increasingly impacting in tangible and immediate ways on the everyday lives of the Scottish people, the significance (and then the status) of Scottish-produced news and current affairs programming will inevitably rise. Indeed one might speculate that the campaign for the so-called 'Scottish Six' – a Scottish-produced evening news programme that 'opted-in' to London – was merely mistimed and that the increased impact of decisions made by Holyrood on our society will result in a more compelling argument being made and perhaps even a daring 'devolution' of broadcasting authority being implemented.

Scottish identity and Representation in Television Drama

What do you do when democracy fails you?
The Proclaimers, 'What do you do?', *Sunshine on Leith*, 1988

Identity is also tested, advanced, reaffirmed and deconstructed in contexts other than politics and current affairs. As Dewar's highly rhetorical speech at the opening of the Parliament argued, devolution 'is about more than our politics and our laws. ... [It] is about who we are.' In terms of broadcasting, drama, comedy and indeed sport remain crucial in the creative distillation, exploration and representation of our cultural identities, of 'who we are'.

In the 1970s – but with roots stretching back over the century – Scottish drama was all-but dominated by a version of Scotland, a type of narrative and a set of characters, that has been described as the 'urban kailyard'. The introspective, aggressively working-class, urban, industrial and post-industrial community that this subgenre described was male-dominated to the point of misogyny and coalesced around the archetype of the 'hard man'. The locus of the drama was central Scotland and in particular Glasgow and its environs (including Greenock and Paisley). Images of the industrial cityscape and the men who worked in it has been described, and sometimes even interrogated, across the range of Scottish media: in the fine art of Stanley Spencer, Ken Currie and Peter Howson; in the dramas of Bill Bryden, Peter McDougall and Aileen Ritchie; in novels as diverse as those of Margaret Thomson Davis, Jeff Torrington, James Kelman and Irvine Welsh. With shocking ease, and seeming near completeness, the figure, his stories and iconography was absorbed into television drama. The bleak, post-industrial setting and the angry, violent figure of Jake McQuillen in Peter McDougall's *Just a Boy's Game* (BBC, 1979) encapsulated the narrative, *mise en scène* and characterisation of contemporary urban drama produced in Scotland, emerging as an assured archetype for subsequent television texts.

It is certainly an identity of huge ubiquity. Variations on the theme of the mean urban streets proved pervasive, preferring to be read not just as indigenous but also as authentic. The characterisation, narrative and milieu extended to a potent subgenre which recast the hard man as detective and established a compelling version of this contemporary Scottish identity as a suffering truth-seeker caught in a bleak, corrupting, insular, near-manichean urban environment. While Glenn Chandler's *Taggart* (Scottish Television, from 1983) is the obvious example from contemporary television, the character has an important televisual antecedent in Eddie Boyd's Daniel Pike, and strong literary parallels in William McIlvanney's Jack Laidlaw, Ian Rankin's John Rebus and, more recently, Chris Brookmyer's Jack Parlabane. Although *Taggart* remains the Scottish industry's most successful television creation, its most recognised brand, the desire to repeat the popular, if perhaps overly familiar formula, of urban and masculine angst is inescapable: Rankin's Edinburgh detective is the most recent example of the figure to be adapted for television in the eponymous *Rebus* (Scottish Television, 2000). Nevertheless, other writers have attempted a rather different approach to the same set of identities most popularly in John Byrne's ironical deconstructions of Scottish popular culture *Tutti Frutti* and *Your Cheatin' Heart* (BBC, 1990), in Ian Pattison's raucous and satirical *Rab C. Nesbitt* (BBC, 1989–99), and in the more recent comedy sketch show *Chewin' the Fat* (BBC, from 1999), with a team of writers that includes the show's lead performers Greg Hemphill, Ford Kiernan and Karen Dunbar.

Set in Glasgow *Taggart*'s iconography of bleak cityscapes and decaying heavy industries and its traditional *dramatis personae* of hard men and long-suffering women was seen as quintessential of Clydeside Scotland. Yet it is a text that has evolved in a number of ways in the years since its first broadcast. Most obviously the narrative focus of the series changed following the death of Mark McManus, the actor who played the eponymous Jim Taggart. The resulting changes, which included killing off the fictional character but retaining the strong branding of the series' title, shifted the tone and the narrative tension of the piece.[7] The series drew increasingly less on the semiotic and narrative codes of Clydeside Scotland and the legacy of the urban hard man, attempting to modernise its topographical and gender representations. The central dynamic is now between a male and female detective, both clearly middle class, with a supporting pairing of a younger gay policeman and the more stereotypical macho bend-the-rules type of cop. The series continues to be concerned with the play and representation of masculinity but the potential identities available here are much more diverse. These shifts in the available gender tropes parallel and are matched by a revisioning of the city itself: indeed it has been argued that 'many storylines have exposed divisions between those living in the affluent "new" Glasgow and those whose material lives remain untouched by the city's vaunted transformation' (Sillars, 1999: 250). This resetting and expansion of the dramatic potential of Glasgow seems likely to be sustained in two forthcoming series – *Tinsel Town* and Stephen Greenhorn's *Glasgow Kiss* (both BBC, 2000) – in which the city continues to reinvent itself as modern, post-industrial, European, media-savvy and hip. In pointed contrast to the limiting and narrow versions of the city and its people that is sustained by the urban kailyard, we might detect in recent television drama a greater variety of potential Glasgows. Ironically, and simultaneously, douce Edinburgh – a surprisingly less frequent setting for drama than is Glasgow – is recast in a rather different direction with the crime-filled and violent world of *Rebus* imaging the Scottish capital in its televisually unfamiliar guise of 'no mean city'.

In all these debates about place, and indeed about gender, Byrne's *Tutti Frutti* remains a useful reference point for television's reimagining of

Scotland in both topographical and narrative terms. *Tutti Frutti* is a series which raises many problems and questions related to script, production context, use of music, nostalgia and Scottishness, constituting as it does a sustained investigation of many of the conventions of Scottish identity. In a text that presents a wide repertoire of Scottish masculinities, Vincent Diver, the self-styled 'Iron Man of Scottish rock', is the most stridently and conventionally masculine, seen wearing leathers, striking an aggressive pose of seemingly assured virility and power – he is a rock-and-roll parody of the urban hard man. Vincent maintains a disintegrating and barren relationship with his wife, Noreen, and an unequal sexual relationship with the infatuated Glenna. Ultimately, however, Noreen's angry revelations of Vincent's sexual impotence exposes the delusive nature of the myth and iconography of the hard man as played out within Scottish culture, and affirms the structural role of the woman in the translation and decon-struction of the signs of masculinity.

I have argued elsewhere that one of the key narrative concerns of the series is the nature and the politics of belonging, definitions and engage-ments with the theme of family, masculinity, the new boy and rites of initiation (Scullion, 1995).

Sillars agrees that the series is about gender but also highlights its active deployment of humour. From *Whisky Galore* (1949) to Stephen Greenhorn's so-called 'road movie for the stage' *Passing Places* (1997), the self-reflexive negotiations of whimsy have been a significant trope in Scottish drama of all kinds: 'In their stories of capable women and inept men and their parodic deployment of traditional notions of class and iden-tity [... the whimsical demonstrates] how dominant models are open to reworking and re-creation' (Sillars, 1999: 250); and all these elements thread through and shape *Tutti Frutti*.

However, one of the other key concerns of the series is its exploration and depiction of topographic Scotland. The series of six one-hour episodes is structured around the twenty-fifth anniversary tour of the fading Glas-gow rock group, The Majestics. The six-week tour meanders across the country, with the band playing gigs in the smallest of venues, in miners' welfare halls and second-rate night clubs, in Shotts, Methil, Ardrossan, Buckie and Aberdeen, the tour culminating in a grand event at Glasgow's Pavilion Theatre, a venue with strong associations with popular and even working-class Scottish entertainment.

For this series 'Scotland' is imaged as a source of narrative tension (being played out in the opposition of the urban and the rural) and as the heightened landscape of The Majestics' near-mythic progression. The urban Scots of *Tutti Frutti* are utterly out of place in the world of small-town and rural Scotland that the tour encompasses. In narrative terms the spaces of Scotland are either 'Glasgow' or 'not Glasgow', and no matter where the band might be if it is 'not Glasgow' they are exposed and vul-nerable and lost. In visual terms, however, topographical Scotland is presented in significant diversity (that is visually the rest of Scotland is much more than the 'not Glasgow' space that the narrative depends upon). The tour covers a huge variety of Scottish landscapes – the streets and tenements of Glasgow are there but so too are the straight empty roads cutting through the green flat lands, the small towns surrounded by pit bings, the distinctive architectures of west coast harbours, and the exposed fishing towns of the north-east. This 'other' Scotland is framed as a strange frontier land, an alien and (outwith the concerts themselves) a near-deserted place – a running joke in the series is that each of the tiny hotels and guest houses in which the group stays is deserted, staff are always missing or just out of ear shot. When they do encounter the indigenous population they are, at least to the urbanites' view, either mild eccentrics (such as Lachie the Radio Buckie DJ) or utterly deranged psychotics (for example, the blonde woman who stabs Vincent in Buckie and the owners of the Ardrossan Paradise Club who threaten to 'knee-cap' the band). Rural and small-town Scotland is cast as an unknown and dangerous place where violence happens frequently and unpredictably and grotesquely. In contrast Glasgow is a much more domesticated place, it is a place of heritage and of nostalgia, of shared memory and of familiarity.

Tutti Frutti was the subject of both popular and critical interest because it was, in the late 1980s, and with the notable exception of *Taggart*, one of the very few Scottish-produced drama series to secure a high-profile network screening. Since then there has developed a healthy diversity in production. Attempts at populist networked programming including *The Justice Game* (BBC, 1989–90), *The Advocates* (Scottish, 1992–93), *Strathblair* (BBC, 1992–93), *Dr Finlay* (Scottish, 1993–96), *The Tales of Para Handy* (BBC, 1994–95) and, of course, the continuing *High Road* (Scottish, from 1980) have won varied degrees of success. These genre pieces – detective shows, legal dramas, nostalgic rural escapes – complemented a more distinctive raft of writer-led projects. In this category original series such as Jed Mercurio's *Cardiac Arrest* (BBC, 1994–96), Donna Franceschild's *Takin' Over the Asylum* (BBC, 1994) and *A Mug's Game* (BBC, 1996), and Frank Deasy's *Looking after JoJo* (BBC, 1997), as well as series based on adaptations like *Hamish Macbeth* (BBC, 1995–97), Daniel Boyle's reworking of the novels of M. C. Beaton, and *The Crow Road* (BBC, 1996), Brian Elsley's adaptation of Iain Banks's novel, and single dramas such as David Kane's *Ruffian Hearts* (BBC, 1995) and Rona Munro's *Bumping the Odds* (BBC, 1997) have continued to expand the representations of Scots and Scotland, at their best testing identity and challenging convention.

In contrast to this critical and even ironic dynamic, the first major Scottish television drama production after devolution seemed to offer an unexpectedly dated not to say sanguine, and in Beveridge and Turnbull's term 'inferiorist', version of the nation (see Beveridge and Turnbull, 1997: 4–15). It is not that post-devolution drama in Scotland should only be about devolution, or about politics, or even about representation, but it was surprising that Michael Chaplin's *Monarch of the Glen* (BBC, 2000) was so little concerned with contextualising or understanding its historical moment or in challenging the preferred images and identities of Scotland. Instead it was a series that constructed Scotland for export purposes and for the international broadcast market-place: wonderful scenery, grand houses, well-known lead performers and couthy story-lines. The series is based on work by Compton Mackenzie. It is, however, more directly influenced by *Ballykissangel* (BBC, from 1996), an idealised depiction of Irish rural life, whose prime-time Sunday evening slot it filled. Set in an equally picturesque imaginary Celtic idyll, the fictional estate of Glenbogle is similarly peopled by broadly drawn stereotypes and quirkily named 'characters' (including, in the former category, the eccentric laird Hector Macdonald and, in the latter, Golly the gamekeeper). *Monarch of the Glen* imagined Scotland in a classic binary opposition with England, presenting Scotland as a beautiful and mythic space, peopled by the fey, the eccentric, the romantic: in a comment that, at the very least, drew connotations with the mythology of Brigadoon, the writer claimed 'There is a charming innocence to it. Viewers will like to visit Glenbogle because it's a place where bad things don't happen. It's a magical place that many will see as paradise.'[8]

Despite the various representations and thematic concerns developed within Scottish culture as being dominated by a mythology of the urban and of masculinity there is a further tendency, particularly prevalent within film, for rural Scotland not to engender the negative psychosis associated with the urban experience but to be magically transformative and psychologically healing. This is quintessentially so in *Brigadoon, The Maggie* (both 1954) and *Local Hero* (1983). In these texts the physical experience of being in Scotland and, of course, being connected with a woman who functions as the personification of Scotland, returns urban man to his contented, complete and natural self.[9] *Monarch of the Glen* eagerly replayed this familiar narrative of the crisis of the urban man in tandem with the equally familiar narrative of the return of the native. (See Derek Wall's discussion of green activist identity on British television for a similar questioning of the values of modernism and materialism.)

The series sees the laird's anglicised son Archie leave London to return to his family's failing Highland estate. There two very different women, two very different versions of the nation, offer themselves: on the one hand is Lexie, the unpredictable and exuberant free spirit of fey and physical Scotland; on the other, Katrina the good woman of rational and democratic Scotland who is both a schoolteacher and, in the course of the series, elected as a local councillor. These figures are framed by the main narrative obstacle to Archie's successful reidentification as 'Scottish', Justine, his English lover. The series' play of national identities is told in a narrative of romantic intrigue, because at root the drama is not about which woman Archie will choose but which national identity.

Justine is set in linguistic, physical and narrative opposition to the Scottish women. Where Katrina wears muted colours and soft fabrics, Justine wears monochromatic tailored clothes. Where Katrina's ambition to be elected a local councillor is couched in a discourse of public service and a desire to overturn the feudal structures of the estate, Justine's ambition is financially and socially motivated. Justine is similarly contrasted to Lexie: whereas Lexie is exuberant and bold, Justine is retrained, measured and even calculating. At the climax of the first series Archie has resisted the advances of Lexie, who (for reasons of class and education as much as narrative tension) has been removed as a potential sexual partner and recast as merely a friend and confidante, just another of the local eccentrics. He seems about to commit to Katrina when, in the context of an elaborate firework show, Justine arrives on the estate as a kind of *deus ex machina* declaring not just love for Archie but also commitment to life with him in Scotland. In narrative terms the scene acts as a cliff-hanger for a second series but it also reaffirms the binary opposition Katrina and Justine, of the Scottish woman and the English woman, of Scotland and of England.

Although a popular success (it received an early recommission with a new series being filmed in summer 2000) the narrative and the cast of characters of *Monarch of the Glen* were far less challenging of traditional conceptions of Scotland and Scottish identity than was the slightly earlier *Hamish Macbeth*. This series undertook a much less predictable investigation of place and popular culture, and successfully (and pleasurably) acknowledged the economic realities of life in isolated and rural Scotland and the fey and the whimsical aspects of Scotland's media identities with the self-deprecating reflexivity that also marks *Tutti Frutti* or *Rab C. Nesbitt* as witty interpretations of the identities of Scotland. However, despite the ironic version of the rural that might be seen in *Hamish Macbeth* or *Tutti Frutti*, despite the satirical version of urban Scotland that marks *Rab C. Nesbitt*, despite the somewhat surreal irony behind the repertoire of Scottish pop-cult characters in *Chewin' the Fat*, the depiction of Scotland as escapist Highland idyll or as a city in crisis remains at the heart of television's predictable readings of the nation. As Sillars neatly concludes in her examination of television drama and devolution:

> While *Hamish Macbeth* [like *Tutti Frutti*, *Rab C. Nesbitt* and *Chewin' the Fat*] wittily demonstrates how Scottish-produced drama can play with dominant imagery in often creative and challenging ways it does not address the questions of whether indigenous production can begin to move beyond these discourses; how it might engage with the politics of a changing cultural identity; and how these changes might be represented to a wider audience. (Sillars, 1999: 251–2)

Conclusion

> Devolution does not mean a parochial Scotland. It does not mean a return
> to the kailyard. Inwardness is not the Scottish experience of the past. It is
> not the Scotland I know. It will not be the future.
>
> From the speech of Donald Dewar at the 'Ireland and Scotland:
> Nation, Region, Identity' conference in Dublin, 29 September 2000

In the context of a society rediscovering itself through a new democracy, a rigorous review and reappraisal of the conceptions and images of Scottish identity is surely necessary. Just as it seems important that current affairs and news producers reconsider what broadcasting Holyrood might mean, so writers and drama producers might also have to respond to the implicit challenge of devolution by adopting a renewed dramaturgy, perhaps predicated upon reassessing and recreating the existing cultural codes and conventions, exposing the emotional uncertainties beneath totemic structures but certainly, and most importantly, taking knowing responsibility for the nature and the effects of our own culture, rather than falling back on preferred and predictable representations and narratives.

While one might argue that some Scottish media and art forms have anticipated and responded to our new legislative context with clarity and purpose, one is yet to see evidence that the makers of Scottish television have seen devolution as the radical intervention that it certainly is. One might convincingly argue that Scottish novelists, theatre-makers and film-makers – for example, A. L. Kennedy, Des Dillon and Chris Dolan, David Harrower and David Greig, Lynne Ramsay and Peter Mullan – have aimed to meet these implicit challenges, and have done so by being *both* international and outward looking *and* essentially and immediately committed to work within and about Scottish society; and it is certainly the case that it is political devolution and the creation of the new Scottish Parliament that insists that these two dynamics can no longer be interpreted as mutually exclusive. In the diversity of new Scottish novels, plays and films such as Kennedy's *Everything you Need*, Dillon's *Itchycooblue* and Dolan's *Ascension Day* (all 1999), Harrower's *Knives in Hens* (1995) and *Kill the Old, Torture their Young* (1998), Greig's *The Cosmonaut's Last Message to the Woman he Once Loved in the Former Soviet Union* and *The Speculator* (both 1999), Mullan's *Orphans* (1997) and Ramsay's *Ratcatcher* (1999), we see artists challenge expectation, orthodoxy and, above all, themselves. None of these texts is overtly about devolution. None is simplistically about representation nor indeed identity. Instead, all allow the fantastical and the imaginary and the mythic to coexist with the prosaic and the tangible and the documentary: the very same mapping of Scottish national identity that one sees in Dewar's treatise on Scottish national identity.

In the ambition of the new Parliament and in the work of some of our leading artists we might see that a central motif of contemporary Scottish culture is critical awareness and questioning, openness and outward-looking, fantastical imagining and critical rigour. Broadcasters have yet to demonstrate an engagement with these critical and reflective discourses, have yet truly to engage with the radical potential of devolution, have yet to respond to the ambition of Dewar's heightened and poetical vision of contemporary Scotland.

Notes

1. In referring to the 'speak of the Mearns', Dewar is acknowledging the diversity of dialects and languages in Scotland and, in particular, the distinctive Scots of the Mearns, the area Kincardineshire on the east coast of Scotland around Stonehaven. It is a language of a rural community, also connoting a marginalised and dwindling culture.
   MSP is the abbreviation for Member of the Scottish Parliament.
2. See Cairns Craig, 'Myths against history: tartanry and kailyard in nineteenth-century Scottish literature', in Colin McArthur, ed., *Scotch Reels: Scotland in Cinema and Television*. London, 1982, pp. 7–15; and, David McCrone, *Understanding Scotland: the Sociology of a Stateless Nation*. London: Routledge, 1992.
3. See, for example, McCrone, *Understanding Scotland*; Craig Beveridge and Ronald Turnbull, *The Eclipse of Scottish Culture: Inferiorism and the Intellectuals*. Edinburgh, Polygon, 1989; and, Tom Nairn, *The Break-Up of Britain: Crisis and Neo-Nationalism* 2nd edn. London, 1981.
4. From *The Scotland Act: Chapter 46*. London, 1998. In addition the full text of the Act is also accessible at <http://www.hmso.gov.uk/acts/acts1998/19980046.htm>.
5. In the Scottish parliamentary elections each elector casts two votes, one for a constituency MSP and one for the party of their choice. (In fact on election day 1999 electors cast three votes: the two described above to elect representatives to the parliament; and a further one in a traditional first-past-the-post ballot to elect representatives to local councils.) Seventy-three of the total 129 members are elected from constituencies on a traditional first-past-the-post electoral system: and these constituencies are the same as the seventy-two Scottish constituencies represented at Westminster, with the exception that Orkney and Shetland are divided, each electing its own MSP. Thereafter fifty-six additional members are selected on a proportional basis from party 'lists' drawn up for each of the current eight European Parliament constituencies. Each of these electoral regions returns seven MSPs through this 'Additional Member System'.
6. On the evening before the election the BBC ran a vox-pop news feature. A camera was set up in a Glasgow taxi and the driver quizzed his passengers on their knowledge of the election procedures – how many votes did they have, what colour was each of the ballot papers, how did the 'list' work? The set up was intriguing – colluding in a series of myths about class, accent, social awareness, devolved politics, and taxi drivers. Those conversations broadcast in the package suggested that the level of ignorance about election procedures was significant. But perhaps more problematically, the jokey sequence was not followed by an explanation of system but by a debate about the success or failure of the Scottish Office's campaign to raise awareness about the election. Whilst this was certainly a valid debate to have the evidence of the vox pop surely suggested that a public-service broadcaster might just have had an additional role of explanation and clarification.
7. In passing, the death of the Taggart figure also excluded the character of Taggart's wife who, as a wheelchair user, was one of the few physically disabled characters to appear in a prime-time networked drama.
8. Michael Chaplin quoted in publicity material generated by BBC Scotland, Ecosse Films and Newtonmore tourist office. See <http://www.newtonmore.com/monarch/m1.htm>.

In passing, one might speculate to what extent *Castaway* (BBC, 2000) – which places a community of thirty-six volunteers on Taransay, a small and remote island in the outer Hebrides for a year – might allow the resetting of the rural experience of Scotland within the rather unexpected discourse of reality.

9. These images and representations are debated in Colin McArthur's classic anthology *Scotch Reels* and revisited in his essays 'The Scottish discursive unconscious', in *Scottish Popular Theatre and Entertainment* eds, Cameron, A. and Scullion, A. Glasgow, 1996, pp. 81–9. He also notes that aspects of the rural identities of Scotland parallel popular culture's use of Ireland and the Irish in his essay 'The cultural necessity of poor Irish cinema', in *Border Crossing: Film in Ireland, Britain and Europe*, eds, Hill, J., McLoone, M., and Hainsworth, P. London, 1994, pp. 112–25.

CHAPTER 5

STORM CLOUDS OF THE MILLENNIUM

REGIONAL TELEVISION NEWS IN AQUITAINE AND THE WEST OF ENGLAND[1]

Michael Scriven and Emily Roberts

The end of the second millennium has witnessed a far-reaching debate on the future of national identity within Europe. National identity is challenged from within by increasing demands for regional autonomy and the representation of minority groups. It also faces the growing sphere of influence of the European Union, and the growth of the global marketplace. These developments encroach upon the political, cultural and economic prescriptions that constitute an integral part of the group identity that national institutions, along with hegemonic forces, have chosen for the nation. In the context of France and Britain, this has been reflected in a concern for the future of national terrestrial television, given the clarion call for regional television, and the culturally globalising and localising potential of digital television.

With the above debate in mind, this chapter explores the regional television of Aquitaine, France and the West of England at the end of the twentieth century. It begins with a brief background to the policy adopted towards regional and local television by the BBC, ITV, FR3 and M6, and assesses how this is reflected in the regional television policies of BBC West, HTV West, FR3 Aquitaine and M6 Bordeaux.[2] It then progresses to a consideration of the depiction of the millennium celebrations on the regional news of Aquitaine and the west of England between November 1999 and January 2000. It will be argued that the organisation of the millennium celebrations reflects the subordinate relationship of the regions to the nations; a fact that is mirrored in the relationship between regional and national television. Regional television is shown to be trapped in a double bind. On the one hand, it tries to bolster an institutionally approved notion of regional identity, firmly placed within a national context. On the other hand, a pivotal aspect of its public service brief is to reflect the views of the regional community, that resents the formal signifiers of regional pride foisted upon them over the millennial period. The consideration of millennium celebrations on regional television highlights the similarities between the status of regional television and the regional celebrations, which are both in a subordinate, mimetic and dependent relationship to their national counterparts.

National Policy, Regional Television, Aquitaine and the West of England

The move towards increased regional representation on national terrestrial channels has been a significant development in televisual policy in both Great Britain and France over the past few decades (see Sergeant, chapter 2). 'Télévision de proximité' (grass-roots television) has become a buzz word in France and a guiding principle in Britain, as television channels respond to the challenges of digital technology. Desktop digital editing allows for cheaply produced regional and local television. At the same time, however, advances in digital technology make more frequencies available for private regional and local channels. The growing recognition of regional identity has also given impetus to the drive for regional television, although this is tempered in both France and (less openly) in Britain by a fear of national fragmentation. Regional opt-out slots in the programming schedules of the BBC, ITV, FR3 and M6 are oases of regional representation within the dominating framework of national television.

FR3 Aquitaine, a regional subsidiary of the national FR3 channel, covers Périgourd, Les Landes, La Gironde, Dordogne and Les Pyrénées Atlantiques. It caters to a rural as well as an urban audience, and encompasses part of the Basque country. The Basque news service, *Euskal Herri*, established in 1992, is based in Bayonne. The six-minute daily Basque news programme is classified as local television by FR3, rather than as a national regional or even a regional service. It is conceived as 'the mirror of a geographic entity, and proposes to restore the role of this territory within a regional and transfrontier environment'.[3] It is significant that the word nation is never used; the tricky issue of Basque separatism is therefore avoided. Perhaps it is the fear of a transfrontier regional nation, not encompassed within the French nation, that is behind the demotion of Basque television to the status of local television.

FR3 Aquitaine claims that the Basque news programme has been a success, Euskal Herri attracting 70 percent of the available market, with 80 percent of the television audience being aware of its presence on the programming schedule. Basque affairs are also addressed within the regional Aquitaine news, although there is a decided emphasis upon the violent activities of the ETA Basque separatists, in protest against the French and Spanish governments' refusal to grant them independence as a nation. This is often dealt with in a censorious way, although occasionally dubbed interviews with masked ETA members have appeared in regional news (e.g., FR3 Aquitaine, March 1999).

In contrast to the somewhat limited approach to Basque representation adopted by FR3, M6 makes no attempt to cater to a specifically Basque audience. It keeps to its policy of providing 'télévision de proximité' for local urban audiences, rather than more diverse regional or national regional audiences. As it does not receive state funding to underpin its regional service brief, as is the case with FR3, M6 is more preoccupied with achieving good televisual audience figures that will enhance its ability to attract advertising revenue. According to its 1998 figures, its local news approach has proved popular, with 2,230 million watching the local news programmes across the nation.

The reception area of M6 Bordeaux is limited to Bordeaux and its surrounding area, encompassing Libourne and Arcachon; and the M6 Bordeaux local news broadcasts attracted an audience of 200,000 in 1998. FR3 Aquitaine has come to mimic the six-minute local news formula, providing a six-minute programme devoted to Bordeaux – broadcast at the same time as Euskal Herri in the Basque country – immediately before the FR3 Aquitaine half-hour regional news.

ITV prides itself on the innovative regional structure that it has enjoyed from its inception. Like M6, it is a privately funded company, and it is therefore aware of the importance of attracting a viable audience that will appeal to advertisers. Unlike M6, however, it has chosen to offer a regional service that reflects its federal regional structure, rather than adopting the local urban centre representation approach. HTV West nonetheless emphasises its intention to engage with the regional community at a grass-roots level, with charity work and programmes such as Crime Stoppers. The artificiality of representing a region in all its diversity is unwittingly signalled by HTV West's own description of its role: 'HTV West is the only thing that links Gloucester to Swindon to Bristol to Taunton'.

The BBC highlights its public service brief, serving the nation through both its national and its regional services. It sets its sights upon establishing a clear identity that distinguishes it from its competitors, that will also win it loyal viewers. Part of this initiative is to answer the viewer's demand for programmes that reflect their grass- roots experience, without focusing overmuch on the main cities.[4] The need for BBC Regional Broadcasting to respond to a changing sense of regional identity was highlighted by the process of devolution in Scotland and Wales, as the BBC *Annual Report and Accounts 1996–1997* acknowledged.

The BBC West regional news service, like that of FR3 Aquitaine and HTV West, aims to represent the region as a whole, rather than a localised urban environment. BBC West and HTV West do not have to contend with an internal national region, although they serve a diverse audience that encompasses both urban and rural communities, and counties and cities with a strong sense of their own specific identity.

The regional news follows the prototype of the national news, even in the case of M6 Bordeaux. A new format has not been devised to reflect the different needs of regional television; perhaps an indication of regional television's lack of confidence and self-perception as a poor relation of national television.

The practice of opt-out slots for regional television makes the distinction between regional and national television nebulous, in terms of a perceived distinction by the audience (Trelluyer, 1990). Despite the renewed interest in regional television, it is still placed very much within a national framework, both in France and Britain.

The state channels of FR3 and the BBC regard regional representation as an integral aspect of their national public service brief. They serve the nation through the regions. Both private terrestrial channels have significant opt-out slots earmarked for regional and local news services. ITV, the BBC and FR3 extend their regional service to encompass current affairs documentaries and fictional and children's programme productions. In contrast to ITV's commitment to the principle of regional television, M6 espouses local television as a popular and therefore profitable offshoot. One significant difference between Britain and France can be seen in the representation of 'national regions' in France, and the nations of Wales and Scotland within Great Britain. Terrestrial television in Wales and Scotland – both state and privately funded – gives a fuller representation of the nations, although the nationally produced programmes are still set within the framework of British national television (see chapters by Scullion and Williams). Even this limited service and the arguably derogatory practice of continuing to refer to a newly devolved nation as a 'national region' contrasts favourably with the terrestrial regional television service available to the French national regions of the Basque country and Brittany, for example, that only receive a six-minute daily broadcast in their own language.

All of the channels, both state and privately funded, are exploring the possibilities of grass-roots television. This type of broadcasting engages with the local community and represents their own experience. This approach can be regarded as a safe option, insofar as it bypasses the dilemma of the dual role of representing internal diversity while simultaneously promoting national unity. Reflecting individual experience that can stand for both regional interests and the interests of the common man or woman, does not jar with the brief of maintaining the domination of the nation as a locus of group identity.

The dual role of encouraging a sense of regional identity and pride, while simultaneously observing the subordinate status of the region in relation to the nation, is the central dilemma of regional television. The millennium celebrations in Britain and France, celebrated regionally within a national context, both reflect and demonstrate this dilemma. The representation of these celebrations, with their emphasis on pageantry, monument construction and the reassertion or invention of tradition, reflects time-honoured practices used by the nation-state to create a focal point for national unity in the shape of national pride. The regional celebrations follow this same pattern. The coverage of the millennium on the regional news of Aquitaine and the West of England reveals how the channels seek to fulfil their ambivalent role as both instruments of national consciousness, fostering regional self-awareness within the clear framework of the nation-state, and mouthpieces for regional communities.

National Millennium Celebrations

The advent of the new millennium captured the imagination of the media across the world. It assumed the status of a deeply symbolic event that could be used to embody national and regional identity. Its focus on prestige projects, pomp and pageantry did not engender a mass outpouring of regional and national pride, perhaps a reflection of the popular cynicism surrounding the artificiality of this artificially constructed focal point of group identity. In contrast to the boundless enthusiasm and optimism of the millennium initiatives and projects, the popular reception of celebrations surrounding the millennium and its innate and acquired symbolism was often shot through with an underlying pessimism, symptomatic of a generalised and public millennial disillusionment.

In his speech unveiling the 'Millennium Experience' in 1997, hinging on the construction of the Millennium Dome in Greenwich, Peter Mandelson underlined the importance of Greenwich as the 'home of time'. 'That', he said, 'is why the rest of the world will be looking to Britain – the new millennium will literally start here. It is a chance for Britain to make a big statement about itself and the rest of the world.'[5] The 'Millennium Experience' therefore functioned as an exercise in the expression of national identity, a record of contemporary Britain at the turn of the millennium, and a public relations exercise, intended to impress other nations.

The Millennium Commission, which was set up to coordinate the millennium projects and celebrations across Britain, described its role primarily in terms of the promotion of the self-expression of British communities. It complemented its funding of prestige projects – designed to enhance the cultural, technological or aesthetic profile and employment prospects at a local, regional and national level – with the encouragement of a vast array of community activities and initiatives. Finally, it helped to coordinate celebrations on 31 December 1999 itself.

France began its millennium preparations later than Britain, choosing to favour 'a wide variety of events that are dispersed all over the country. In this way, it is possible to avoid heavy budgets on a "universal exposition" scale'.[6] 'Mission 2000', which worked under the authority of the French Ministry of Culture and Communication, emphasised the preparations for the festivities on the night. Cultural events, rather than prestige projects, were favoured. This contrast between the two nations is a reflection of the financial constraints upon the celebrations in France,[7] and the fact that Britain enjoyed a windfall from the profits of the National Lottery, established in 1994, a proportion of the proceeds of which were earmarked for the millennium celebrations.

The French celebration was designed to provide both a reflection of the past and visions of the future. Mission 2000 claimed to promote the exploration of 'ways in which the beginning of the new millennium should be lived'.[8] Two major initiatives deserve mention; the planting of a 'line of trees representing the Parisian Meridian', and the 'Gates of the Year 2000'.[9] The representation of the Parisian Meridian recalled France's glorious and influential past in the international arena. It was the site of a mass picnic across France on Bastille Day. The 'gates' symbolised a 'passage into a new era', a radical departure from the old.[10] People across France were encouraged to walk symbolically under 'gates' that were either 'virtual' gateways, made with lasers or fireworks, specially created gateways, or city gates already in existence.[11] The linking of the crossing of the threshold into a new future, the commemoration of the foundation of the Republic, and France's glory days as an international player suggest that the ideal of France's future would be a renaissance of its past. This would signal a new era in France's position on the world stage, although its Republican values would remain intact.

The national preparations for the millennium can be regarded in a number of ways. They were designed to promote events and celebrations which represent the cultural vitality and diversity of the nations; that is, to put forward a positive vision of their national identity both in its entirety and in terms of its constituent parts. They were an outward reflection of the nation-state's perception of its own identity and prestige, designed for consumption overseas as well as internally. In Britain, the approach of the new millennium inspired the construction of prestigious monuments designed to represent Britain's current wealth and success. The promotion of the millennium was designed to enhance community networks, operative at a regional, as well as national, level. Local and regional celebrations, however, are placed firmly within a national context. They are clearly inspired by the structure of traditional celebrations of national pride.

Regional Television and the Millennium Celebrations

The use of the past in the representation of localised territorial identity is abundantly in evidence in the regional news millennium coverage examined. The coverage focuses on the re-enactment of traditions, and the renovation of long-standing architectural heritage, often Christian in nature, in both the French and the British context. The regional news therefore serves to bolster the institutionalised understanding of territorial identity being rooted in a shared pride in heritage.

Church bells are also linked to the millennium, with bells in a Wiltshire village as well as Bayonne in Aquitaine being renovated specifically so that they could ring in the New Year (HTV West, 23 December 1999; FR3 Aquitaine, 21 December 1999). The HTV West coverage of the Wiltshire village observes that this renovation was 'bringing village tradition back to life', with the churchwarden commenting that this is 'surely a good omen for the start of the third millennium' (HTV West, 23 December 1999). The church renovations symbolise the resurrection of a traditional, church-based way of life. They are associated with the resuscitation of rural life and by extension identity, something to be desired in the third millennium. There is a clear implication that these values have fallen into relative disuse in recent times. It is worth noting that these values are not covered in the M6 Bordeaux broadcasts, which focus exclusively on urban, rather than rural, identity. It can be surmised that more cosmopolitan urban identity does not need to have recourse to the social codes of the past.

As well as renewing traditions, the Year 2000 is also marked by a new spin on traditions. December 1999 witnessed the exceptional alteration to the centuries-old tradition of presenting the Queen with a 'Holy Thorn' from Glastonbury Abbey, to adorn her table. In an unprecedented move, the 'Thorn' was delivered personally by a Somerset schoolboy, to 'mark the millennium' (HTV West, 15 December 1999; BBC West, 15 December 1999). The regional televising of this event firmly links the region to the church, the monarchy, and, through the personal delivery of the Holy Thorn to Buckingham Palace, the nation's capital, London. This regional tradition is therefore placed firmly within the context of nation as a whole.

The two thousandth anniversary of the birth of Christ also inspired a more overt connection between Christianity and the millennium celebrations, in the shape of a large-scale Christian celebration, planning for the year 2000, which received £30,000 of national millennium money. In an interview, the Bishop of Tewkesbury states that the celebration would see different denominations of the Christian church coming together across divisions. The event would be 'one of the largest millennium events in the region' (HTV West, 20 December 1999). Apart from providing an opportunity for the renewal of interest in Christianity, the millennium appears to be an occasion for those associated with a sense of community and solidarity that overwhelms difference.

The link between regional heritage and the Church is further indicated by the choice of a Saxon church as the venue of a project recreating Wessex as it was one thousand years ago (HTV West, 22 December 1999). Interactive computer displays were employed to bring heritage to a technologically aware generation, thereby bringing together the past and the contemporary world. The voice-over comments that the Saxons paid little attention to the advent of the new millennium, and expresses the hope that 'this will not be the case this time'. In this respect, the broadcast is actively soliciting the viewers to get involved in the celebration, and to differentiate between themselves and their less sophisticated and communitarian forebears.

Pre-existing monuments to past glory were also revamped as part of the millennium celebrations. M6 Bordeaux focuses on the incorporation of Bordeaux's prestigious architecture into the celebrations. One of the 'gates' in Bordeaux was renovated in anticipation of its role in the 31 December festivities (M6 Bordeaux, 23 December 1999). This ties in with a national initiative, situating the local celebrations very much within the framework of national celebrations. The illumination of Bordeaux's *Grand Théâtre*, previously known as the *Opéra*, is a less ambivalent symbol of the region itself (M6 Bordeaux, 20 December 1999). In the West of England, there was a renewed attention to the region's maritime and trade heritage, with a campaign to renovate a dredger (BBC West, 22 December 1999), and to preserve the Lydney docks (BBC West, 13 January 2000). The region's nautical trading past, centred around Bristol, is being salvaged as a source of pride in its distinct identity.

Regional television depicts the way in which cultural heritage, in its varied forms, was brought alive at the time of this symbolic intersection of the 'end' of one era and the 'beginning' of another. It reflects the drive, initiated by both national and local authorities, to prove that the past was not suddenly rendered redundant by the advent of a new millennium. Regional identity sought legitimacy through its foundations in a proud and noble history. As Hobsbawm comments, these traditions 'are responses to novel situations which take the form of reference to old situations, or which establish their own past by quasi-obligatory repetition' (Hobsbawm and Ranger, 1992: 2). The televisual reminder of these traditions and heritage at the symbolic moment of the millennium demonstrates a deeply conservative desire to emphasise a continuity with what Hobsbawm, in his discussion of invented traditions, would term 'a suitable historic past' (Hobsbawm and Ranger, 1992: 1).

This emphasis on the continuing relevance of the past is coupled with the coverage of the activities of the young to commemorate the millennium. A sustained focus on the youth of the region is designed to represent idealism, hope for the future, and the continuity of the community into the future. On 21 December 1999, FR3 Aquitaine covered schoolchildren filling a time capsule with objects which best represented their lives, 'bearing witness in an instantaneous form to the end of this century for the children of the next century'. The children, who stood for the future, buried an unchangeable, immutable testament to the present for future generations. The spirit of the moment was enshrined in a different way in Tetbury in the West of England, in the shape of commemorative 'millennium' medallions depicting famous landmarks. The money raised was earmarked for the maintenance of historic buildings and the provision of private educational grants for children (HTV West, 21 December 1999). Although these medallions were designed to mark the importance of the moment of the millennium as a moment in time, they impacted upon the future, ensuring private education for gifted youngsters. They also hark back to the past, through the depiction of landmarks, and the decision to use a part of the proceeds to maintain historic buildings in the town. The marking of the present was therefore contextualised in terms of the past and the need for continuity into the future.

On 10 January 2000, both HTV and BBC West ran an item on a performance by Bath youngsters, entitled 'Our Town Story', which was to be performed at the Millennium Dome. The BBC West reporter covering the events rounded up the story by proclaiming that 'all these performers know they will be flying the flag for the West Country' (BBC West, 10 January 2000). The 'pageant' of events and celebrations surrounding the millennium is designed to project an image beyond the region, as well as to bolster the region's self-perception and sense of identity at the turn of the twentieth century. The age of the performers serves to emphasise the youthful vibrancy of the region.

The eve of 31 December itself was the subject of organised celebrations all over the world. In France, this moment was often referred to as 'the passage to the year 2000'. This term embodies a moment of transition and also suggests the notion of a rite of passage to be shared by a community. This sense of a movement towards a new, distinct age is combined with an acknowledgement of the past, as well as contemporary difficulties, in the special eight-minute local news bulletin dedicated to the New Year's Eve celebrations, broadcast on 1 January 2000 by M6 Bordeaux.

The programme begins with a peaceful image of the Garonne and a stately bridge, in 'the first morning of the year of our Lord 2000 on the banks of the Garonne, where New Year celebrations took place yesterday'. Footage of the popular celebrations in Bordeaux is also provided, centring on the Place de la Bourse. The programme continues in the vein of complete novelty and contemporaneity with an item on the first baby to be born in the region in the year 2000. A following item, however, shows an elderly couple celebrating at home despite being deprived of a power supply by storm damage. This represents the current difficult situation faced in Gironde. The old couple link the present to the past as they draw parallels between their present experience and their memories of the Second World War. The final item addresses the significance of the millennium, in terms of the conceptualisation of the future: 'Now that the threshold of the Year 2000 has been crossed, we must seek out new horizons to fuel our imagination'. That is, now that the future has become the present, our expectations of change in the future must once again be moved forward. Imagining the future, it seems, is an important aspect of constituting an imagined community. Seen in this light, the millennium as an instant in time – that is 31 December 1999 – is only significant in the countdown to millennium eve as a symbol of change. Once it has occurred and continuity has been seen to triumph, it is stripped of this meaning, and a new receptacle for the concept of a new beginning must be sought.

The bulletin embodies the tension between the appeal of complete novelty and the desire for continuity and pride in past and present achievements. Its sustained focus upon individual experience at grassroots level, which can be taken to represent more universal celebrations of a common event, illustrates M6 Bordeaux's use of 'télévision de proximité'. The imagery of tranquillity, continuity, hope and stoicism is an effective propagandic promotion of an idealised local Bordelais identity that could represent almost anywhere in urban France.

BBC West also places the emphasis on the representation of individual experience of the New Year's Eve. It encouraged viewers to send in their home videos of their millennium night, retaining the News West 2000 logo at the beginning of the item that was employed throughout the build-up to the millennium. This 'proximity television' approach to the brief of regional television has been increasingly adopted as a model by regional television in France and Britain alike.[12] It conveniently resolved the ambivalence of the millennial moment as both a time to celebrate continuity, and to anticipate alteration to the existing status quo. This representation of Millennium Eve is significant in terms of what it reveals about the local community, their practices and their aspirations *at that moment*, rather than in terms of the seismic social or cultural changes it could herald. However, the insistence upon the inter-generational nature of the celebrations, and the coverage of the 'millennium promise' to forge a better future, indicate that the 'millennial moment' is never and can never be fully isolated from the temporal context of the past and future.

The 'pageantry' of the millennial moment **is** accompanied by a desire to help to shape the future in a more positive image. This is reflected in FR3 Aquitaine's decision to present a 'retro-prospective' series in the run-up to the end of 1999. Originally, the nine-part series was designed to cover nine subjects: genetically modified foods, the reduction of the hours of the working week to 35; communication technologies; the Maurice Papon scandal; the preparations for the year 2000; social reforms, medicine, and women. In the event, the full series did not run, as the severe weather eclipsed all other news from the 27 December onwards. The series examined national or global phenomena within the context of regional experience.

On 22 December, the series begins with a consideration of progress in the field of medicine. An overview of new medical equipment and medical problems in the region is provided. The following interview with a professor of neurology addresses how medical needs might change in the future. The issue of the ageing population – a national phenomenon particularly prevalent in Aquitaine – is highlighted: 'is this what the year 2000 holds?' Although the emphasis is initially on advances already made, the interview shifts attention to a vision of a future demographically different from the present.

The series continues with an examination of the impact of new communication technology on society. The item begins and ends with a universal discussion of the possibilities of the internet as a tool for communication, commerce, training and free democratic speech. The middle section gives regional examples of the global phenomenon of new technology (FR3 Aquitaine, 23 December 1999).

The third item in the series tackles the legal reforms that have been undertaken in France. This 'revolution' in the justice system embraced the election of magistrates, the end of industrial tribunals as they currently function. This would put an end to a system that has been in place for 436 years. In the coverage of a legal conference held in the region, the speaker commented that 'the magistrates of the third millennium will be more independent, and those tried will be better protected' (FR3 Aquitaine, 24 December 1999). There would, therefore, be a significant break from the 'bad old days', timed to coincide with the advent of the third millennium. Once again, a national occurrence is examined within a regional context, an approach typical of regional television.

Pessimism and Indifference: The Real Millennium Bugs

The pessimism surrounding the new millennium, as depicted on regional television, centres on the fear of novelty and change, the erosion of present mores and the loss of the past. It can be read as a popular reaction to the propagandist aspects of the millennium celebrations, as they are planned by the state and regional authorities, and depicted by the media. Notable expressions of this pessimism were the sense of anti-climax that meets the moment of transition itself, the implied failure of the celebration of the region's past to inspire, and the distrust of new technologies. An anxiety concerning the meaning of the 'millennium' underpinned the sense of anticlimax that meets the marking of the millennial moment. The regional news evening programmes in the West of England and Aquitaine addressed the failure of the celebrations of Millennium Eve to come off without a hitch. The disappointment of one Swindon family is revealed in an interview concerning the cancellation of one of the county's biggest events just over a week before New Year's Eve. (BBC West, 23 December 1999). The regional impact of the failure of the much-heralded 'l'effet deux mille' (year 2000 effect), the anticipated spending spree that would boost the economy, is indicated through interviews with the region's restaurant owners and travel agents (FR3 Aquitaine, 17 December 1999). The tendency appears to have been for celebrations to take place 'en famille', rather than, the implication is, as part of a larger, communitarian event. The non-arrival of the 'the year 2000 effect' was compounded by the severe weather.

Even before the impact of the storms was felt, the millennial period was feared as a potential source of disaster due to the possible effects of the much-hyped millennium bug. The regional television news in Aquitaine joined forces with the Nuclear power-station in Blayais to reassure the regional public concerning extra precautions in the event of a power failure. (M6 Bordeaux, 17 December 1999; FR3 Aquitaine, 17 December 1999). Ironically, it was not the millennium bug, but the storms, that resulted in a power failure that affected the plant over the New Year period. In the West of England, the regional news items addressing the issue of the millennium bug emphasised the preparations of the emergency services for Millennium Eve. Fire-fighters would be on alert, and emergency generators would be prepared and set up in regional hospitals. The regional news channels would exercise their public service brief, in terms of seeking to exorcise public fears. A French survey conducted by Mission 2000 in 1997 confirmed the assumption that technology, and by association the future, was a source of great popular concern in France in the build-up to the new millennium. It found that 'the perception of the future is uniformly negative', with technology being perceived as the potential source of 'social dehumanisation', 'ecological degradation', and some serious misjudgements on the part of medical research.[13] The same report later describes technology as being, somewhat unsurprisingly, 'notable for its absence from projects surrounding the celebrations'.[14]

Pessimism also hounded prestige projects undertaken by the Millennium Commission. The negative reception of the Millennium Dome is well documented, leading to both the Culture Secretary and Dome Minister attempting to 'distance themselves from the flagging attraction' (*Guardian*, 13 July 2000).

The controversy surrounding the worth and misfortunes of these millennium projects inspired the BBC to set up an internet discussion forum entitled 'Millennium landmarks – are they cursed?'[15] Comments ranged from a number of indictments of the London-centric nature of the millennium projects, to criticisms of the 'dumbing down' effect of the projects, to a cynical suggestion that the millennium industry was created to cover up long-term industrial and agricultural decline. One critic compared the millennium initiatives with the costly and overblown prestige monuments built during the decline of the Roman Empire: an interesting comparison, which suggests that while they are intended to express the nation's confidence in its present achievements and gleaming future, they in fact embody the nation's insecurities, and the fears surrounding its present decline and future failures.

In the West of England, an ambitious millennium project also provoked controversy. The project linked the regeneration of the harbourside (of which @t-Bristol is an aspect) with an extravagant fountain feature in the city centre. However, the fountains were closed for repairs 'a fortnight after the razamatazz' of the opening ceremonies (BBC West , 11 January 2000); this could hardly be what the council wanted for the start of the millennium, as HTV West commented in its coverage (HTV West, 11 January 2000). Regional television coverage emphasises that ironically, rather than symbolising the region's success and prestige, the millennium projects are a public embarrassment.

The failure of these particular millennium celebrations and millennium projects to satisfy the public perhaps hinges on their promotion of the future. This emphasis upon an unknown future plays into the hands of those who see the new millennium as synonymous with social and cultural change. Fears of what the future holds for 'traditional' ways of life manifest themselves in the HTV West coverage of the situation of rural post offices. Backbenchers and MPs of rural constituencies are opposed to the transferral of responsibility for benefit distribution from post offices to banks, which could sound the death knoll to small post offices, which are a lynchpin of rural life and identity. As a Labour MP comments in a studio interview following the report, the latter are the 'hub of rural communities', and a threat to their future is a threat to the survival of rural life (HTV West, 12 January 2000).[16]

The plight of a regional garage owner eloquently expresses this fear of the erosion of symbols of aspects of national and regional identity, this time by the European Union rather than by government policy. The Exmoor man is being forced by EU regulations to convert his petrol pumps from gallons to litres. As he finds the cost of conversion to be punitive, he is refusing to change (HTV West, 21 January 1999). He has garnered local support, as well as sympathetic coverage from the regional news, with reporters making a point of filling their cars in front of the cameras. When an aspect of the region's heritage, in this case the old-fashioned pumps, is threatened by EU and national legislation, the regional television channels prioritise their role of representing the grass-roots experience of the regional public.

Regional television news coverage indicates public disillusionment with the millennium hype. The new millennium was simultaneously equated with both new technologies and the inevitable dangers and failures of these new technologies. Regional television both attempts to sing the praises of new technical developments in line with institutional attitudes, and to reflect popular concerns.

The equation of the approach of the Year 2000 with apocalyptic change received a boost from the double whammy of disasters that afflicted Aquitaine in the last days of 1999. The natural and man-made disasters that besieged the South of France at the turn of the twentieth century were perceived by some as symptomatic of what the new millennium could hold, if man's assault upon the environment is not halted. As the regional newspaper *Sud Ouest* commented, 'with the oil slick coating our coast and a hurricane ravaging our forests, the second millennium seems to be ending on an alarming note. Will this alarm be heeded and will the third millennium be one of rediscovered environmental awareness?' (*Sud Ouest*, 31 December 1999).

The oil slick received extensive coverage on the regional television news, with both M6 Bordeaux and FR3 Aquitaine providing bulletins of the development of the oil slick on a daily basis. It was portrayed as an unwelcome harbinger of the future, if attitudes and practices are not altered. The local politician in charge of the region's response to the disaster described himself as 'an active pessimist', taking the line of preparing for the worst before it happens (FR3 Aquitaine, 20 December 1999). Protection and anticipation were seen as paramount, in the face of this unpredictable threat, which drew the region together to present a united front.

The televisual depiction of regional unity in the face of a shared threat was magnified by the arrival of the severe storms that ravaged the South of France on the 27 and 28 December 1999.[17] The reaction to the damage inflicted by the storms was one of solidarity with the victims of the extreme weather, tinged with pessimism and fear for the future economic implications of the devastation. The coverage of both M6 Bordeaux and FR3 Aquitaine illustrates the devastation wrought by the 'storm of the century' with tales of personal suffering and ruined livelihoods. Fears concerning the future agricultural and economic implications of the storm damage in the region regularly cropped up. Morale-boosting stories of *fraternité* are emphasised to lighten the mood; on 31 December, for example, FR3 Aquitaine covered a local radio station which has mobilised accommodation and invitations for the New Year's Eve celebrations of the *sinistrés*, those 'devastated' by the storms. Suffering is depicted as acting as a force that galvanises networks of collective identity, strengthening their bonds.

The storm victims are shown demonstrating dignity and stoicism in adversity, in a way that is designed to inspire pride in the region's response. The victims are described as 'trying to meet misfortune with a brave face' (FR3 Aquitaine, 31 December 1999); in the flooded village of Blaye, 'the population ... are trying in spite of everything to make their town look presentable again' (FR3 Aquitaine, 28 December 1999). The importance of keeping up appearances in difficult times is a reflection of the village's awareness of its own self-image, and the image that it projects beyond its confines.

According to the editorial approach adopted by the regional and local news of Aquitaine, it is in times of trouble that the mechanisms of regional identity swing into action. Economic, social and geographical differences in the region were put aside as the communities in the affected areas drew together to help those afflicted and to present a united front in the face of adversity. The disasters that affected the region provided a more effective and immediate focal point for a sense of community and cohesion and regional pride than the much-hyped 'millennium', in all of its manifestations. Regional television reflected this through the use of proximity television, and chose to underline the importance of community.

Conclusion

The 'millennium' was marked across the world, with fifty-one television channels, including the BBC and TF1, collaborating to produce '2000 today', which was dedicated to marking the last day of 1999.[18] As René Pucheu comments in his article devoted to the depiction of the millennium: 'The artificiality of the Year 2000 at least brought us the scene of the globalisation of the human race' (Pucheu, 2000: 29). The coverage of the 'millennium' on regional television news therefore encapsulates how regional identity is negotiated in relation to national and global cultures. As with the language surrounding national millennium events, projects and hype, the regional rhetoric is at its most uneasy when it is focusing on the present and the future, rather than the groundrock of the past. This could provide a partial answer to René Pucheu's rhetorical question: 'What does this orgy of memories and pseudo-memories signify?' Pucheu, 2000: 27).

The millennium celebrations were nonetheless a reactionary attempt to foster a sense of regional and national unity that bypassed the recognition of internal ethnic and cultural diversity, attempting to promote national and regional identity through the (time-honoured) use of pageantry, monument construction and the celebration of tradition. The failure of these devices is strikingly revealed by the different reactions to the storms that coincided with the millennium period. It is notable that the reaction to the storms in Aquitaine demonstrates that the 'law of proximity' – which dictates that in times of danger that demand an instant and coherent response, the rule is to help or turn to one's neighbour before all else – eclipses the 'global village' ideal of the world united in the celebration of the millennium. Although at the turn of the millennium the regions were encouraged to consider themselves as part of a nation and on a larger scale as part of a global society, the importance of geographically defined territorial affinity asserts itself in the solidarity following the storms. It is, therefore, at its most powerful not at moments of celebration and self-congratulation, but at moments of shared fear in the face of present difficulties and future repercussions.

The televisual coverage of the millennium celebrations reveal the paradox of the split role of regional television. Its very *raison d'être* is to represent the feelings of the local and regional communities. It also, however, attempts to adhere to its public service brief to promote geopolitical unity. This is demonstrated by the promotion of the state and regional government-inspired celebrations that accompanies the coverage of regional rejection of the millennial hype. This negative popular reception of millennial hype is a manifestation of popular resentment of manipulation by the state, local authorities and the media. Perhaps the advent of the digital millennium will herald a move away from the attempt by the regional and national media to engender regional pride artificially, towards a more concerted attempt to represent more accurately the diversity of British and French regional and national societies, in the past, present and future.

Notes

1. We would like to thank the Arts and Humanities Research Board for a research grant which enabled us to conduct essential fieldwork in Bordeaux for this chapter.
2. The sample was taken between 15 December 1999 and 15 January 2000. Unfortunately, due to fears concerning the millennium bug in both Britain and France, and strikes conducted by FR3 over the institution of the thirty-five hour working week, it is a comprehensive but not a complete sample.
3. 'Le miroir d'une entité géographique et propose de restituer le rôle de ce territoire, dans un environnement régional et transfrontalier.' http://www.france3.fr/fr3/region/aquitain/info.html. Consulted 11 October 1998.
4. See *Going Digital: the challenge for BBC regional journalism.* BBC Regional Broadcasting, 1996.
5. Quoted on http://www.bbc.co.uk/politics97/news/06/0626/millennium.shtml consulted 22 June 2000.
6. Source for the above: millennium information website, <http://www.tour-eiffel/base_offline/manif/pg_1063_uk.html> consulted 28 January 1999.
7. Mission 2000 was instructed to limit its financial investment to 400 million francs, which would be bolstered by money from city and regional councils, as well as private investment. Quoted from 'an 2000, site officiel pour la célébration du 3ième millénaire'. Ibid., consulted 6 July 2000.
8. Ibid., consulted 6 July 2000. This is not to say that technology formed a large part of the preparations for the millennium, as Mission 2000 themselves acknowledged.
9. <http://www.tour-eiffel_offline/manif/pg_1063_uk.html>, consulted 28 January 1999.
10. <http://www.tour-eiffel_/base_offline/manif/pg_10222.uk.html>, consulted 28 January 1999.
11. See <http:www.2000enfrance.com/sites/portes_province/actu/actu.htm>, consulted 8 June 2000.
12. See the special edition of *Dossiers de l'audiovisuel* no. 57, (September/October 1994), dedicated to the subject of 'télévision de proximité'.
13. See <http://www.2000enfrance.com/cfm/magazine_fiche.cfm?reference=sondage_04>, consulted 8 June 2000: 1.
14. Ibid., p.2.
15. See <http://newsvote.bbc.co.uk/hi/english/talking_point/newsid_788000/788015.sth>.
16. This led to the 28 June 2000 announcement of reforms to 'prevent all avoidable closures of rural post offices', ranging from the modernisation of the network, bursaries to local offices to the continued provision of benefits and pensions at the local post office. <http://www.number-10.gov.uk/news.asp?NewsId=1062>, consulted 4 July 2000.
17. See Roche, M., *L'Année 1999 dans* Le Monde: *les principaux événements en France et à l'étranger.* Paris, 2000, for a summary of the newsworthy events in December 1999.
18. See *Les écrits de l'image: les saisons de la télévision,* no. 25, December 1999: 95, for more details.

SECTION II

MINORITY AND 'OTHERED' IDENTITIES

SECTION II

MINORITY AND 'OTHERED' IDENTITIES

Michael Scriven and Emily Roberts

The previous section demonstrated that there is a state-endorsed coales-cence between dominant hegemonic structures of identification, governance and groupings, and the portrayal of territorial identities on television. This is, however, more tenuous in the case of Wales and Scot-land, as the newly devolved national identities in these 'national regions' are in the process of seeking self-definition, in terms of their modern, rather than traditional, group identity. As Sergeant emphasises, there is a move towards representation of smaller units of group identity. The regions are nonetheless struggling to find a more authentic source of group identity, removed from the prototype of national identity. The priv-ileged status of geopolitical forms of identity becomes evident when they are juxtaposed with other forms of minority and 'Othered' identities.

The burgeoning presence of minority or 'Othered' group identities on the small screen accompanies the self-assertion of the regions on national television in Britain and France. This section addresses a range of group identities, from socio-cultural ethnic identities, to identities determined by political choice, sexual orientation and socio-economic positioning. The first two chapters provide a comparative study of ethnic minorities on French and British television. They are supplemented by industry per-spectives, contained in annexes I and II. The following two chapters provide an insight into group identities that have asserted themselves in interesting ways in Britain and France respectively: the *banlieusards* in France, and Green activists in Britain. The final chapter provides a com-

parative study of the portrayal of homosexuals on British and French television. The coverage of a wide cross-section of minority or 'Othered' group
identities in two nations reveal that despite the obvious differences
between these group identities, the portrayal of group identities that subvert the white, middle-class, heterosexual norm is characterised by similar
processes of conceptualisation. On the one hand, the group is normalised,
its special identity is denied, in an attempt to play down its perceived
threat to normative national identity. On the other hand, the group's differences are sensationalised, and the group is subsequently rejected as a
locus of fear and danger. Although these group identities are becoming an
established aspect of the national televisual landscape in France and
Britain, their treatment is still highly ambiguous. An acknowledgement of
their presence in the national arena is not tantamount to an acceptance
of their right to retain their integrity as autonomous groups with a specific identity worthy of respect.

Minority identities pertain to groups that are deemed to be sufficiently
different from the prescribed hegemonic norm as to engender discomfort
or even a degree of distrust, that manifests itself in their televisual representation. In extreme cases, these minority positions can become
'Othered', in the sense that their difference is viewed as such a threat to
the hegemonic status quo that it is perceived as deviance. Homosexual
identity has long borne the brunt of this negative perception, as has the
marginalised identity of the *banlieue* population in France, and the politically defined anti-establishment Green activist identity in Britain. Several
approaches mark the representation of group identities that are considered to constitute minority positions in a complex or even contestatory
relationship with the overarching national identity.

The first two chapters explore the more problematic relationship
between the French Maghrebi and British Asian socio-cultural groups, and
the overarching structure of 'the nation', in the context of televisual representations of ethnic minorities. The multi-ethnic nature of France and
Britain has necessitated a painful and revealing probing of the practice of
situating national identity in the 'glorious past', so beloved of national
iconography, but so rooted in imperialism. (Husband, 1994: 4). Television
has its role to play in the refashioning of geo-political identities to reflect
multicultural realities, as British and French governments and television
companies have recognised. However, it would be premature to consider the
'first, faltering steps' of representation of ethnic minorities on mainstream
terrestrial television as 'great strides' (Frachon and Vargaftig, eds, 1995: 3).

The *Fonds d'Action Sociale* (FAS), which functions under the auspices
of the Ministry of Social Affairs, underwrote a number of television programmes aiming to serve and represent ethnic minorities. This did not
necessarily signal a brave new era of ethnic minority-friendly television;
Akli Tadjer, who wrote or co-wrote two sitcoms depicting French Maghrebis, remarks upon the 'graveyard' slots allocated for his programmes,

despite a favourable critical response and a laudable integrationalist agenda (see annex I).

Joanna Helcke is guarded in her appraisal of the impact FAS's promotion of pro-integration 'multicultural' programming, and its aim to sensitise the general population to ethnic minority issues. She detects a tacit assumption that 'integration' is reliant upon a change of attitudes and practices in the immigrant population, rather than on the part of society at large. The programmes that do depict Maghrebis are allocated slots that do not attract a mass audience, with the effect that Maghrebis continue to be overwhelmingly absent from national terrestrial French television.

The director of the IM'Média ethnic minority-based media production company, Mogniss Abdallah, acknowledges that although French television has some way to go in terms of representation of ethnic minority groups, Britain should not be held up as the example to emulate:

> The British experience of multi-cultural programming and openings for independent producers seemed like the stuff dreams are made of compared to the way French broadcasting ostracizes immigration and social experiment, but we should beware of turning it into a myth. The BBC cannot get rid of a highly institutionalized, slightly paternalistic and complex-ridden style of race relations. (Abdallah, 1995: 56)

This can be clearly perceived in the institutional attitude towards programmes such as *Goodness Gracious Me (GGM)*. Whereas programmes such as *GGM* have raised the profile of British Asians in Britain, television is still 'lagging behind society and failing to reflect the multi-cultural nature of the country' (*Guardian*, 8 December 1999). As recently as March 2000, a BBC promotional website was listing *Goodness Gracious Me* among the 'risky new ideas' that it had developed.[1] As Marie Gillespie notes in her chapter on *Goodness Gracious Me*, the programme is not afraid to probe taboos that the older generation of Asians find uncomfortable, such as sexual relations and the decision of some to deny their cultural roots in an effort to assimilate. In her discussion of the cultural significance and reception of the programme by Asian viewers, Gillespie explores the role and practices of 'ethnic comedy'. The use of satire, caricature, inversion and parody subvert commonly held racial (-ist) stereotypes concerning Asian identity in a challenging and empowering way. She concludes that, although *Goodness Gracious Me* has achieved impressive results in terms of raising consciousness concerning racist attitudes towards Asians, multicultural broadcasting still has much to do. (See interview with Nina Wadia, an actor in *GGM*, in annex II for further information.)

The process of normalisation of perceived difference, which manifests itself as a drive for assimilation in Joanna Helcké's interpretation of Maghrebi sitcoms, can be detected in the portrayal of other minority or 'Othered' groups. In his chapter on the portrayal of *banlieue* identity on French television, Chris Warne addresses the portrayal of this socio-economic group comprising a variety of ethnic groups in it, which has developed its own specific form of cultural expression. He focuses on the relationship between television and the growth of French hip-hop culture, and its perceived links with the issue of social exclusion in the poorer suburbs (*banlieue*) of France's major cities. Hip-hop originally graced the French small screen as an object of curiosity, embodying exotic 'Otherness'. This objectification of the *banlieue* youth, although superficially appearing to be well-intentioned and tolerant, indicates the positioning of the *banlieue* youth as 'Other' to an assumed norm. This portrayal of difference cedes to one of deviance, as the *banlieue* youth became connected with fear of the social problems of the poor suburbs. This has grown into a distrust and criticism of the perceived subtext of sexism and violence that underpins the lyrics and music videos of hip-hop bands coming from the *banlieue*. As the relationship between television and hip-hop culture has deepened, rap groups have come to mobilise and exploit the medium that once objectified them.

In the following chapter, Derek Wall outlines the changing nature of Green activist representation, as a source of inspiration for fiction, as a form of propaganda, and as a focal point of distrust and fear on British terrestrial television. The Green activist on television is often 'deradicalised' to render them more socially acceptable. Wall highlights the complex relationship between television and activists. While some reject it as an instrument of the establishment, others recognise its power, and the potential of recruiting new members to the cause through exposure on mainstream television. Like the hip-hop artists described by Warne, some Green activists have explored the possibilities of 'grass-roots' video production as a more representative medium for the portrayal of their needs and true sense of their own group identities being explored. Minority or 'Othered' groups, the objects of curiosity and fear, are reclaiming their own representation through the manipulation of existing media and televisual devices.

Murray Pratt's chapter examines the 'heteronormative' pressures evidenced in the representations of homosexuality on both French and British television. Through a process of 'normalisation' described by Pratt as 'banalisation', the homosexual figure is often seen to espouse the heterosexual ideal of a monogamous relationship that provides a socially acceptable prototype for gays to mimic. Alternatively, aspects of the homosexual figure's life that may titillate an audience weaned on heteronormative values are emphasised, to the exclusion of more general observations that could lead to a greater understanding of the challenges facing the homosexual community. This can be due to the pressures of gaining good viewing figures for the programme. Although certain programmes, such as *Queer as Folk*, a Channel Four production, have been promoted with the gay market in mind, 'the colonising structures of male heterosexuality' can still be perceived. The figure of the homosexual is always framed as deviating from the acceptable norm. The televising of homosexuality, however, even in a 'normalised' or sensationalist mode, opens up opportunities for reinterpretation and self-definition as a group.

Both British and French televisual representations of minority or 'Othered' groups are often underpinned by the desire to 'normalise' the group. Helcké, Wall and Pratt comment on the process of stripping minority or 'Othered' groups of the specificities that form their unique identity. Alternatively, the group is demonised for its Otherness. Despite their failings, however, programmes that depict minority groups at least introduce previously ignored or omitted groups into the public sphere. In certain instances, there are indications of the diversity within the minority group identity itself. The televisual image of the group can be reconfigured by the minority or 'Othered' viewer. Even a bastardised form of representation on national television can help move towards an acknowledgement of the cultural diversity within the nation-state; although it is far from ideal.

What does the future hold for group identities on television? The practices of normalisation at one extreme and sensationalisation at the other indicate a desire to retain the normative national values of national television in France and Britain, rather than to embrace the conception of the nation as a federation of different but equal group identities. Some members of minority and 'Othered' groups are looking elsewhere for means of unmediated representation. New developments in digital technology and audio-visual communications allow minority groups some scope for self-expression. With time, this could offer a more accurate representation of their own conception of their identity, challenging dominant attitudes towards 'Othered' minority groups.

Note

1. <http://www.bbc.co.uk/info/news/2000/ch oice/choice2.shtml>.

CHAPTER 6

THE REPRESENTATION
OF MAGHREBIS
ON FRENCH TELEVISION

Joanna Helcké

When the French football team won the World Cup in 1998 hopes of a new society embracing ethnic plurality were widely voiced and the media loudly proclaimed France's multi-ethnic team to be 'a model of successful integration'.[1] Yet little more than a year later, the media – and television in particular – stood accused of excluding ethnic minorities and of providing television viewers with a whitewashed diet of programmes. In September 1999, the pressure group, *Egalité*, called on France's minority ethnic population to boycott the country's most popular terrestrial channel, TF1, and stated that 'in the streets, the stadiums and at school, the population is multi-racial, and it must also be so on the small screen'.[2] Indeed, whilst ethnic minorities form an established part of French society, even a cursory look at television reveals that they still remain distinctly absent from France's audiovisual landscape.

It is within this general context that the question of how France's Maghrebi population is represented on French television will be broached. The purpose of the present chapter is three-fold: firstly to examine briefly the dominant images of Maghrebis on television. The second section will discuss the French government's attempts – within the framework of republican, universalist thinking – to use television as a tool for promoting the 'integration'[3] of ethnic minorities. The final section will expand on this theme through a more detailed analysis of the representation of Maghrebis in the TV sitcom, *Fruits et Légumes*, one of the biggest investments of the *Fonds d'Action Sociale* (FAS)[4] in the 1990s and the only series starring a Maghrebi family in recent years.

Dominant Images of Maghrebis from the 1970s to Today

France's Maghrebi population constitutes the main minority ethnic group in the country, and yet people of North African origin rarely grace the small screen. Despite their relative absence from television, the portrayal of Maghrebis has shifted considerably over the last thirty years. To a certain extent, these changing representations are a reflection of the evolving nature of France's Maghrebi population, from the predominance of male, immigrant workers in the 1970s, to the importance of today's second and third generations. Thus, in the 1970s, Maghrebis tended to be seen in 'factual' television programmes, and the focus was essentially on male workers and issues relating to their living conditions in France, such as employment and housing (Hargreaves, 1997). An analysis of the French press from the 1970s to the 1980s shows a similar situation, revealing that in the former decade, immigrants were portrayed in economic and social terms, without being attributed any cultural and religious dimensions (Hamès, 1989). During this period, Maghrebis were voiceless faces brought into the homes of the French public by a medium – television – that was essentially directed at the majority population.

Along with the increased politicisation of the debate surrounding immigration – fuelled by the rise of the extreme right-wing *Front National* – ethnic minorities have become progressively more visible on television. As commentators have pointed out[5] this raises the question of what role television played during the 1980s in the emergence of Le Pen's party. From the early 1980s, Maghrebis, and immigrants in general, were increasingly conspicuous on the small screen as objects of news and in current affairs programmes (Hargreaves, 1992a). In terms of the representation of Maghrebis during this period, there was a noticeable shift from the 1970s image of the immigrant worker largely devoid of any cultural markers, to that of the *Muslim* Maghrebi. Both Hargreaves and Hamès have argued that this Islamicisation of the portrayal of France's North African population was due to a number of developments which took place towards the late 1970s and in the early 1980s (Hargreaves, 1992a; Hamès, 1989). Within France the political élite was gradually having to come to terms with the fact that many Muslim immigrants were not there on a temporary basis: their families had come to join them, and this decision to settle entailed the creation of a network of places of worship. Meanwhile, beyond France's borders, the Iranian revolution of 1979 was the culmination of a more general Islamic revivalism which was widely perceived as a threat by the West. These events and developments were compounded in 1983 by immigrant workers at the Renault factories in France going on strike, one of their demands being prayer-rooms within the workplace. The result, argues Hamès, was that France's Maghrebi population was no longer portrayed 'in terms of social class, national or linguistic origin. One description alone summarises or cancels out all others: Muslim' (Hamès, 1989: 84).

The Islamicisation of the representation of Maghrebis has, in the 1990s, moved up a gear and sped into the fast lane of fundamentalism. Increasingly, during the last decade, France's North African population has been associated with *intégrisme* (Islamic fundamentalism) on screen. The equation of Islam with fundamentalism on television has been reinforced by events such as the headscarf affair in 1989,[6] the Gulf War in 1991 and, in particular, the near-civil war in Algeria with its ramifications in France (Ouali, 1997). In 1995, France found itself embroiled in the Algerian crisis when a series of bomb attacks in French cities was undertaken by a group of second-generation Algerian youths linked to the Islamists fighting against the Algerian government. Not only did these attacks reopen the wounds of the Algerian War of Independence but they also strengthened the association in the French public's mind between Maghrebis and Islamic fundamentalism. This terror campaign came to a sensational, and highly public, end when the prime suspect – Khaled Kelkal – was shot dead by the police on television.[7]

The death of Kelkal, who came from a marginalised suburb of Lyon, highlights another recurrent theme in the 1990s portrayal of Maghrebis on the small screen: violence. Over the last decade, second-generation Maghrebis living in France's *banlieues*[8] have become the focus of intense and hyperbolic media coverage, as suburbs across the country have witnessed spates of joy-riding as well as riots sparked off by *bavures policières*.[9] Television reporting of these incidents has tended to reinforce both 'the negative image of the young rioting immigrant' (Ouali, 1997: 23) and the widespread belief that France's Maghrebi population is 'unassimilable'.

Moving away from 'factual' programmes to the other end of the televisual spectrum, France's Maghrebi population is still largely excluded from fiction, such as soaps and sitcoms (Prencipe, 1995; Hargreaves, 1997). To engage an audience successfully, these genres have to build a rapport between the fictional characters and the viewers. With audience ratings the priority, commercial channels have, on the whole, been unwilling to cast characters of minority ethnic origin. Of the few series which have featured Maghrebis on a regular basis, not only were most broadcast on public service channels but they were also partially financed by the government, via the FAS. The general dearth of fiction starring Maghrebis, and in particular, the absence of programmes aimed specifically at minority ethnic groups, is very much a 'by-product' of France's universalist approach to immigration: television made for minorities would be seen as hindering 'integration' (Prencipe, 1995; Ouali, 1997). Nevertheless, within the framework of universalism, the FAS has – over the last three decades – made a timid contribution towards France's televisual landscape. It is to the role of this government agency in shaping the relationship between France's minority ethnic population and television, that we now turn.

The FAS and Its Audiovisual Policy

Created in 1958, the FAS is the principal public agency responsible for facilitating the 'integration' of minority ethnic groups in France. It carries out this role through the financing of a wide range of projects designed to assist the immigrant population. Since 1975, it has sought to harness the power of television by supporting programmes devised to improve ethnic relations. Over the last twenty-five years the FAS's audiovisual policy has evolved from the financing of programmes that targeted specifically the immigrant population, to supporting programmes aimed at sensitising the general public to the minority ethnic presence in France.

One of the FAS's earliest, and most successful, contributions to the French audiovisual landscape was the magazine programme *Mosaïque* which ran for eleven years starting in the mid-1970s. This weekly programme catered essentially for France's immigrant population although it was defined as being for the general public. In spite of *Mosaïque*'s undoubted popularity – it secured an audience of between four and six million viewers (Humblot, 1989) – many criticisms have been levelled at it. Like most subsequent programmes supported by the FAS, *Mosaïque* was broadcast at what Humblot refers to as a 'ghetto' time slot: 9 am on a Sunday (Humblot, 1989: 7). As Hargreaves comments, the positioning of the FAS's programmes at such inconvenient times of the day merely serves to reinforce the marginal status of the immigrant population (Hargreaves, 1992a). According to Humblot, more worrying still was the unstated aim of the programme: although *Mosaïque* provided France's immigrants with a much needed weekly dose of their own cultures, the underlying objective was to prepare immigrants and their families for repatriation, in line with the government's then policy of *l'aide au retour*[10] (Humblot, 1989; Hargreaves 1997). Thus, rather than providing ethnic minorities with a cultural space on television, the FAS's first significant step into France's televisual landscape aimed to prepare immigrants for their return 'home'.

By the early 1980s *Mosaïque*'s audience had dwindled considerably and a major re-evaluation of the FAS's audiovisual policy took place.[11] In view of the evolving nature of the immigrant population – with families now settled and a second generation born and socialised in France – it was suggested that *Mosaïque* and other FAS-supported programmes should be directed more at the younger generation. As a result of these discussions, *Mosaïque*'s format was changed slightly. However, audience ratings continued to fall and in 1986 it was shelved. A number of other FAS-financed magazine programmes – again aimed primarily at France's minority ethnic population – followed *Mosaïque*, although none was a ratings success and all were relatively short-lived. As Humblot observes, the irony of these programmes is that whilst their key objective is to encourage the 'integration' of immigrants, their very existence highlights the status of the minority ethnic viewer as different (Humblot, 1989).

Faced with the fact that its programmes had, on the whole, been less than successful, the FAS undertook a second review of its audiovisual policy in the early 1990s. A report summarising the outcome of discussions suggested that programmes supported by the FAS should be aimed at two types of audience: first-generation immigrants so as to promote their 'integration', and the general public in an effort to sensitise them to the minority ethnic presence in France (Hargreaves, 1993). As a result of these recommendations, a daily magazine programme – *Premier Service* – was broadcast on FR3 at 7 a.m. With the immigrant audience in mind, *Premier Service* included, for example, a section giving legal advice, whilst a section on the foreign origin of words commonly used in the French language was aimed primarily at majority ethnic viewers.[12] Although a great deal of thought went into devising *Premier Service*, it proved to be even less watched than previous FAS-financed magazine programmes, a situation which Hargreaves partly attributes to the anodyne nature of the programme (Hargreaves, 1993). His analysis of *Premier Service* highlights a consistent tendency to avoid anything that could prove controversial, thus resulting in a programme so bland that few viewers could identify with it.

In line with the FAS's second priority – that of sensitising the general public to the minority ethnic population in France – financial support has also been provided for the making of programmes aimed at majority ethnic viewers. These have ranged from one-off productions screened at peak viewing times, to soaps and sitcoms. *Sixième Gauche*, the first ever French soap to feature a Maghrebi family, was broadcast in 1990 and produced with the financial assistance of the FAS. The series focuses on two neighbouring families – one French and one Algerian – and the friendship which develops between them. Throughout the fifty episodes, the Algerian Ben Amars are portrayed in an unrelentingly 'positive' light, with the parents speaking flawless French and the eldest children in high-flying jobs (Hargreaves, 1992b). As Hargreaves points out, the result of this 'positive' portrayal is that 'throughout the soap one has the impression that the Ben Amars have been fashioned according to the French public's need to be reassured about the immigrant population, whereas the Villiers [the French family] are not answerable to anybody' (Hargreaves, 1992b: 103). Similar criticisms can be levelled at the Badaoui family, which features in the more recent FAS-financed sitcom *Fruits et Légumes*. It is on the representation of Maghrebis within this series, and the FAS's influence in shaping the depiction of this minority ethnic group, that attention will now be focused.

Fruits et Légumes: From Script to Screen

Fruits et Légumes was broadcast daily on France 3 at 1.30 p.m. from 25 July to 26 August 1994. Behind the pictures on the screen lay three years of negotiations between the different production partners of the series. The creation of any television programme requires the collaboration of a number of different parties: a production team must be assembled, financial backing must be secured – often from a number of sources – and once the programme has been produced, a television channel must be willing to broadcast the programme. In the case of *Fruits et Légumes*, this production partnership was further complicated by the involvement of the FAS. In seeking financial assistance from the FAS, the production company – Cinétévé – had to consider not only the commercial, technical and artistic aspects of producing the series but also the FAS's social aims. Thus, the production process of *Fruits et Légumes* involved a complex, and sometimes arduous, coalition between the script-writers, Cinétévé, France 3 – the television channel – and the FAS.[13]

The Production Partnership

At the beginning of 1993 France 3 stated to Cinétévé that it would be willing to accept a new series if it were 'a sitcom in the form of a French-style *Cosby Show*'.[14] Having achieved this indication from France 3, Cinétévé now had to see whether the FAS would co-finance the series, as without the latter's support, production of such a sitcom could not proceed. By the summer of that year the FAS had been given ministerial authorisation to co-finance the project, and work was started on the series.

Whilst the writers, Cinétévé and France 3 were aiming to produce an entertaining sitcom that would be a ratings success, the FAS wanted the series to feed into its 'integrationist' project. In particular, it stated that 'the FAS's objective through the financing of this series [is to] contribute towards the integration of immigrant populations and those of immigrant origin'.[15] Whilst these two objectives are not necessarily incompatible – a convivial atmosphere throughout the series could well encourage the audience to be receptive towards a more serious message – they were sufficiently different to cause friction between the parties involved. Moreover, although Cinétévé, the script-writers and France 3 were, essentially, striving towards a shared goal, they each had their own distinct agendas regarding the production of the programme.

The 'Bible'

When producing a fictional series, it is customary to start with the drafting of what the French call the 'Bible', this being a document which summarises the fundamental characteristics governing the programme. Given the importance of this document, it was the subject of long discussions during which the various production partners – and in particular the FAS – put forward their objectives and specific requirements regarding *Fruits et Légumes*. Following receipt of the first version of the 'Bible', the FAS made a number of stipulations that did not correspond entirely with the initial concept proposed by Cinétévé and the script-writers. For example, the FAS expressed regret regarding the near-absence of French origin characters. This had been a deliberate choice on the part of Henri de Turenne and Akli Tadjer – the writers – due to their previous experience scripting *Sixième Gauche* where they felt that 'our French characters were either insipid or, if we wanted to stereotype them as racist, loathsome'.[16] The FAS, however, expected 'native' French characters to play a greater role in the series, 'integration being a process in which immigrants and 'Gauls' play an equally important part'.[17] A further demand made by the FAS was that each episode should broach 'real-life situations, including intergenerational conflicts within the family and among other characters, confrontations which though troublesome, eventually lead to integration'.[18] The authors, on the other hand, felt that 'the sitcom genre, unlike the documentary, is not made for raising serious issues. ... Our message is subliminal'.[19]

In answer to the first of these concerns, a number of 'native' French characters were incorporated into subsequent versions of the 'Bible'. The most important of these characters was Suzanne who was to become a close friend of Farida Badaoui, the mother in the Algerian family. Her role throughout the series was to encourage the latter 'to free herself from her husband Amar's domination'.[20] However, in spite of the authors' assertion that the Badaoui family 'clearly lives in a French environment', [21] majority ethnic roles are rarely more than secondary in the broadcast version of the series. In accordance with the FAS's second wish, an updated 'Bible' stated that 'the situations will be generated by societal problems which are specific to Beurs [young French people of Maghrebi origin] and to immigrants'.[22] However, no concrete examples of this are given and only a few months later, two characters mentioned in earlier drafts and who would have been particularly apt to illustrate the ethnocultural dimension of the minority ethnic presence in France – an Italian priest and an imam born in France – disappeared without explanation from the 'Bible'.

The Scripts

When scripting the series, the authors were very conscious of the need to create an Algerian family that was as engaging as possible, as otherwise, it would neither be possible to establish a convivial atmosphere, nor the identification process that the FAS hoped for. The script-writers were, therefore, extremely careful regarding their choice of subject matter for the episodes: not only was the issue of Islam avoided because it was felt that many people of French origin fear this religion but also themes relating to drugs and criminality. The FAS, however, proved to be even more prudent, insisting that one episode in particular, *La Perle de Tipaza* (The pearl from Tipaza) be abandoned because it focused on a marriage of convenience, designed to circumvent immigration controls. Whilst this censorship was the most extreme case of the FAS's influence on the script-writing, a number of other disagreements over the scripts emerged, these sometimes leading to significant changes being made.

One such example concerns the first version of an episode called *La Quinzaine Africaine* (The African fortnight) which centred on a polygamous West African family, and was criticised by the FAS for portraying polygamy in too favourable a light. When commenting on the script, the FAS emphasised not only that polygamy was incompatible with French law but also that it was 'the cause of numerous problems, both within the host country, and within polygamous families in France'. [23] As a result of this unfavourable remark, in the broadcast version of the episode, Farida is seen having a conversation with the wives in the polygamous family, during which she delivers a little speech on the reasons why she considers polygamy to be an unacceptable practice.

The authors did not, however, always yield under the criticisms levelled at their scripts. A character with a secondary role, Momo (short for Mohammed) worried the FAS because of the description of him in the script as a 'yobbo and a vandal'. [24] To avoid any characters of Maghrebi origin being depicted in a negative light, the FAS wanted Momo to become Maurice, a youth of French origin: this change never took place. Nevertheless, the comments made by the various production partners required significant changes to be made to the first set of scripts. It was only once the authors were fully aware of the constraints within which they were working, that they were able to proceed at a much faster pace by avoiding any situations and dialogues that might have led to controversy. Recording of the series began in March 1994 and the final touches to the last episode were only made shortly before the end of filming two months later.

The Broadcast Version

To what extent did the broadcast version of *Fruits et Légumes* satisfy the FAS's objectives? This is a complex question, arising from the fact that tensions existed between the stated aims of the FAS and unspoken, sometimes contradictory, attitudes which appear to have been implicit in its thinking. It is when the FAS's stated objectives are compared with the requests it made and the end-product, that inconsistencies come to light. These cannot be fully understood without an appreciation of the ambiguities that surround the idea of 'integration' in the debate over public policy towards immigrant minorities in France. Immigration became one of the most divisive issues in French politics during the 1980s. Fearing that these divisions were primarily benefiting the extreme-right Front National, mainstream parties began to build a consensus around the notion of 'integration' which became the watchword of public policy under governments of both left and right during the 1990s (Weil and Crowley, 1994). As the principal public agency responsible for assisting minority ethnic groups, the FAS has played a key role in promoting 'integration'. Despite the apparent cross-party consensus around this concept, it has in fact been beset by ambiguities (Bonnafous, 1992; Hommes et Migrations, 1994; Revue française des affaires sociales, 1997).

The word 'integration' has been used in many different and sometimes contradictory ways. Three of these are of particular note in the present context. Some politicians, particularly on the right of the political spectrum use it as a virtual synonym for 'assimilation', that is, the adoption of majority ethnic norms by groups of immigrant origin, together with the abandoning of their distinctive cultural practices. Others regard 'integration' as a process of mutual acceptance by majority and minority groups, which in some cases may include adaptation and change on both sides. A third perspective focuses on the idea of participation of minorities in 'mainstream' society, without this necessarily implying cultural change. Traces of all three approaches are present in the objectives formulated for *Fruits et Légumes* by the FAS.

In its most succinct and categorical statement of objectives, the FAS told Cinétévé that its 'aim through the financing of this series [is to] contribute towards the integration of immigrant populations and those of immigrant origin, and to encourage a development of the French public's mentalities towards a greater acceptance of difference'.[25] This would appear to point to 'integration' of the second type, with the emphasis falling on the acceptance of cultural differences rather than on changing majority or minority groups. In pursuing this goal, the FAS wanted the series to engender sympathy and identification on the part of majority ethnic audiences vis-à-vis minority ethnic characters. In this way, the programme would have a performative function: it would not simply represent the 'integration' process but would positively facilitate it by encouraging suitable attitudes among majority ethnic viewers. At other times, however, FAS officials appear to have thought more in terms of simply portraying successful 'integration' on screen. For this reason, they asked the programme-makers to include more majority ethnic characters. Yet at other times, FAS officials spoke of the need to represent cultural conflicts both within the minority ethnic family and its relations with the majority ethnic population. In principal, such an outcome might be achieved through 'integration' as a process of mutual acceptance by majority and minority groups. In practice, however, the FAS appears to have assumed that cultural change was necessary on the minority ethnic side but not among the majority population. It can be argued, therefore, that although this was never explicitly stated, there was an implicit presumption in favour of assimilation.

The evidence pointing towards this implicit assumption is of two types. Firstly, as noted above, a number of story-lines and incidents were either inserted or eliminated at the insistence of the FAS, and these suggest a need for minority ethnic adaptation to majority norms rather than the opposite. Thus, regarding *La Quinzaine Africaine* (The African fortnight), it will be remembered that FAS officials wanted the episode modified in such a way that polygamy was depicted in a less positive light. As a result of the FAS's intervention, in the broadcast version Farida is seen lecturing the Senegalese family staying at her home on the reasons why she considers polygamy to be an unacceptable practice. This is a conspicuous instance of cultural change being depicted on screen, and clearly the movement is expected to be on the minority side towards majority norms.

A second key feature of *Fruits et Légumes* which implicitly points to the FAS's assimilationist assumptions lies in the de-ethnicisation of the Badaoui family. According to the press dossier drafted by the programme-makers to accompany the broadcasting of the sitcom, Amar (the father in the Badaoui family) 'clings to his cultural roots and traditions'.[26] This considerably overstates Amar's conservatism. In practice, he and his wife, Farida, are both very much at ease in French society. Whilst many first-generation Maghrebis are illiterate and have to rely on their children to deal with administrative documents, Amar and Farida both speak impeccable French, and can read and write perfectly. Moreover, Farida – played by the glamorous former television presenter, Nadia Samir – is seen sporting plunging necklines and short skirts, clothes that it would be unlikely to see a first-generation Maghrebi woman wearing.

The Badaouis' high level of de-ethnicisation is emphasised in the episode, *Amar ce héros* (Amar the hero), where Amar rescues his French neighbour from a gas leak in her home. Convinced that Amar has saved her life, she telephones the newsroom at one of the television channels and they send a film crew to interview him. The journalists were planning a report on 'the Arab hero', only to discover that Amar's grocery shop was not 'ethnic-y enough' and that he 'didn't look like an immigrant'. In an attempt to give the news report a more 'genuine' feel, the journalists make Amar wear a fez and rearrange the products on the shelves around him, in such a way that he is surrounded by packets of couscous and dates. The interview is, however, so lacking in 'authenticity', that it is never broadcast.

In short, therefore, the Badaouis 'differ little from the average French person and will soon become completely French' (Humblot, 1994). It could be argued that de-ethnicising the Maghrebi characters maximised the chances of a French audience identifying with the Badaoui family. On the other hand, mutual respect for differences, to which the FAS paid lip-service, could only occur if there were differences – beyond the physical appearance of characters – to be seen on screen. Whilst the average French viewer may have overcome an initial hurdle by watching *Fruits et Légumes*, there is still a long way to go before the French public is exposed to the sympathetic portrayal of real cultural differences.

Conclusion

Today, television is the single most important source of information and entertainment for a mass audience, and undoubtedly plays a significant role in shaping popular attitudes. In view of this, those aiming to facilitate the incorporation of ethnic minorities into French society cannot afford to ignore the potential – both positive and negative – that this medium has. Yet at the dawn of the twenty-first century, French television is still a rather pale-faced affair in comparison with much of European television and France's Maghrebi population finds itself largely relegated to the margins of the French audiovisual landscape. Ironically, North Africans are represented either as *too* different in 'factual' programmes, or as *no* different in FAS-financed fiction and, although well-intentioned, the FAS's heavy-handed intervention has done little to redress the ethnic balance on the small screen. Thus, as the frontiers of audiovisual technology are pushed back, minority ethnic viewers have turned increasingly to satellite and cable television to supplement their unsatisfactory diet of terrestrial TV. This increased flexibility cannot, however, blot out the shortcomings of a national television network accused of being 'allergic to colour'.[27] It is perhaps not surprising, therefore, that *Egalité* have raised the possibility of introducing quotas, an 'Anglosaxon' spectre that haunts the French political élite.

Notes

1. *Libération*, 10 July 1998. NB All translations are the author's.
2. Calixthe Beyala, spokeswoman for *Egalité* and renowned author, quoted in *Le Figaro*, 24 September 1999.
3. Due to the ambiguous currency of this term in France, it will only be used in relation to the government's policy towards immigration, the quotation marks indicating the circumspection with which this concept must be handled.
4. The main public agency responsible for encouraging the 'integration' of ethnic minorities in France.
5. See, for example, Ouali, 1997.
6. The headscarf affair refers to an incident where three Muslim girls were excluded from school because they wore headscarves. This provoked widespread debate and a great deal of media coverage. For an analysis of this event see Gaspard, F. and Khosrokhavar, F. *Le foulard et la République*. Paris, 1995.
7. For a more detailed discussion of the media coverage of this event, see Hargreaves, 1997.
8. These suburbs can be equated with Britain's inner city areas.
9. These are so-called 'police errors', which have led to the deaths of numerous youths – mainly of Maghrebi origin – from the *banlieues*.
10. The *aide au retour* policy was initiated in 1977, and consisted of providing immigrants with a FF10 000 financial incentive to return to their countries of origin.
11. See Humblot, 1989, for a more detailed discussion of the 1982 Gaspard report and its recommendations to the FAS.
12. For a comprehensive analysis of *Premier Service*, see Hargreaves, 1993.
13. For a detailed analysis of the making of *Fruits et Légumes* see Hargreaves and Helcké, 1994.

14. Interview with Fabienne Servan-Schreiber, director of Cinétévé, 6 January 1994.
15. Letter from the FAS to Cinétévé, 17 March 1994.
16. Interview with Henri de Turenne and Akli Tadjer, 7 January 1994.
17. Letter from the FAS to Cinétévé, 7 October 1993.
18. Letter from the FAS to Cinétévé, 7 October 1993.
19. Interview with Henri de Turenne and Akli Tadjer, 7 January 1994.
20. 'Bible', January 1994.
21. Interview with Henri de Turenne and Akli Tadjer, 7 January 1994.
22. 'Bible', September 1993.
23. Letter from the FAS to Cinétévé, 17 March 1994.
24. Quotation from the script of *Les Loulous de Zouzou* (Zouzou's yobbos), December 1993
25. Letter from the FAS to Cinétévé, 17 March 1994.
26. Press campaign dossier, July 1994.
27. Libération, 5 October 1999.

CHAPTER 7

FROM COMIC ASIANS TO ASIAN COMICS[1]

GOODNESS GRACIOUS ME, BRITISH TELEVISION COMEDY AND REPRESENTATIONS OF ETHNICITY

Marie Gillespie

Comedy and Ethnicity

Despite differences of emphasis, theorists of comedy seem to agree that most humour is based on some form of degradation since there is always a butt to a joke. All jokes have a tripartite structure: the comic source or teller, the receiver/s and the object of humour. There are formulaic jokes, jokes that trade on insider knowledge, and jokes that change with different audiences. Those who share a joke share a certain intimacy and thus jokes confirm closeness (Cohen, 2000). Those who share a joke belong to a community, however temporary, of people alike enough in outlook and feeling to be joined in sharing a joke – as we shall see is the case with young British Asians and the British Asian sketch show *Goodness Gracious Me (GGM)*.[2] It is the social intimacy and pleasure of laughter which explains why we tell them and what they are for. But jokes are also exclusionary. Jokes define social categories and group boundaries incorporating some as insiders and others as outsiders, delighting some and offending others. Jokes which trade on stereotypes of national, racialised and ethnic categories give pleasure and offence simultaneously. But the key question remains: who is laughing with and at whom and why?

Methodologies for Analysing Representations of 'Race' and Ethnicity

In the past, explorations of media representations of 'race' and ethnicity have analysed ethnic groups in terms of negative and positive images – as if it were simply a question of replacing negative with positive images. But positive or negative for whom, and in what context? The telling of the tale, the teller, the context of its telling and the social and power relations between participants play a critical role in determining who laughs with and at whom and why. Joking relations flourish in both difficult and 'safe' areas of social life, and are frequently used to defuse potentially conflictual social relations. The terms 'honky', 'nigger' or 'paki' may be used inoffensively among white, 'Asian' and black peers. Similarly, ritual exchanges of Irish and Jewish jokes among friends may confirm intimacy. We are not necessarily promoting stereotypes or unpleasant attitudes by telling such jokes. Dubious jokes can be funny and the kind of moral rectitude promoted by certain forms of political correctness will not wipe the smile off your face if you find it funny. For the joke to work you need knowledge of the stereotype but this is not necessarily to endorse it.

However when national television institutions employed performers like Bernard Manning and Jim Davidson in 1960s and 1970s, and gave them a platform to express xenophobic and racist attitudes and to tell jokes about the criminality, the stupidity or the mere existence of blacks and Asians in Britain, the institutionalisation of racist regimes of representation entered public life in a new way. So what approach can we take to the analysis of media representations of 'race' and ethnicity that does justice both to the aesthetics of comedy and to the politics of 'race' and difference?

In the 1960s and 1970s, studies of 'race' and the media often invoked white ethnicity as the taken-for-granted norm against which black and Asian ethnicities were analysed (see chapter 10 for an analysis of this phenomenon in the context of gay identities). More recently an approach which understands ethnicity as constructed and contested, relational and contextual has been adopted. This has helped dispense with unproblematised and essentialised notions of minorities and with studies focusing exclusively on the portrayal of specific ethnic groups. Since we are all ethnically located, the idea that only media texts which foreground 'race' or ethnicity are relevant is clearly absurd. Musser argues for a more adventurous approach involving a shift from looking at individual groups with the aim of affirming their identities to taking 'a more ironic look at the larger question of ethnic identity itself' and the complex and contradictory negotiations which take place in the interaction of institutions, texts and audiences (Musser, 1991: 41). In a similar vein, Shohat (1991) has argued for a methodology which seeks to analyse ethnicities-in-relation, 'submerged ethnicities', absences as well as presences, and repressed racial and ethnic contradictions in mainstream texts.

The following analysis of television comedy and ethnicity will focus on the comedy show *Goodness Gracious Me* and will explore how ethnic caricatures operate in a wider system of comic and racialised representation (Hall, 1995). It will explore the use of comic techniques of satire, parody, comic inversions, forms of verbal humour but it will situate textual analysis in wider institutional and national frameworks of production and reception.

British Television Comedy, 'Race' and Racism

British television comedies provide symbolically potent representations of racialised group identities, and their development offers a barometer of state discourses and policies on 'race' relations – from integration and assimilation to pluralism in the political sphere, and from equal opportunities and positive discrimination to cultural diversity in the cultural sphere. This chapter will sketch the national, institutional and multicultural contexts which framed the production and success of *GGM*.

Since the 1960s British TV comedy has slowly moved away from images of comic 'Asians' as the butt of white script writers' jokes to comic representations produced by Asian comics themselves. It is worth noting that the actors and script writers of *GGM* were brought up with these images on television. They demonstrated how the programmes could be read 'against the grain' by Asians, and used as a source of inspiration and something to react against. According to Meera Syal, one of the British Asian creators of *GGM*, the emergence of a new generation of Asian comedians reflects the confidence of this generation at ease with being British and Asian and 'barely noticing the seam'.[3] *GGM* draws not only on Jewish but also a very British (rather than Indian or Punjabi) tradition of humour. In many ways it reflects the television diet of its Asian producers and performers who grew up in 1960s Britain. For example, it uses some comic techniques of the early 1960s' comedy *It Ain't Half Hot Mum*, a series set in a British army camp during the Second World War (that has recently been revived on British television), a testament to its enduring popularity.

Meera Syal claims that her parents loved it but that she was horrified by the Punk Wallah character played by Michael Bates who 'blacked up' for the part.[4] Sanjeev Bhaskar, a fellow actor in *GGM*, found that after initially feeling appalled by the character, he began to appreciate Bates' ability as a comic actor, with a good working knowledge of and improvisational skills in Punjabi and Urdu.[5]

Bates was born and brought up in India. Throughout the series he talked mainly in Urdu and Punjabi only delivering punch lines in English. The humour, as in *GGM*, played on insider knowledge of these languages which delighted parents and grandparents unaccustomed to the sight, let alone the sound, of an Indian on mainstream British television. This partly explains the series' popularity among Asian parents and grandparents.

Moreover, as Bhaskar points out, the butt of the joke was usually the English class system and in most scenarios, as in *GGM*, Indians came out on top. Anil Gupta, BBC producer of *GGM*, also remembers his family's positive reception of the show as a fair portrayal of Indians at that time. It was written from a more informed point of view as is *GGM* which is written from the experience of being Asian in Britain, but makes no attempt to write *for* British Asians.[6]

Sitcoms of the 1970s like *Till Death Us Do Part*, written by Jewish script writer Johnny Speight, attempted to expose the blind bigotry and xenophobia of the English working class at a time when policy makers were promoting integration and Enoch Powell repatriation. However, although racism was the object of laughter, it was easy for the racist imagination to identify and laugh with the racist bigot, Alf Garnett, rather than at him. This aspect of the popular reception of the series highlights the problems of tackling racism through the sitcom genre. Indeed the sitcom itself has been accused of being a racist form (Husband, 1988). But how can we generalise about the ideological progressiveness, or otherwise, of comic forms *per se*? To label a series as racist tends to close down discussion and render it analytically obsolete (Medhurst, 1989). However, whatever one's view, after forty years the sitcom remains a useful point of reference in debates about the politics of 'race' and comedy. The device of conducting comic assaults on racist bigotry, reminiscent of the early films of the Marx Brothers, is exploited by the *GGM* team to comic effect in the series.

The 1970s were held to be a Golden Age in British television comedy but many comedies played the 'race' card for cheap laughs, and exploited the theme of racial tensions by exposing white fears concerning blacks moving into white neighbourhoods. The abusive and insulting name-calling between the chief male protagonists in *Love Thy Neighbour*, using everyday street terms like 'honky' and 'Sambo', was widely appreciated by black audiences. Many interpreted the comic narratives as 'black people getting their own backs on whites', and exposing their preconceptions as ridiculous.[7] But the routines of club comics like Bernard Manning and Jim Davidson, involving jokes based on racist stereotypes reduced blacks and Asians to the status of objects of laughter. Blacks and Asians thus became the 'new Irish'.

Asians and other 'outsiders' also appear as the butt of humour in television comedy series like *Mind Your Language* (*MYL*) where they are portrayed as silly foreigners getting their words mixed up with ridiculous accents. Meera Syal remembers how when at school the catch phrases of *MYL* were replayed in the playground in racist fashion and used to laugh at Asians, herself included – another aspect of British TV comedy which *GGM* reversed with comic effect.[8] Eventually both sitcoms were taken off the air because (as the climate of race relations changed and it was realised that blacks and Asians were in Britain to stay), they were accused of perpetuating racial stereotypes.

Tandoori Nights was one of the first all-Asian comedy shows (1985–87) produced by Channel 4 under its cultural diversity remit. It played out the rivalry of two restaurants, named after major television costume dramas, inspired by Paul Scott's novels set in the British Raj, *Jewel in the Crown* and *The Far Pavilions*. Its comic narratives used the techniques of reverse racism and tackled the issue of Indian prejudices against whites. It introduced new kinds of representations of Asian women, sexy and left-wing, as opposed to stereotypical images of Asian women as passive and submissive victims of archaic cultural traditions and practices. It also addressed inter-racial romance directly. The series poked fun at subjects usually out of the bounds of civilised society such as alleged hygienic customs of Bangladeshis, in the context of 'realistic' dialogues between one rival restaurant owner and another (Naughton, 1985).

Since the 1980s, 'alternative' comedians in Britain, such as Ben Elton, Victoria Wood, French and Saunders and Lenny Henry, have rejected the use of easy sexism and racism as a source of humour. Black British comedians have entered the comedy landscape and altered it irrevocably. British Asians, however, have not been quite so successful in persuading the gatekeepers of broadcasting institutions that 'Asians' can be funny.

'Crossing-Over' and Institutional Racism at the 'Beeb' (the BBC)

Anil Gupta, the producer of *GGM*, had previously been involved in the mainstream satirical show *Spitting Image* and the black comic show *The Real McCoy* with Meera Syal. They decided to do an all-Asian comedy show.[9] They wanted to bring together a pool of high quality British Asian talent to produce a show that would transcend the Asian ethnic label and have wide cross-over appeal. He organised a series of workshops at the BBC for Asian comedy script writers and through that met Sharat Sardana and Richard Pinto (East End of London schoolfriends) who wrote the scripts of the first series. He hand-picked stand-up Asian comics from the comedy club circuits including Nina Wadia, Sanjeev Bhaskar and Kulvinder Gir.

The writers adopted a deliberate strategy of aiming for multicultural audiences, while not alienating the white audience. The objective was to entice the white audience to watch, and once it was captured, to take the comedy further into new terrain. This kind of 'entry' strategy was essential, according to Gupta, if the show was to make white people 'feel comfortable' about Asians telling jokes. It was a deliberate attempt to break into the mainstream. They did not want the kind of show that would inspire guilt in the white audience with constant reminders of racism and the legacy of imperialism. The team was also keenly aware that if the show was perceived to be targeted at ethnic minorities alone, this would alienate white audiences.[10] They wanted sketches that had universal appeal where the humour worked both ways, even-handedly using both whites and

Asians as sources of humour. It was recognised that Indians, too, have stereotypical and sometimes odd views about the English; for example, that they treat their dogs better than their children, sending the latter to boarding school at the age of three. Sanjeev Bhaskar, actor and writer on the show, claims that *GGM* works as a cross-over show 'because we used our Asianness to get our humour across, not the other way round'.[11]

Despite the screening of *GGM*, Gupta is scathing about the condescending and dismissive attitudes that he has encountered at the BBC. In his early days at the BBC he was introduced to the Head of Comedy by a senior producer as 'the new boy who's here on an Equal Opportunities scheme'. Later on, during a discussion of ethnicity and humour, he reports one senior producer of comedy programmes as saying: 'Black Americans are funny, Jews are funny, but the Chinese – I don't think they are funny'.[12] Another producer at the BBC is reported by Gupta to have said: 'I did not realise Asians had a sense of humour until I saw *GGM*'.

Comic Techniques and Textual Strategies in GGM

The title *GGM* itself refers ironically to the comic texts of an era in which white actors – in this case Peter Sellars in the film 'The Millionairess' – 'blacked up' and impersonated ethnic minority characters. Sellars adopted ridiculously exaggerated traits of behaviour, language and speech, exclaiming with idiotic frequency the refrain 'Goodness Gracious Me' from the film song in a distorted Indian accent. This refrain was used to mock Asian kids in the playground. The naming of *GGM* was perceived as a way of reclaiming that phrase.

Disguising, 'passing', mimicking identities are central to much ethnic comedy which exploits the pressures on migrants to assimilate and adopt new identities in their 'new home', where they are often treated as outsiders. The comic play on what is the real essential identity and what is the artificially adopted identity of immigrants, and the collision of different cultural systems in *GGM*, provides excellent comic material. It is through comic performances of ethnicity that discourses placing immigrants as victims can be smashed, notions of cultural authenticity subverted, essentialised ethnicities ridiculed, and new identities imagined and recreated (Gillespie, 1992; Gokturk, 1999).

Playing with Language and Class

According to Sanjeev Bhaskar, the *GGM* team initially hoped to emulate the way in which Jewish humour and Yiddish vocabulary and idioms have passed into colloquial usage in the States. Jewish humour is noted for the ways in which it uses language and logic to subvert authority (Cohen,

2000). Bilingualism, foreign accents, misunderstandings and word-play are exploited for their comic value. *GGM* has clearly succeeded in adopting these devices, bringing Punjabi words and idioms into popular public culture. At the height of its popularity some of the catch-phrases from the series became common parlance, particularly those used by the Bhangra Muffins. They are a pair of working-class, intellectually challenged street boys, fans of Afro-American hip-hop who are desperately seeking cutting-edge status. They speak a street-wise London argot interspersed with Hindi and Punjabi vocabulary.

Phrases such as 'kiss my chuddies' (kiss my underpants) and 'Ras Malai' (an Indian sweet or anyone you fancy) were to be heard in playgrounds and popular parlance all over Britain among youth of all backgrounds. Sanjeev Bhaskar claims that skinheads have run down the street after him playfully calling out 'Ras Malai'. When he has done school workshops, white working-class kids who might otherwise be prone to delivering racial slurs ardently learn the *GGM* Punjabi catch-phrases from their peers.[13] The Minx Twins are the female counterparts of the Bhangra Muffins. Once again subverting stereotypical conceptions of meek subjugated Asian femininity, they are tarty, brash and desperately seeking boys, and everything they say ends with the London/Southall tag 'innit'? Working-class, specifically British-Asian behaviour, 'dumb' speech and mannerisms are the butt of the humour (Gillespie, 1992). The Bhangra Muffins appeal mainly to the younger audiences who enjoy the following kind of exchange:

A – Hey man, there's a global, pan-continental, interracial Ras Malai festival going on. In fact in the year 2050 everyone on the earth will be brown 'cos of inter-racial mixing

B – Yeah, so what you're saying is right that everyone's gonna be Asian?

A – Yeah, that's what I'm saying

B – That's gonna be a massive problem.

A – What are you chattin' about now?

B – Well if everyone in the world is gonna be Asian who can I smoke in front of without my mum finding out?

A – That's a small price to pay for racial harmony man but you gotta think about the positive aspects of Asia World.

B – What's that, man?

A – Well, for example, all shops will be permanently open and you won't have to spend ages waiting for a doctor 'cos you will be one.

Here is a utopian fantasy based on the premise of a world dominated by Asians; a comic reversal of the status of the Asian working class as a minority group in the UK. The image of prevailing racial harmony is (with triumphant bathos) immediately undercut by the resultant surveillance society where transgression of parental norms becomes impossible. The stereotypes of Asian cornershops and doctors are exposed, and used to good comic effect in this vision of Asia World which is as naïve as the stereotypes used to describe it.

Turning the Tables: Reclaiming Punchline Power Through Comic Inversions

A central comic technique used in *GGM* is the subversion of existing stereotypes through the device of comic inversion. For example, a group of Indian students come to England for a holiday in search of authentic English villages. They complain bitterly about the homeless beggars on the streets and the awful food. Another sketch shows a new white English employee in an Indian firm plagued by the miserable failure of his colleagues to pronounce his name ('Jonathan') correctly. This highlights the absurdity of the inability of white British people to pronounce Indian names correctly. The aim, according to Gupta, is to subvert and challenge stereotypes: 'but we could not do it if they did not exist. When the number of stereotypes is too small – when there is only one main stereotype of Asians then that is a problem. That was the case in this country when Asians were seen mainly as working in cornershops'. The proliferation of stereotypes concerning the Asian community preceded the broadcast of *GGM*, perhaps as white British people came to recognise – yet still reject – the diversity of the British Asian minority.

One of the most famous examples of this kind of comic inversion alludes to white racism in Indian restaurants, in the sketch entitled *Going for an English*.

Going for an English

(The setting is Friday evening in downtown Bombay at a Berni Inn. The pubs have just shut.)

A – I'm totally off my face. How come every Friday night we end up in a Berni Inn?

B – 'Cos that's what you do, innit? You go out, you get tanked up and you go for an English. ...

C – I'll have prawn (mispronounces) cocktail with it. What are you having Nina?

D – Could I just have a chicken curry?

ALL – Oh no, its an English restaurant you've got to have something English, no Spices Shisis.

D – I don't like it, too bland.

C – James (calls waiter and mispronounces his name as Jam ess) What have you got that's not totally tasteless? There you are steak and kidney pee!

D – No no it blocks me up I won't go to the toilet for week.

C – That's the whole point of having an English.

GGM turns a stereotypical British experience around in this sketch. Britain boasts an Indian restaurant in every town. It has become the British national dish *par excellence*. 'Going For an Indian' has become a quintessential British experience. New kinds of dishes like the Balti, designed to cater for British tastes, are an excellent example of invented tradition.

Satirising Class Snobbery and Family Rivalry

One response adopted by some migrants in the face of racism and cultural difference in the host country is that of fast-track assimilation and/or to deny one's cultural background. The pretentious striving to be part of the upper middle-class English élite in behaviour, dress, manners and speech is open to comic exploitation as the following 'Cooper' sketch demonstrates:

A – Hello, hello so glad you could make it, come in!
B – So sorry we're late, got held up on the golf course.
A – What is your handicap these days?
B – Still my footing I'm afraid.
A – You must be Vina.
C – Actually, I prefer to be called Vanessa.
A – Oh Vanessa! You never told me your wife was so beautiful Surjit!
B – Still got the old charm you silver-tongued devil. Incidentally, it's not Surjit it's St. John (pronounced Sinjin). So at last I get to meet the lovely Mrs Kapoor.
D – Pronounced Cooper.
B – How's that son of yours Subrash?
D – Sebastian, oh he's abroad at the moment spending a year in India.
B – Good God! Why India of all places?
D – Apparently he's gone to find his roots, you know what these crazy youngsters are like, he says we're losing our cultural identity here in Chigwell.
B – Oh my god, what's this? A brick? Hang on, there's a message on it. It says 'Pakis go home!'
ALL – Quite right!

This sketch performs a comic inversion of typical generational relations, and shows how mechanisms of disidentification and misrecognition work to deny racism in those desperately seeking cultural assimilation, rather than maintenance of cultural integrity. This is where the comic and the serious, if not the tragic, come close together.

Ethnic Caricature

The series draws upon a range of stock characters familiar to British Asians, whose idiosyncrasies are played out across episodes. *Hunky La Funga* is the archetypal Bollywood macho male, conceited, phoney, stupid and deeply uncool. *Smeeta Smitten the Showbiz Kitten* opens each sketch with 'Miaow pussycats!' and claims to loiter in the 'litter tray of the stars to unearth hot juicy turds of exclusive gossip for your delight'. These characters satirise the sham flamboyance and glitter of Bollywood stars, and the gossip columnists of the ever popular Hindi film magazines. *Mr Everything Comes From India* is the ultimate chauvinist who is forever pointing out the Indian origins of everything English – 'verandhas, polo, shampoo, bungalow, all Indian!' Also Father Christmas: 'big beard, fat man, terrible suit. Indian!' In fact everything comes from India except Apache Indian (a British Asian pop act) and Balti cooking (a type of curry unknown in India but popular here). Ironically, he proclaims: 'They're from Birmingham'. Then there is the thrifty matriarch *Mrs Bedi 'I can make it at home for nothing'*. 'Why would anyone want to pay perfectly good money for something you can make at home for nothing? Heh ha?'

Although these characters speak specifically to British Asians, they also embody more universal characteristics that transcend ethnic difference. Pomposity and cultural chauvinism can be found in most cultures.

Parody

The team are talented singers and they regularly include a song and/or dance act. They have spoofed a number of pop songs with their own lyrics which again have caught on in the manner of catch phrases. These include 'I'm a Barbie Girl' which translates into 'I'm a Punjabi Girl' and parodies prevalent stereotypes of Asian girls as passive, oppressed creatures. They have also reworked Pulp's hit 'Common People' into 'Hindi People' which parodies the 'Asian Cool' trend of pop stars like Madonna, while at the same time satirising the dependence of young Asians on their parents, and their parents' willingness to put up with them:

> Take a medical degree graduate at 33
> Move back in with mum and dad
> Even though they drive you raving mad
> You sure you want to live like Hindi people?
>
> I wanna live like Hindi people
> I wanna eat what Hindi people eat
> I wanna dress like Bindi people
> I wanna wear Mendhi on my feet.

In a similar vein, a young Asian man tries to rebel against his parents by becoming a doctor not a pop singer and refusing their offers of cocaine. This reflects the growth of 'Asian cool' and the new interest in careers in media. The show is also unsparing towards whites' attitudes and stereotypes as it is to Asians. In another sketch there is the Indian woman fleeing her violent husband. She arrives at a women's refuge, pursued by her husband brandishing an enormous knife. The worker, however, refuses to intervene in case that would be 'culturally oppressive'. The cultural relativism of white liberals is thus attacked in this aggressive but hilarious comic assault.

White liberal society has responded positively to *GGM* and what it is trying to achieve. The series has been promoted by the BBC and mouthpieces for British society in general as a token of harmonious 'race' relations. But what of British Asians?

Reception of GGM among British Asians

What follows is a summary of some general patterns of response from British Asians of all ages who were interviewed.[14] First and foremost, the series is seen to create a generational division. It is understood by all age groups to appeal mainly to young British Asians (ten to thirty-five years) born and brought up in this country. Its very Britishness is thus stressed through its appeal to second-generation British Asians. Those parents who do enjoy it tend to be younger, and their pleasure in it is understood to expose their 'Westernised' and liberal values. The series can thus serve as an indication of the underlying values among parents:

H – Like the guy who eventually tells his parents he's gay and that his white friend is his partner and they go 'well, couldn't you find yourself a nice Indian boy?' (laughter) it really brings home their real values which come out as hypocritical you know .. that's all they're concerned about that you don't go out with a white person ..

S – Like I'm Hindu and if there came the option. .. they'd go for the Hindu first, the Muslim next but no way English, no way! (laughter)

P – it shows how ridiculous those values are.

Some parents protest that *GGM* corrupts their children's minds, others feel that it mocks grandparents and the elderly excessively, thus flouting a key norm of unconditional respect for elders. In treating all things Indian as 'Pindu' (backward or peasantish), some say that it plays into the hands of racism. Many parents claim that the show started out very well, with its timely exposure of white racism and Asian comic caricatures. However, in later series it lost its critical edge and took taboo subjects too far, becoming overly preoccupied with sexually explicit and bawdy humour that prevented families from watching it together. But as one young girl said, 'nothing's going to be good without offending someone'.

It is the direct exposure and airing given to taboo subjects such as homosexuality and the norms of endogamous marriage that so delights its fans. The rivalrous mothers who compare the size of their sons 'dundaars' (penises) sends up the Oedipal attachment of sons and mothers so reminiscent of Jewish humour. But most of my interviewees recoil at the Punjabi Adult Porn Phone Line where a son reaches orgasm on the phone to the impersonated sounds of his mother's voice. By the third series many found that 'they were scraping the barrel for cheap laughs'. Punjabi humour is known for its 'quick fire repartee and bawdiness, but this is not Punjabi humour', according to one parent. He claims that *GGM* has reinforced regional stereotypes of Punjabi Sikhs as terrorists, obsessed with Bhangra music. Numerous complaints about alleged mockery of a Hindu wedding ritual by Hindus were upheld by the Broadcasting Standards Commission. The *GGM* team said they missed the point. The object of humour were the second-generation kids who practise rituals without bothering to find out about their symbolic meanings. The hostile reactions of some more fundamentalist Hindus has apparently resulted in a death threat to the team. This gives some indication of the different degrees of provocation felt, and the hugely variable responses to *GGM* among British Asians.

GGM is seen to bring out not only the religious and class differences between families but also, paradoxically, the commonalities. Sharing the jokes creates intimacy and cultural group identification:

P – The programme brings out a lot of things that are so common in Asian families that you tend to forget about [due to an emphasis on religious and other axes of differences among British Asians] and the way the programme keys into that is really amusing.

G – like suitcases on the top of wardrobes, plastic covering carpets, crazy family picnics and parents over-reacting at things.

Amarjit – and fruit cream on every dessert (laughs).

Status competition and rivalry among parents over their children's achievement and upward mobility is one of the key targets. As Sarita says 'It's always like you've got to do one better you know, it's quite common'. But parents are also the butt of humour due to their failure to assimilate and understand British ways: 'like the one where the dad turns up and says, "Kids I've got a pet for you" and he brings a cow into the kitchen'. Here the incongruous concepts clash to great comic effect.

Across the interviews, young British Asians are able to reel off sketch after sketch and appropriate the comic narratives to express aspects of their own lives and the lives of British Asians more generally. But perhaps what is most appreciated are the comic assaults on racism. They are widely held to be affirmative and to bolster confidence, helping young people to reject discourses of victimhood, alienation and marginalisation. As one interviewee put it, '*GGM* does cover the difficulties of our lives as Asians but it makes you feel inspired to go out and assert yourself and not to be afraid to challenge anyone in authority. .. we do love our parents but we can't always agree with their ideas so that inevitably creates conflict'. Therein lie the identificatory processes acting within *GGM* that both amuse and ultimately empower the British Asian viewer.

Re-branding Britain 'Multicultural'

GGM has come to occupy a central position in British popular culture as the series which broke boundaries in British 'race' relations in terms of their relationship and representation of the Asian community in particular. Though not a politically correct show, some claim it has done more for antiracism than a thousand earnest documentaries. White British people, from liberals to skinheads, have laughed at the hypocrisies and the arrogant prejudices of the English or British. The British establishment have also used the series to signal the re-branding of a multicultural Britain, and to mark and symbolise a new era of tolerant British 'race' relations: 'with no help from marketing departments, Britain is re-branding itself: ... "mainstream" is no longer synonymous with "white"'.[15]

The show ignited a public debate. Murdoch's conservative newspaper *The Times* (7 January 1998) published a leader article celebrating *GGM* as a British comedy classic and lauding it as the 'oil of race relations ... for when blacks, whites and Asians can laugh together the sting is taken from prejudice or crude generalisation'. According to *The Times*, *GGM* is eclectic, based on old traditions of quirky British humour which have been readily accepted and updated by the *GGM* team:

> The British sense of humour is something that even foreigners, depressed by the weather and despairing over the food, agree makes life in Britain worth living. ... The famous sense of humour has also emerged as the secret ingredient in that other little trumpeted success, Britain's increasingly successful race relations record.... It would be unthinkable in America: race relations are too brittle and the tyranny of political correctness too pervasive. Old Britain and its more recent immigrants are lucky. When both laugh at each other, both like each other better for doing so.[16]

Such assertions have to be considered in the light of a paradoxical feature of British society: the simultaneous tendency towards, on the one hand, multiculturalism, and on the other hand, mounting racism and nationalist chauvinism. Stephen Lawrence's murder and the subsequent McPherson Report highlight widespread institutional racism in the police force, and the rise in racially motivated attacks and violence. A report by the Runnymede Trust reveals the endemic Islamophobia in British society. The reports, coupled with the relative poverty, deprivation and lack of access to opportunities and resources among Pakistanis and Bangladeshis also suggest that we have no reason to be complacent.

Despite considerable advances made in multicultural broadcasting in Britain, both in mainstream and specialist television units, there is plenty of evidence that ethnocentrism and subtle forms of racism persist. There are few examples of overt racism thanks to established codes of practice, self-censorship and the prevailing climate of political correctness. However, broadcasting institutions need to be proactive in the antiracist struggle since the achievement of a truly multicultural society cannot be left to market forces or 'natural evolution' alone; but the pursuit of ratings increasingly makes producers play safe. With the success of *GGM* the BBC can claim to have 'done its bit' for British 'race'-relations; but has it and is it enough? The future of multiculturalism in broadcasting, despite the achievements of shows such as *GGM*, is still uncertain. Now that the third series is over, what will replace it? Will the writers and performers find more work, and if so, will they always have the 'Asian' comic label attached to their names? What is the future of integrated casting? Will we arrive at a moment when we simply do not notice that half the cast of a comedy show is Asian or black? Will the numbers of blacks and Asians at the top echelons of television companies increase? Is the mobilisation of essentialist categories such as Black and Asian in the battle to secure scarce resources simply reinforcing categorical groupings which are, in the long term, counter-productive? Time alone will tell. [17]

Notes

1. *Front Row*, BBC Radio 4, 10 November 1998.
2. *GGM* first appeared on BBC Radio 4 in July 1996 in an 11.25pm slot and was popular with the middle-aged, middle-class white audience. In 1997 it received a Sony Gold Award (a prestigious radio award), having captured an audience of 2.83 million. It transferred to BBC2 television in 1998 and was no less successful. It got an average of three million viewers which, for a new BBC2 comedy series, is an excellent rating. 85 percent of the audience were not Asian. Given a population of 1.26 million Indians, Pakistanis and Bangladeshis, this is more a matter of arithmetic than an upsurge of interest on the part of white viewers. *GGM* had gone mainstream. (These statistics are reported in *Guardian Weekend*, 20 February 1999.) The second and third TV series were given a prime slot on Friday night at 9.30 p.m. in recognition of its success and status. According to Meera Syal, the television show was watched mostly by white males aged between eleven and twenty. She claims: 'You know you've made it when you get a response from middle England'. But the show has been hugely successful with Asian audiences too – a group that the BBC had failed previously to reach in any great number. More than half of the potential Asian audience watched the second series. Though no breakdown figures are available, judging from audience profiles at their nation-wide live performances, these audiences are young (mainly eighteen to thirty-five), middle-class, and, like Meera

Syal and the rest of the team, very relaxed with a hyphenated British-Asian identity (cited Hotline, November 1998).

3. See <http://www.wmin.ac.uk/media/pgjnet/sarah-gill/meera.html>, page 2.
4. *Front Row,* op. cit.
5. *Front Row,* op.cit.
6. *Laughing Matters*, BBC Radio 4, 22 February 2000.
7. *Laughing Matters,* op.cit.
8. *Laughing Matters,* op.cit.
9. *Laughing Matters,* op.cit.
10. *Guardian Weekend*, 20 February 1999.
11. *Guardian Weekend*, 20 February 1999.
12. 'Making or Breaking Stereotypes.' Talk and Discussion by the *GGM* team in the 'Inspirations and Aspirations Series' organised by Dhooleka Raj, at Lucy Cavendish College, University of Cambridge, UK, held on 10 May 1999.
13. As above.
14. This section draws upon extensive interviews with fifteen British Asians of all ages conducted over 1998–2000.
15. *Guardian Weekend*, 20 February 1999.
16. *The Times*, 9 January 1999, p. 9.
17. This chapter is based upon research that was conducted as part of the Economic and Social Research Council's Transnational Communities Programme. The project, 'Axial Writing: Transnational Literatures, Cultural Politics and State Policies', (Grant number L214 25 2030) was conducted between 1998–2002.

CHAPTER 8

CURIOSITY, FEAR AND CONTROL

THE AMBIGUOUS REPRESENTATION OF HIP-HOP ON FRENCH TELEVISION

Chris Warne

The question of social exclusion has dominated political debate in France for more than a decade. Evidently, television has played a key role both as a medium for this debate, in setting its parameters and establishing its visual representation. Of particular focus has been the question of the *banlieues*, or outer-city housing estates, that have emerged as the particular sites for the litany of social problems associated with exclusion (poor housing, reduced educational and employment opportunity, high levels of crime and violence, concentrations of ethnic minority groups). However, as many observers have pointed out, the anonymous and universalised media-propagated picture of social deprivation that is conjured up in the social discourse on 'the problems of *banlieue*', fails to address either the need for a particular explanation of what are often complex, localised problems, or the need to find localised solutions (Boyer and Lochard, 1998: 91–107). Thus no one single, identifiable group emerges from the rather amorphous conglomeration of 'outsiders' (whether they be immigrants, drug-pushers or young rioters) that appears to populate these 'areas in difficulty'. It is for this reason perhaps that over the same period, many in the television media have seized on the emergence of hip-hop in France, firstly as a way of understanding life in the *banlieue* (hip-hop artists and practitioners become valuable witnesses in coverage of the question), and secondly as a way of presenting the problems of social exclusion as an individual drama that can be understood and empathised with.

The result has been that the equation 'hip-hop equals *banlieue*' is now more or less taken for granted in many quarters (Calio, 1998). As such, it is an equation that is both exploited and disputed by practitioners of this cultural form themselves. On the one hand, several rap groups present themselves as the bearers of an urgent message on the decay of French society at its outer margins (as revealed in phrases like 'nous sommes les hauts-parleurs de la banlieue' ["we are the housing estates' megaphone"] or 'le rap, c'est le CNN des cités' ['rap is the CNN of the projects']). The pre-eminence of the visual media is evident in this metaphor. On the other hand, many dispute an equation that threatens to relegate a viable and autonomous set of cultural practices to the status of mere by-product of poverty and social miserabilism. This alternate exploitation and rejection of an association between rap and *banlieue*, that is to a large extent the product of television coverage of the phenomenon, shows that the culture itself is not only media aware, but to a large extent media dependent. An examination of aspects of the representation of hip-hop on French television since the mid-1980s should therefore shed light on the relationship between a dominating institution on the one hand (the institutions of televisual media in France) and a minority group on the other (the loose collective of hip-hop musicians, artists and practitioners). Despite the latter's initial marginal position, it has nonetheless succeeded in both attracting attention to itself, and to an extent, in questioning television's practices.

Three moments can be identified in this televisual representation (the moments of curiosity, fear and censorship). They can be identified as three particular moments in a chronology, corresponding to three particular periods of television's continued fascination with French hip-hop. However, in a less strictly chronological sense, it could be said that these three moments recur as impulses in *all* representation of hip-hop on French television. It is the contradictory interplay between these impulses that in part explains the rather ambiguous relationship that has developed in France between television and hip-hop as a minority group.

The Moment of Curiosity

The first prolonged interaction between television in France and hip-hop culture came in 1984, with the weekly broadcast of *Hip-Hop* on TF1. It was initially conceived as a stopgap before a reorganisation of the Sunday schedule to take account of competition from the newly privatised channels. For a short while at least, the programme became the vanguard for a period of media fascination with hip-hop, and with forms of hip-hop dance in particular (breaking, body-popping), collectively described in France as the *vague smurf* (the smurf wave). The programme was very much at the initiative of Marie-France Brière, the new head of light entertainment at the station. She had been aware of the new popularity of hip-hop at her previous post at the independent Radio 7, where a regular slot devoted to black dance music had become the focus for a network of young dancers, rappers and musicians. The DJ for that slot, Sidney, was himself a trained dancer, and had already visited New York and embraced the new forms of street dance emerging from the Bronx. It was through his contacts with Brière that he became the presenter of *Hip-Hop* (Bocquet and Pierre-Adolphe, 1997: 53–63). The greeting with which he opened each programme ('Bonjour les frères et les sœurs' ['Hello brothers and sisters']) both created the tone for the programme as a whole, and revealed the optic through which this new form of culture was being presented. What was emphasised was the playful, ludic side of hip-hop, its ability to unite young people of all cultures and colours in a new international family, celebrating their 'natural' energy and inventiveness. The format evolved a little during the year of its broadcast, but remained broadly focused around a dance lesson, where Sidney and a colleague demonstrate a particular aspect or move of break dancing, and where the programme climaxes in a competition between two young hopefuls, who have to demonstrate their aptitude in a series of set moves, before being given free rein in a short freestyle piece. If Sidney presided over the televisual proceedings in a paternalistic fashion, the family affair was reinforced by the presence of 'older brothers' in the shape of the dance troupe Paris City Breakers, formed as a result of contacts from Sidney's time at Radio 7, and who acted as the judges of the competition.

The programme, then, is strictly located in the genre of light entertainment, and bears many of the hallmarks of youth pop music television from the period (use of a warehouse-like studio, active audience participation from the surrounding scaffolding/stage set). Sidney himself was given a fair amount of autonomy regarding the scripting and content of the shows: however, in focusing principally on the dance aspect of hip-hop, the programme perhaps deliberately eschews any confrontation with some of the issues that were to dominate French hip-hop later in the decade (violence, racism, ethnicity). Even visits to the home of hip-hop in New York are undertaken without any real attempt to contextualise the movement in terms of the social problems of the Bronx. This was undoubtedly to prove a weakness in the programme. Inevitably, as media interest in smurf as a dance fad waned, so too did support for the programme from the institutional forces at TF1. After a year, the programme was pulled. Sidney himself sought to convert his capital as a youth television presenter in subsequent short-lived and less successful projects that dealt more broadly with pop culture. The moment of curiosity was over.

However, despite this institutional disregard for the new movement, television had undoubtedly played a vital role in its development in France. There is a clear distinction here between the purposes of the programme-makers themselves, and the uses made of that programme by members of the audience. Firstly, the programme played a significant local role: the television studios of TF1 from which *Hip-Hop* was broadcast quickly became the assembly point for young people, many from the housing estates on the outskirts of Paris. It was in the course of such assemblies that many of the networks and contacts were formed that were to prove vital in the re-emergence of hip-hop and rap in France towards the end of the decade, not just between performers and artists, but between future promoters, record-label managers and fanzine writers (Bazin, 1995: 23). Secondly, the programme had a wider national impact for a very particular constituency. Many biographies and life-stories of first and second generation hip-hop practitioners in France are marked by a reference to the moment when Sidney's programme was first broadcast: for many young people growing up in the ethnically mixed suburbs, it seems that *Hip-Hop* served as a vital affirmation, for it was in effect the first time that this group were seeing themselves on television, not just as the subject (or object?) of reports into the social problems of the *banlieue*, but as presenters, as active participants and above all as performers (Madec, 1998: 30–1). Thus despite the limited aims of the programme-makers, and despite the lack of priority accorded the programme by TF1 as an institution, it is fair to say that television here played a vital role in forming and promoting a sense of group belonging and group identity, a sense that was to prove essential for the continuation of hip-hop in France in the years that followed, against a background of indifference and even hostility from cultural and media institutions in France (Boucher, 1999: 63–9).

The Moment of Fear

The year 1990 marks a turning-point in the general debate about the *banlieue* in France. A year after the euphoric sense of unity, inspired domestically by the bicentennial celebrations and internationally by the fall of the Berlin wall, and two years after François Mitterrand's overwhelming re-election as president 'of all the French', a series of events called into fundamental question the national solidarity that was supposed to have developed around the new political and social consensus of the post-Cold War. In November, at Vaulx-en-Velin in the Lyons suburbs, riots broke out in response to the death of a young motorcyclist after he was involved in a collision with a police car. In the same month, demonstrations in Paris organised by high-school students to protest against proposed reforms of the exam system, ended in violence as shops were looted, cars hijacked and set alight, and police injured as they tried to restore order. These two spectacular moments served to draw further attention to the question of youth gangs which had simmered in the popular Parisian media throughout the summer, where reports centred on the existence of exotically named, ethnically segregated groups engaged in violent confrontation over territory, a violence that seemed to culminate in staged confrontations in the Défense and Les Halles areas of the city (Negroni, 1991). By highlighting the continued existence of a marginalised, alienated youthful group drawn from the housing estates and projects of France's larger cities, the riots also seemed to offer an interpretation for the wave of graffiti and tagging that had engulfed Paris and its public transport networks since the mid-1980s. This was surely the same group expressing their alienation in another form (Vulbeau, 1992).

It is well to underline, however, the sense of shock and bewilderment that greeted these events, not just on the part of France's political class; the socialist governments of the 1980s had after all devoted considerable energy and resources to tackling the problems of social exclusion in the *banlieue*. The emergence of the so-called *Beur* movement from the same areas of social deprivation in the 1980s had been read by many as a positive sign that the previously alienated and excluded children of immigrants were now positively engaged in constructive dialogue with the political processes and institutions of the Republic (see chapter 6 for an analysis of the representation of French Maghrebis on French television).[1] Thus it is bewilderment that dominates early television news reports of these phenomena, a bewilderment increased by the sense of strangeness that the average metropolitan journalist felt on entering the suburbs for the first time. The media interest in gang warfare had in any case been launched not by television, but by the written press. Thus, to the general sense of bewilderment must be added a sense that television is playing 'catch-up' on this issue, following the lead established by other forms of media. A report for TF1's eight o'clock news by Allan Rothschild in August 1990 is typical in this respect. Visiting the Cité des Bosquets in Montfermeil in the Seine-St-Denis suburbs to follow up police reports of feuding gangs, Rothschild frames his report by a description of the estate as rundown, inhabited by a plethora of different nationalities. The bored youth of this estate need only the slightest excuse to engage in violent confrontation between races (the many nationalities have now become two ethnicities, 'black' and 'beur'). There follows a series of vox pops, clearly in response to the leading question 'have you seen the gangs?', for the most part conducted at an apparently 'safe' distance, with the journalist addressing inhabitants on their apartment balconies or through their windows. Thus the sense of prison evoked in his opening with reference to the estate's 'six barres d'immeuble' ('six tower blocks', but 'barre' can also be a prison bar) is reinforced by the framing of the inhabitants themselves. They are pictured imprisoned by the problems of the estate, and by the violence of the young gangs. The sense of an untraversable distance between journalist and interviewee is reinforced by the clear exaggeration of some replies to his questions. One youth in particular willingly talks of violence and bloodshed with an assumed wide-eyed naïvety: such is his exaggeration that his companion stalks off snorting with apparent contempt for the interview process. Thus no concrete evidence for the existence of the gangs is produced (there are no interviews with gang members for example, or with police officers who may have arrested gang members), but the picture of growing ethnic tensions on France's housing estates is apparently confirmed by a readiness to complain about one's neighbours, and by the final shot of a youth playing with a knife.

A similar sense of the dangerous strangeness of these new youth tribes is evoked in a report on tagging and graffiti for TF1's news magazine programme *Envoyé Spécial* in April 1990. Clearly the mission of the programme is to get to what underlies this phenomenon. However, before this explicative mission can be fulfilled (and the skill of the journalists in deciphering the signs revealed), the very incomprehensibility of the phenomenon is first evoked, either with the interjections of bewildered passers-by ('Non, non, c'est du turque? C'est du romain, c'est quoi, vous savez, vous?' ['I've no idea, is it Turkish? Is it Roman, what is it? Do you know?']), or with shots of graffiti-filled walls in metro stations, the alienating impact of which is enhanced by the isolated (and by implication vulnerable?) female passengers pictured sitting in front of them. One of the four groups who are the focus of this report (KTA) spend their time in the Paris catacombs, and their familiarity with, and agile navigation of this mysterious terrain is in direct contrast to the reporting crew, who are shown struggling with their equipment through the network of darkened passages and tunnels. The ethnographic aspect of this report, with the journalists in the role as intrepid explorers of the urban jungle, is further reinforced by its presence within a programme that devotes much of its content to the analysis of foreign news;[2] but as presenter Paul Nahon explains in the preamble to the screening of the report, this expedition into the unknown also calls for a reconsideration of tagging. He invites the viewer to suspend judgement, to ignore the impulse to dismiss graffiti as simple vandalism. By the end of the piece, tagging is indeed read as a sign, but not simply of alienated youth, but rather of a youth in movement, inventing their own language and style, and in so doing, uniting themselves with the young of 'toutes les grandes villes de la planète' ['all the large cities in the world']. French television is helping to record the emergence of a new youth identity.

This revalorisation of tagging as a resistant subculture coincides with a wider movement in television reporting of the young of the *banlieue* throughout 1990 and 1991 (Boyer and Lochard, 1998: 109–15). As noted in connection with the report on gang activity, the discourse on the 'dangerous youth of the suburbs' was not invented by television, but to some extent inherited from the written press. Perhaps in a desire to establish intermedia differentiation, or from a willingness to engage in self-criticism, there emerges a distinct attempt to avoid painting the situation in the *banlieue* as being completely desperate. It is for this reason no doubt that hip-hop is seized upon. In turn, hip-hop practitioners used television as a means of expressing themselves. In seeking a new angle, television exploited the existence of groups of rappers, dancers and artists, marked by a genuine articulateness, as ideal material for a re-evaluation. A series of reports towards the end of 1990 unfailingly presents hip-hop as a positive way forward for a group experiencing the pressures of social exclusion and deprivation. No doubt such encounters were seized upon by particular groups themselves as a valuable form of self-promotion (hence the recurring presence of the later to be nationally famous rap group NTM in several of these reports); and no doubt once such contacts were established, they provided a convenient access point into the strange world of the *banlieue*. A report on TF1's eight o'clock news following the violent demonstrations of November in Paris set out to establish the identity of the 'casseurs' ['rioters'] who had led the violence. While no rioter could be found, a rap group (le Clan MC) from Seine-St-Denis, who had featured a fortnight earlier in the context of a quite different report on the re-emergence of French rap, was approached by journalist Thomas Hugues for their explanations of the rioters' motivation (though they had not been present themselves at the demonstrations). Thus to a certain extent, television is seeking to play a distinct role from other sections of the media. There is a desire to overcome the moment of fear, first through the foregrounding of a strategy to get 'behind' the spectacle of violence, and to understand the concerns of the participants, and secondly through a strategy of building contacts with this strange world by picking up on a cultural movement that could be presented as the positive face of a difficult situation.

However, for this strategy to be successful in the longer term, it would depend to a large extent on the willingness of hip-hop artists and practitioners to play the role cast for them by television, namely that of the saviours of their estates. As noted above, undoubtedly the attraction of media attention was tempting for many of the individuals, artists and groups that were solicited by a series of news reports, televised debates and documentaries on the *banlieue* and its problems throughout the early 1990s. In these interviews, many of these groups demonstrate a keen awareness of the processes involved in creating the televisual spectacle, choosing either to adopt a policy of deliberately playing up to the camera, or of trying to take control of the direction of the programme through adopting disconcerting or even aggressive postures. In the longer term, however, some began to be wary of such media attention, first from a realisation of the dangers of reducing themselves to simply an aspect of the now rather monotonous discourse on '*la banlieue*', and secondly from a refusal to be cast in the role of the brave, but naïve heroes of a situation which was neither of their making or their solving (as Joey Starr of NTM was to put it, 'nous refusons le rôle du bon nègre' ['we refuse to play the role of the good negro']). Perhaps it is not surprising then, that in rejecting the terms of the dialogue that television offered to them as a minority group, certain hip-hop artists and practitioners found themselves caught up in another moment of television's encounter with hip-hop in France, that is, in the moment of censorship.

The Moment of Censorship

On more than one occasion during the 1990s, rap songs, videos and even concerts were at the centre of calls for censorship and control. Perhaps the most notorious of these occasions was the so-called NTM affair of November 1996, when the group were sentenced to a six-month prison sentence (later reduced to three months suspended on appeal), and forbidden from performing in France, also for a six-month period, by the magistrates court in Toulon. The charge against the group had been brought by an alliance of several police associations -from both the left and the right – who had been outraged by the nature of the group's participation in an antiracist concert held at La Seyne-sur-Mer in July 1995, organised to protest against the advance of the extreme-right National Front in a series of local elections, most notably the election of mayor at Toulon. NTM had taken the opportunity of this concert to launch into a tirade against the police, denouncing them as the 'real fascists', and expressing their urge to 'fuck the police, and piss on the justice system'. It was for these words then that the group were condemned (for the crime of insulting an officer of the state) and not for the lyrics of one of their songs. However, the debate that ensued was dominated by the theme of freedom of expression, with politicians of both left and right queuing up to express their concern at, or approval of, the judgement. Television coverage of the event quickly latched onto this freedom of speech angle, despite the fact that the group themselves refused to employ the freedom of expression plea as part of their own defence. Thus, some issues received less attention from the televisual media than in some press coverage of the affair. For example the question of the difficult relationship between the police and portions of the young populations of the *banlieue*, or the particular political circumstances in Toulon that would allow a single magistrate to pass such a judgement.

Why then should the affair so rapidly be turned into a debate about censorship and freedom of expression? Several reasons can be found to explain this. Firstly, the promotion of rap undoubtedly gets to the heart of the ambiguities surrounding the role of television in a democracy – as an instrument of free speech, or as a normative hegemonic force – and in particular the influence that it may or may not have over the young. Because hip-hop targets a young audience, anxiety is expressed in some quarters as to what rap's often direct treatment of violence – and to a lesser extent in France – its apparent predilection for sexist imagery and macho attitudes, might have on that constituency. Obviously, current affairs coverage finds itself at the heart of this dilemma as to whether it should portray things 'as they are', or whether account should be taken of the sensibilities of the potential audience, and in the commercial sector, of potential and actual sponsors. Such ambiguities are obvious in 'background' reporting of the NTM affair, where the group's previous encounters with the authorities were routinely cited. An interview for A2's eight o'clock news in November 1996 with Olivier Richard, the director of programmes at the cable channel MCM, reveals that they were cautious about programming the groups 1995 video 'J'appuie sur la gachette' ['I pull the trigger'], which in recounting the suicide of a young unemployed man, graphically shows the moment of suicide with a pistol shot to the head; and yet the whole interview is carefully staged and conducted in an edit suite, with the offending image clearly visible and frozen on two monitors behind Richard. Similar rather disingenuous flouting of the unwritten codes of propriety in television characterised the national cable channel Canal Plus's coverage of the affair, who adopted a frankly supportive attitude to the group, according them plenty of respectful air time in which to present their case. Again the commercial imperative is present in this championing of the underdog, as directors of the channel were doubtless aware of the need to avoid alienating their own core constituency, which undoubtedly overlaps with the audience for rap in France.

If the NTM affair, and other less notorious confrontations between French rap and the censors, reveals something of the ambiguous relationship that television has maintained with hip-hop in France, it also allows us to begin to address the other side of the relationship, which is how members of the movement practise the televisual media once they find themselves immersed in them. As noted in connection with the re-emergence of hip-hop in the early 1990s, hip-hop practitioners have often showed a keen awareness of, and a willingness to play with, the processes at work in the construction of the television news agenda. The NTM affair itself revealed a particular rap group who were choosy about their allies and supporters, whether in or out of the media, and choosy too about the moments when they would express their reaction to the judgement. However, as hip-hop has developed in France, so have the opportunities for members of this minority group to control the camera more directly, in particular through the medium of the pop video. Something of the nature of how this minority works out its relation to the medium of television can be seen in an analysis of two of NTM's videos, both of which have been the subject of forms of control and censorship, though short of a complete ban. Television has had an ambivalent relationship with hip-hop to date. The NTM pop videos, presumably designed to be screened on French terrestrial as well as specialised cable or satellite music stations, exploit this ambivalence in an aggressive way, confronting dominant social taboos surrounding sex and suicide.

The first video, 'J'appuie sur la gachette' made in 1995 and mentioned above, was given limited air-play because of its graphic treatment of suicide. The second, 'Ma Benz' ('My [Mercedes] Benz') made in 1998, was the subject of a restriction order limiting broadcast to after ten o'clock at night, placed by the body responsible for the regulation of the broadcast media in France (the Conseil Supérieur de l'AudioVisuel or CSA), on the grounds that the video 'degraded the image of women'.

In both cases, the clear intention of the group is to be provocative. However, this provocation is achieved in two very contrasting ways. In the first case ('J'appuie sur la gachette'), it is guaranteed by the exploitation of images that while stylised, are hyper-realistic in their portrayal of a violent suicide. The opening shot is a textual warning about the potential to shock of what will follow. The group make no apology however: they have done no more than relate a true story, knowing that 'on occasion, truth is stranger than fiction' ['la réalité parfois dépasse la fiction']. The video is shot in a near black and white, and the action takes place either in the cramped circumstance of a shadowy cell, or in the similarly claustrophobic surroundings of a council flat. Intercut between shots of the group performing in this environment, the story is developed of a young boy at odds with his indifferent father, of the same individual as a young man who is the victim of a violent police raid on the flat (a gun is held to his head, an image that is reprised at the moment of the suicide), culminating in his mental collapse and suicide. His increasingly fragile mental state is conveyed through increasingly fast cutting (by the end of the song, an almost stroboscopic cut occurs on every beat of the bar), but also by disorienting camera effects and interferences. The group's stance is clear: while performing, they stare accusingly at the camera, inviting the viewer to share not only the sadness of the story, but also some of the guilt for daring to be indifferent to its occurrence. Their stance mimics that adopted by some *banlieue* youth in documentaries and news reports.

In the second case ('Ma Benz') an opposite strategy is employed. If the images in 'J'appuie sur la gachette' are marked by an exaggerated realism, 'Ma Benz' is marked by a fantastic translation of 'naked' masculine desire. The link between the commercial promotion of cars and female sexuality is taken to a shocking extreme. Mid-shots and close-ups of black models in provocative poses on cars as if in a peep-show are intercut with tracking shots of the rappers on the circular stage, themselves performing: they struggle with each other to be at the front and in full shot, as if fighting to get a better view of the spectacle, but also to be the star of that same spectacle. Further intercut are brief shots of each of the rappers entwined in sexual pose with one of the models, on car-seat-like sofas arranged around the stage. It is as if the 'don't touch' barrier imposed on the peep-show audience has been traversed by the group. From being outsiders, spectators at a party to which they were not invited, they are now participating in the realisation of their own fantasy, a participation enabled by commercial success in general, but by the material acquisition of a car in particular.

The provocative side of this celebration is the implication that the female models are simply another aspect of this material acquisition, and it was this objectification of women that brought the judgement of the CSA. However, it could be said that the provocation occurs at a deeper level: in their appropriation of the televisual media, the group are simply pushing to an exaggerated extreme one logic of television discourse, that is, the commercial promotion of a product via a blatant association with male sexual desire. Similarly, in 'J'appuie sur la gachette', the group push another logic of television to its extreme, but in this case, the logic of news reporting, and its aim to transparently represent the realities of the world, no matter how indigestible. It is almost as if hip-hop is taking its revenge on the television medium, repossessing it and putting it to hip-hop's own uses. This repossession of a media form that has previously served to define the *banlieue* youth is reminiscent of the use of video by other minority groups, as a means of achieving self-representation. Having been positioned first as exotic, a curiosity of the urban jungle, secondly as an aspect of a social danger (no matter how positive an aspect), this minority group are now daring the institutions of television to face the consequences of their own practices: will they admit to ownership of a monster that they have helped create, or will they resort to control and censorship? Much of the ambiguity of television's relationship to hip-hop in France stems from what has become a perpetually indecisive response to this question.

Notes

1. *Beur*, the *verlan* (backslang) for *Arabe*, is a term that has come to be generally applied to those born in France but of North African origin. For an insider's critical account of the misapprehensions surrounding this movement, see Bouamama, 1994.
2. For a probing account of the way that the other is both fetichised and exoticised in *Envoyé Spécial*, see Buxton, 1995.

CHAPTER 9

GREEN ACTIVIST IDENTITIES ON BRITISH TELEVISION

Derek Wall

What are the chances of a runaway from a children's home forming relationships with both the PR of a local Middlesbrough factory and a young
woman campaigning against the industrial pollution from said factory,
which killed her brother? ... What started as *Kes* has now become *Edge of
Darkness*. I feel like I'm in Thatcher's Britain again. ... This is a brave commission in a world where cosy thirty-something dramas reign. ... Someone's
conscience up at BBC Towers is clearly being eased by it all.
> Review of *Nature Boy*. *Evening Standard*, 17 February 2000.

I watched the opening of the recent BBC drama, *Nature Boy*, and thought
it was good, but I never got past the first episode. My schedule is just too
hectic.
> Darren Johnson, Green Party candidate for London mayor,
> *Guardian*, 17 April 2000.

This chapter stemmed from an interest in Green activist identity formation; namely, the question of how individuals became radicalised,
transforming their identities and joining militant collective movements
that mobilised against some of the most obviously destructive manifestations of capitalist growth from Twyford Down to the World Trade
Organisation agenda talks in Seattle. The considerations that follow consequently aim to address the relationship between Green activist identity
and television. Popular television in Britain has a history of drawing upon

images of environmental activism and in turn helping to create new activist identities. Different motivations ranging from hostility to sympathy, as well as the need to generate story lines, have inspired such programming. The content of the programmes is sometimes altered as a result of production processes. The programmes themselves are also subjected to reinterpretation by green activists, who are also taking matters of representation into their own hands by making their own programmes.

It has become increasingly evident that direct action inspires forms of popular culture that might in turn be recycled back to fuel 'real life action' by Green activists. In the context of this chapter, the term activist is taken to refer to an individual who acts as a 'political entrepreneur' mobilising resources and tapping into networks to build protest. Accounts of activists stress their commitment to 'high risk' protest rather than more mundane participation (McAdam, 1982). Equally an activist is likely to have moved through a process of intense and profound identity transformation (Melucci, 1996; Roseneil, 1995).

While much research has been undertaken in an attempt to theorise environmental news creation, the examination of the production and consumption of other types of television portraying environmental activism is rare. This chapter seeks to redress this imbalance through the consideration of Green activist identity in mainstream television drama and comedy.

Environmental Activism in Britain

Environmental activism in Britain is not new. In the 1930s members of the British Workers Sports Federation held a mass trespass on Kinder Scout, an area of beautiful moorland monopolised for grouse shooting. Their campaign for working-class access to the environment helped create pressure for the creation of national parks and conservation legislation (Rothman, 1982). Victorian feats of activism included an episode where the Open Spaces Society hired contractors to tear down fencing around common land. A number of factors including the student revolts of the 1960s and the globalisation of environmental problems help account for a steady increase in Green direct action since 1970. Since the early 1970s radical social movements engaged with environmental and peace issues have blossomed in the UK. In the 1970s radical environmentalism was translated into the doomsday syndrome of Malthusian fears of rising population, ecological catastrophe and scientifically manufactured disaster (Rudig and Lowe, 1986; Veldman, 1994). Activists occupied Oxford Street in 1971 to campaign for a ban on cars, and blockades were used to attempt to halt nuclear power (Wall, 1999). In the 1980s the earlier Campaign for Nuclear Disarmament was revived, but unlike in the 1960s when it had first mobilised, the peace campaign was more strongly influenced by environmental activism. The slogan 'atoms for peace' was rarely heard and feminists particularly at the Greenham Common peace camp made ecological demands (Roseneil, 1995). Militant action by animal liberationists also grew during the 1980s (Ryder, 1989). In the 1990s environmental protest was focused against motorway building at sites including Twyford Down in Hampshire and Leytonstone, East London. Activists belonging to loose social movement networks such as Earth First! and Reclaim the Streets often established colourful camps, sat in trees, and tunnelled beneath construction sites (Wall, 1999). In the new millennium environmental protest has broadened and deepened with action against genetically modified crops and globalisation.

Environmental Activism and Popular Television in Britain

Since 1970 popular television (as well as radio) seems to have been saturated with images of radical environmentalists often engaged in protest action or practising alternative lifestyles. Indeed Kimber and Richardson observed that 'the environment has insinuated itself into such programmes as *The Archers* and *Softly Softly* and has become entertainment' (Kimber and Richardson, 1974:1). In 1999 the BBC TV comedy *The League of Gentlemen* portrays the monstrous proprietors of the 'local shop', the incestuous husband and wife Edward and Tubbs who kidnap and torture road-builders who threaten their gothic abode high on the moor above Royston Vasey. In this instance, Green activism is invested with sinister undertones. Decades earlier in 1975 the gentler *Good Life* showed the gentler, more socially acceptable face of Green activism, with middle class environmentalists Tom and Barbara aiming for suburban self-sufficiency. During the late 1990s *The Fast Show*, a vista of swiftly delivered sketches included the satirical figure of 'Dave Angel – eco warrior'. With less obvious irony Ben Elton, author of a range of eco comedy novels such as *Stark*, acted as a 'new age traveller' in an episode of *The Thin Blue Line* on Christmas Day, as well as working on the script. Another episode of this show portrayed a road protest camp, complete with a military intelligence *agent provocateur*.

The issue of Green activism has therefore received substantial attention in sitcoms and comedy shows, an indication of its all-pervading influence upon the British media, which in turn could signal its encroachment upon the popular imagination. It has been portrayed positively, negatively and satirically. Radical environmentalists have not, however, figured in comedy solely on the BBC. The long running Granada soap *Coronation Street* has included Spider, a character loosely based on Swampy, a real-life activist who campaigned against the new Manchester Airport runway. Detective series including *Pie in the Sky* and Ruth Rendell's *Road Rage* (1997) have also included intimate illustrations of anti-roads camps and their protagonists. The drama/soap *London's Burning*, which centres on the fire service, included a story line where a brigade member helped support an anti-roads camp before being forced into betrayal.

Green activist issues have also been aired in science fiction series. Green science fiction has incorporated numerous episodes of *Dr Who* as well as *Doomwatch* and the post-apocalyptic *Survivors*. Another televisual genre that has covered Green activism is that of the thriller. These have included *Edge of Darkness* in 1985, starring Bob Peck, which showed the consequences of a raid by Gaia, a group of Green activists who infiltrate a 'hot cell' or illegal nuclear installation deep beneath North Moor. In the breaking months of 2000 BBC 2's *Nature Boy* narrated its protagonist's odyssey from nature reserve to protest camp to genetically modified crop laboratory.

Three distinct motivating problematics can be detected in the depiction of environmental protest on popular British television programmes. First, Green activism is used as a source of inspiration. In this way, Swampy becomes Spider in *Coronation Street*, or the difficult first line of the new television project proposal for a script is born out of a news story about an anti-roads camp. Protest provides a ready-minted set of archetypes that can be used as material for increasingly over-worked media workers who have to deliver scripts to ever-tighter deadlines. *Nature Boy* with its vivid and hermeneutical sensitive portrait of a protest camp is a case in point. The narrative focus in episode three is on what Doherty has termed 'manufactured vulnerability' with the collapse of a tunnel dug to prevent the construction of a new runway (1999).

Second, programmes have been produced as 'deliberate propaganda', advocating a radical green case. Discussing a *Dr Who* television programme broadcast in June 1973, its producer Letts noted the overt political agenda behind the programmes:

> *The Green Death* came about after Terrance Dicks and I had read a series of pieces in an environmental magazine *The Ecologist*, about the pollution of the Earth by man (sic). The article was very disturbing and made me wish we could do something positive about it ... we had no intention of attacking high technology or big business in themselves but, rather the attitude that the maximisation of profit is the only good; that economic growth must be maintained at all costs. ... Alternative technology, on the other hand, is to be used in the service of humanity, in the search for a more humane way of living. ... *The Green Death* was a quite deliberate piece of propaganda. (Howe et al, 1994: 59–60)

The information provided by a minority interest environmental magazine is processed into mainstream television entertainment that will reach a mass audience. Troy Kennedy Martin, who wrote *Edge of Darkness*, was equally dedicated to pursuing explicitly Green themes:

> I wanted to fashion Craven's ancestors ... to make him the reincarnation of the original 'green man' whose destiny was to confront and destroy in the name of the planet the free-market forces of modern entrepreneurial capitalism as represented by the chairman of the Fusion Corporation of Kansas, Mr Jerry Grogan. (Martin, 1990)

The ideal of a return to natural origins is posited against the criticism of the modern world, with its prioritisation of materialism and profit above all else. The depiction of green themes can encapsulate the dominant Green ethos behind the programme, perhaps a reflection of the prevailing form of Green activism at the time of writing. This is the case in the thriller *Survivors*. Brosnan noted *Survivors'* articulation of the pervading pessimism and class biases of early 1970s environmentalism:

> The starting point for the series was the arrival of a plague in Britain that kills almost everyone in six weeks, leaving about 7,000 people alive. The series follows the adventures of various small groups of survivors, concentrating on their efforts to cope without technology and their encounters with other, less sympathetic groups; in fact the series sometimes takes on the aspect of a middle-class, rural paradise, what with the disappearance not only of all those smelly cities but also of the working classes. The overnight disappearance of technology, and in particular the shortage of petrol, is never adequately rationalised (Brosnan, 1981: 586–87).

Third, some programmes appear to have been motivated by hostility such as Rendell's *Road Rage*. It describes murderous anti-road activists who kidnap and threaten to kill hostages in their endeavour to prevent the planned 'Kingsmarkham Bypass'. In direct contrast to the propagandist approaches described above, which depict Green activism as redressing the balance between materialism and the general interests of humanity and the planet, the activists in *Road Rage* are willing to murder for their cause. Their beliefs have therefore eclipsed their humanity. This indicates the conservative bias of the novel; significantly, Rendell's original novel is dedicated to 'Chief Inspector Vince Coomber of the Suffolk Constabulary who gave me good advice and corrected my mistakes'.

Television production is a complex process influenced by socio-economic forces as well as internal production dynamics. The original intentions of script authors dealing with Green protest movements such as Troy Kennedy Martin are transformed in production. Bob Peck's character in *Edge of Darkness* moves from an identity based on a career in policing to one of activism. Tapping into networks to get information concerning his daughter's death, he comes to resist the nuclear state. Martin noted how the director, perhaps wisely, rejected his idea that his protagonist would not merely be transformed from a police officer to Green activist but would turn into a tree at the end of the final episode. Symbolism was sacrificed in the interests of realism, so as not to lose the credibility of the narrative and the cause in the eyes of the viewers.

The reception of such television programmes by activists and potential activists also demands consideration if we are to understand how such programmes influence identity formation. Many of the activists interviewed were hostile to even sympathetic portraits of Green activism on television.

They felt that the medium of television which so often trades on heroic figures is problematic, as such élitist and unrepresentative representations might suggest that only the unique few are capable of acting. This lack of realism may alienate more than it involves the audience. Thus *Edge of Darkness* might discourage individuals from taking direct action because direct action is seen as the preserve of cells of superhuman heroes willing to risk all in defence of Gaia. Marshall, a founding member of Earth First UK, noted the following:

> Nothing I have ever seen on television has inspired me; however I am doing a great deal of work on video. I think video has the means to provide a grassroots communication, a form of communication which is appropriate for grassroots needs.
> ... the media takes symbols and exploits them and that's why I think the mainstream media is very dangerous. (George Marshall)

Marshall produced videos as a mobilising tool. The Undercurrents Collective based in Oxford who have produced activist news videos since the mid-1990s followed him.

The activists interviewed were often hostile to television genres, one even declaring television to be 'a terrible thing'. Some even linked an absence of television in childhood to later activism. Yet by placing images of activism in the public arena and charging them with drama or humour, television can produce the cultural raw materials necessary to inspire others to commit themselves to activism. Fiske, for example, has argued that minority or oppositional groups in society are able to decode even hostile accounts, similar to *Road Rage* against the grain in a positive way, reinterpreting images to sustain their own cultural identity (Fiske, 1997). Any representation, it appears, is beneficial to Green activism, even when it is effectively anti-Green propaganda.

An interview with Shane Collins, an active Earth First!er and Green Party candidate for the 2000 Greater London Assembly, illustrates how dramatic television may bolster a green identity:

> [You didn't come across Edge of Darkness?]
> I did and what a brilliant programme it was.
> [Was it formative in your...]
> I suppose it was a bit in that it linked in nuclear with the secret state that I hadn't really, really made that connection before in a big way.. .
> [It was a very deep ecology thing]
> Yeah, I don't think I really took it quite as that. I took it more as...a sort of nuclear priesthood idea the fact that there was you know more than the police force operating in this country and yeah...secret services and all that.

The anti-institutional aspect of this television production has therefore communicated itself effectively to this Green activist. In a similar vein

Alex Begg, a prominent Green Party radical who narrowly escaped death after being crushed by a digger during attempts to block the construction of the M3 motorway at Twyford, observed how programmes watched during childhood, including *Dr Who*, had fuelled later Green concern:

> A formative influence that strike[s] me as being quite influential now are some of the children's programmes that were on. I think *Dr Who* was probably a major influence, you know, this pacifist activist going in there and setting the world to rights, about a sort of activist philosophy, and a respect for living things and a mistrust of machines.

The figure of *Dr Who* is read as a prototype for an activist philosopher, advocating direct action. Another anonymous activist also noted a romantic link between popular culture and Green protest:

> One has got to say that direct action protest is certainly linked in various ways with the sort of fantasy world that one inhabits as a child through books and movies so whether it is *Dr Who* or *Lord of the Rings* or the *Narnia* books or whatever it is. These are a lot of the things that one does as an environmental protester. You are regaining a connection with the raw elements of nature.

Varied forms of popular culture permeate the pores of society and generate symbols that can be recycled into new identities. The impact of Green activist video production as both a means of achieving credible self-representation and a propagandist tool can be complemented by the endeavours of popular television, with its epic depictions of Green activist identity. Television genres help reproduce Green myths that may be transmuted into Green identities. Images may be decoded by audiences who might on some occasions rise up and reclaim the streets.

CHAPTER 10

GOING OUT TO THE STRAIGHT COMMUNITY

TELEVISUAL AND HETERONORMATIVE LOGICS IN REPRESENTATIONS OF HOMOSEXUALITY

Murray Pratt[1]

The discursive framing, mediation and construction of homosexualities in contemporary Western cultures – televisual and otherwise – can be understood as a series of ongoing negotiations which define the boundaries of the national collectivity. As Jacqueline Stevens has demonstrated in *Reproducing the State*, concepts of national and state identity are communicated via the kinship and marriage laws and practices of each social group, to the extent that full forms of citizenship are never unproblematically available outside of the relational structures which these reproduce (Stevens, 1999). Stevens clearly shows how the dynamics of national membership are applied as forcefully in socio-sexual organisation as in issues of immigration and birth right. 'Marriage laws,' she writes, 'make outlaws of same-sex partners ... and alienate their forms of being from political society in a manner similar to the way kinship rules for citizenship (including territorial birth criteria) render certain people aliens in a particular political society' (Stevens, 1999: xv). Coming from a quite different place, the French Philosopher Guy Hocquenghem argues that homosexuality is subjected to a form of political repression due to its tendency to disrupt the clear gender divisions on which 'civilised society' is predicated (Hocquenghem, 2000: 3). 'Sex,' he writes, 'is the first figure in our national identification number', that which makes the very concept of identity possible (Hocquenghem, 2000: 103).[2] According to the national script, the very notion of homosexuality disrupts the clear demarcations upon which the smooth functioning of national units relies, producing, it might be said, homosexuals with identity crises rather than identities. It is to the family unit, Hocquenghem explains, that effective regulation of sexuality is delegated, positioning 'parental responsibility as the weapon of universal responsibility' (Hocquenghem, 2000: 75), He cites a dossier on homosexuality presented by the newspaper *France-Dimanche* from 1972, as offering indispensable reading for the 'all mothers of a family', precisely since it is they who are charged with the task of ensuring that the children in their ward for the nation grow up straight.

Throughout the second half of the twentieth century, the social microgeography of television in the West has been clearly etched, often through clichéd images of happy family viewing carried in advertising, newspapers and on television itself. Replacing the hearth as the focal point of the centrally heated family home, television edged out the wireless as the Möbius strip connecting home life and the wider national perspectives of defining national events as well as the more everyday ideologies of news broadcasts. As such, television viewing came to occupy a privileged place among the technologies modelling family adherence to national consensus. It constituted a post-modern fold in the social fabric such that if, by the 1960s, 'big brother' wasn't watching you, then at least you were watching 'big brother'. Moreover, as generations of British children grew up to learn, you were watching with mother.[3] In the early years of the medium, the neutral consensus of television dealt with homosexuality, in the time-honoured fashion, by simply ignoring it. In Hocquenghem's terms, individuated instances of desire are transformed by 'the great machines of society' (Hocquenghem, 2000: 58) into a desire for repression itself, creating a field of representation which excludes all but the archetypes of the conventional Œdipal family. Yet, as Hocquenghem points out, the representational field remains nonetheless structured around homosexual desire, albeit in the form of a latency which discourses defend themselves against. More recently, viewing habits have evolved (and continue to evolve) in competing directions (portables in teenager's bedrooms, satellite television in pubs, internet and digital broadcasting), due to a variety of economic, technological and social factors. Correspondingly the social functions which they fulfil have become increasingly diverse and subtle.

Heteronormativity

Over the last few decades of the twentieth century, Britain and France, albeit at quite different paces, have undergone seismic shifts concerning the admissibility and visibility of forms of homosexuality within the public domain, which affect the kinds of representations made on television. However, both societies are still largely governed by varying forms of 'heteronormativity', namely the range of everyday practices, discourses and technologies which combine to construct our own and others' identities in terms of heterosexual norms such as marriage, the family and different sex attraction, and expectations that these constructs can be taken for granted. As an ideology, heteronormativity circulates through insinuation, as a doxa beyond contestation or discussion, imposing its edicts as natural and unremarkable, while policing its Others: the rarity of questions such as 'When did you first realise you were heterosexual?', or 'Have you told your parents that you're straight' testify to its ubiquity.

Representations of homosexuality, by contrast, serve to construct and mark the identity as requiring a response, whether it be interrogation, debate or even those silences and avoidances which constitute the trope of the open secret. However, through the entry into discourse which is thus afforded to homosexuality, spaces for contestation and strategies of counter-identification can also be opened up.

By the 1990s, fêtings of each new lesbian kiss or other type of positive gay representations on British, French and other national televisions[4] abounded in the gay press, tending to indicate that the sitting targets of innuendo and camp comedy had become a thing of the past alongside the mutism of the early, family-focused years of the technology. However, while this chapter will focus on some of these 'firsts', as examples of televisual production which could be considered as opening up the field of representation to homosexuality, the backdrop against which each new territorialisation has occurred remains relatively constant. The homophobic disclaimers ('As a married man'), gestures of distanciation by British newsreaders (the consistent and deliberately archaic pronunciation of homosexual as 'hommosexual'), and the panoply of heteronormative assumptions which structure the introduction of game show contestants, all conspire to heterosexualise the television day on a routine basis. Programmes which expressly offer gay content, do so, it will be argued, largely to the extent that they continue to adhere to the function of policing national sexuality, either by confirming or modifying the place of homosexuality within the national consciousness, as the examples from French discussion programmes will show, or in the case of *Queer as Folk* in Britain, by constructing a viewing community which is operated with reference to the economically viable consumer gay model, itself legitimated within the strictures of the straight state.

The Logic of the 'Audimat'

In his essay *Sur la télévision*, Pierre Bourdieu introduces the idea of the 'audimat', or tyranny of viewing figures, which, for him, produces a kind of televisual marketing capable only of offering up 'idées réçues' (received ideas) for re-legitimation (Bourdieu, 1996: 28–9). He applies this concept to the question of debate shows. Caught up in the same logic, debate shows are condemned to replicating existing social structures, rather than contesting them, as they ultimately owe more allegiance to the material conditions of their production than to the topic discussed. The 'journalists' pairs of spectacles', which, for Bourdieu, frame all television according to the demands of the 'audimat' become apparent in one of two ways. Firstly, the debates are 'really false', in as much as the guests all belong to the same circle, 'go for dinner with each other', and who, although taking opposition against each other, do so in 'such a conventional way' that they simply replicate the academic values of their 'côterie', with no possibility of opening out on to wider perspectives (Bourdieu, 1996: 32–3). At the same time, debate shows can also be considered as 'falsely real'. That is to say that a 'series of acts of censorship' is brought to bear on the subject at the level of the organisation of the programme: from the ways in which the terms of the debate are posed, to the presenter's allocation of time to particular guests, and responses to them which mediate a presupposition of the attitude of the average viewer, to the partition of guests between those who are there 'to explain themselves', and those whose job it is to 'offer explanations' (Bourdieu, 1996: 33–9).

French news broadcasts had touched upon 'homosexuality' as a defined mediatic 'issue' for some time. It figured in the coverage of the 1981 Presidential elections; TF1 ran a novelty item on 4 March 1977 about some idyllically long-haired students presenting themselves as a homosexual list for elections in Aix-en-Provence; and as early as 1973 a medical broadcast aimed to investigate the affliction known as 'male homosexuality'.[5] It has been the case, however, that debate shows isolated homosexuality as a social phenomenon of interest to the viewing public throughout the 1990s. Beginning with an edition of Jean-Marie Cavada's *La Marche du siècle* from 1990, entitled 'Homo, comme ils disent',[6] homosexuality figures at regular intervals as the topic of discussion. The format adopted by the 1990 broadcast sets down the tendencies for debate shows which followed, both in terms of an increasing move away from an abstract and intellectualised approach towards a voyeuristic 'reality show' model, and in imposing the structure of discussion guided by short filmed reports offering glimpses into the lives of ordinary gays and lesbians, usually couples.

The 1990 programme sees a round table of invited guests, including author Dominique Fernandez and one of the first sociologists to write about the AIDS epidemic in France, Michael Pollak. They are interrogated by Cavada on a number of issues relating to homosexuality in France, and whose responses are steered resolutely towards the autobiographical despite each having a 'professional' interest in the matter, whether as journalist, writer or sociologist. These discussions are interspersed with video clips, such as a report on Laurence and Corinne, two lesbians struggling to keep custody of the former's children in a photogenic rural setting, which in turn introduce the next set of questions for debate. This edition of *La Marche du siècle* conforms in many ways to Bourdieu's account of the genre. The guests, in the main, belong to varying branches of the gay movement in France,[7] and have a common mission in appearing on the show, despite their differences around tactics and terminology. The programme could also be seen as 'falsely real' in that Cavada resolutely steers each speaker towards the autobiographical tone whenever possible. At one point Fernandez discusses the taboos of earlier decades, preventing homosexuals from finding any outlets of expression other than through literature, a point which Cavada reorientates towards questions about Fernandez's feelings about having been married before, and whether they had children or not. Rather than allowing the interviewees to discuss issues that affect the homosexual community, the presenter goads them to reveal details of their lives that could titillate an audience weaned on heteronormative values. In this respect, the presenter 'represents the viewing public' (Bourdieu, 1996: 35), and within Bourdieu's logic of television as false representation, one of his functions is to trick viewers into misrecognising the ordinary as extraordinary (Bourdieu, 1996: 19). The presenter's role, in this programme as in later debates, is to mediate the 'difference' of gayness within television's parameters to an audience which is consistently positioned as mainstream and straight. Homosexuality, therefore, is considered only in terms of its differences as seen through a universally heterosexual lens.

Cavada's renewed sense of enthusiasm, for instance, as he ends this edition with a long and lively account of next week's show dealing with the war in Afghanistan, serves to position him clearly as a professional, whose interest in homosexuality, like that of his viewers, has been entirely platonic and transient. The appeal used is, in part, to their intellectual curiosity, hence the persistent stress on the expert status of its guests. However, the programme mainly addresses the questions which any legitimisation or recognition of homosexuality might pose to the dominant social model of familial organisation. In other words, the consensual ideology projected by the show is governed by a process of normalisation, or 'banalisation', to use the term which is borrowed from *La Marche du siècle*, and adopted by René Scherer in the title of a speech he gave at the Sorbonne just a few weeks after the broadcast.[8] For Scherer, the concept of 'banalisation' is already paradoxical, impracticable; either it simply refers to the process of recognising minority rights, in which case the minority is still 'marked' as distinctive, or it tends towards the full integration of homosexuality within existing social structures, its erasure, or unmarking as a discursive entity (Scherer, 1995: 24–5). In this latter case, Scherer argues, there will always be aspects of sexuality, such as 'pederasty', or more communitarian forms of identifying homosexuality, which fail to be recuperated in the move towards establishing the gay couple as a valid social grouping. He accounts for the process in the following terms:

> That homosexuality which is banalised never corresponds to lived models nor to our consciousness of it.... The banalised homosexual is faced with a double sided dream in terms of identification: identification with oneself as homosexual and identification with others, those heterosexuals to which he does not belong. He asks himself, 'Why not me?' Why am I not married? Why don't I have children? Why can't I pass the test of normality? But the answer to these questions, rather than deriving from law, is found in the structures of sexuality which give rise to, which produce, one might even say, that within homosexuality which is 'banalisable' or not. (Scherer, 1995: 25, Note 1)

Scherer's reading, drawing on Foucault and closely resembling Gayle Rubin's hierarchy of 'good and bad sex' – namely the division between 'the charmed circle' and 'the outer limits' – again picks up on familial technologies as the 'test' of banalisation, the social boundary which television debates such as *La Marche du siècle* attempt to police (Rubin, 1993: 13–14). Rubin herself indicates that, 'if it is coupled and monogamous', homosexuality begins to 'inch across' the borders of her hierarchy. However, the actual effect of such television programmes that attempts to make (certain forms of) homosexuality respectable, is debatable, in that the extent to which their audience is posited as a voyeuristic straight community should not be underestimated.

According to Bourdieu's thinking, this programme forms a classic example of the ways in which television remains within the categories of that which is of interest to a wide viewing public, a process which he too, interestingly, calls 'banalisation' (Bourdieu, 1996: 50–55). While the focus on homosexuality is clearly predisposed towards the 'banalisable' couple (almost as if to justify the outrage of permitting themselves to discuss homosexuality at all, as a nod, wink and point of entry to their heterosexualised viewers), the debates are far from enacting the normalisation of homosexuals. In Scherer's terms, full assimilation is a structural impossibility. As French debates throughout the 1990s show, this offers a model for understanding the heteronormative logic which demands figurations of homosexuality, while at the same time attempting to control or absorb them by positioning them within, and only viewable from, a heterosexual perspective. *La Marche du siècle* can, therefore, be considered as an exercise in social control. It constitutes 'a false debate', since the underlying topic is not whether homosexuality is an exception (which it clearly is inasmuch as it is debatable at all and the invited speakers are all eminently worth listening to), or banal (which it clearly is inasmuch as they each get on with their lives in their own ways), but rather it is about reining in the right to represent, discuss, question, assimilate or reject the terms of any debate within the terms of straight social norms.

Ordinary Lives

The first edition of *Bas les masques*, presented by Mireille Dumas and destined to become a classic confessional television 'reality show' throughout France, was broadcast by France 2 in 1992 under the title, 'Je suis homo comme ils disent'.[9] Again interspersed with video clips on 'la vie du couple' (two men shopping in a supermarket, preparing dinner – doing nothing exceptional other than both of them being male), this programme puts Denis, a young man from 'la France profonde' (although we later learn that he has recently left his Loire Atalantique village to work for Gai pied in Paris), on the spot and scrutinises his life choices via a range of invited guests. However, what gives the programme the 'scoop' which will elevate an ordinary life to the level of the extraordinary – and then back to the ordinary as other journalists get in there too – (Bourdieu, 1996: 20),[10] is the fact that Denis is not only gay, but also potentially implicated in the family structures of heterosexual organisation. Throughout, Dumas brings the debate back to issues touching upon Denis's family life. On one occasion she follows his comment about him being the only member of his family to accept his sister's divorce with the comment, 'so divorce and homosexuality are more or less the same'. On another, Denis attempts to respond to her question about whether he has had relationships with women by talking about his first experience with a man, only to be interrupted by Dumas asking about how his mother responded to his sexuality. Denis is effectively unvoiced, to the extent that his closing remarks – 'It's not easy appearing here – it's a risk, but you have to *lower the masks*. All I ask is for mothers to take a step back at puberty and think about the sexuality of their children' – reinforce the programme's coquettish flirtation with difference from the perspective of the normal viewing public. By parroting the programme's title, his appearance is effectively reduced to a promotion of straight values. From this point of departure, the debate format is able to delve into taboo worlds in order to create the *frisson* of the extraordinary.

A further moment in the logic of the scoop occurs in 1993, when TF1's *Mea culpa*, presented by Patrick Mené, ups the stakes by offering a similar show, replacing Denis with Thierry, this time from a village in the Beaujolais. Thierry is not only gay but also, shock horror, an ex-husband and father of a six-year-old son. He is also HIV-positive and prone to depression into the bargain, and wears leather jeans in public; another indication of his transgression. The tone here is directly confrontational, with the village doctor, the mayor and (for some reason never particularly apparent) a local viticultor, in particular censuring Thierry for all sorts of reasons and denouncing his 'romantic effusions' in the garden. Now while *Mea culpa* not only sounds like, but actually does enact the worst kind of homophobic bear-baiting imaginable, the effect of the programme is actually double-edged. For, as the show progresses, the homophobia of Thierry's adversaries becomes its real subject. His mother, phoning up on air as one of the whacky pranks which the series favours, is revealed as only concerned about her grandson, almost to the extent that she doesn't care whether Thierry lives or dies. When Mené puts this to her she replies, 'Absolutely'. By contrast, Thierry's 'Aunt Denise' appears in person, and is quickly framed as the down-to-earth provincial who has 'come to terms' ('*assumer*' being a litmus-test word in all these programmes) with her nephew's sexuality in quite unproblematic ways. Here, it is ultimately the gay man who is banalised (although at a price: he ends up accepting that his 'aggression' was unacceptable) while rampant homophobia emerges as the issue at stake. The introduction of a single mother who has had to put up with similar forms of ostracisation indicates that *Mea culpa* is actually more interested in addressing 'intolerance' than taking the very real problems faced by Thierry seriously. Within the logics of both television and the heteronormative, the programme's remit is to create viewer consensus about acceptable social responses to difference, in other words an issue with which 'we all' (as innately repulsed by homosexuality) have to 'come to terms'.

A similar sleight of hand is a familiar strategy in drama series on both sides of the channel. The introduction of gay characters into mainstream series and serials in Britain, from *Eastenders* and *Brookside*, can be seen as serving a social awareness agenda in tackling viewers' presumed homophobic responses. Yet, as with Asian characters, gays never tend to last very long in British soaps. Beth Jordache's controversial seduction of the Farnham's naïve, straight-identified nanny in Channel 4's *Brookside*, for instance, was gradually ditched as Beth's character became caught up in a small matter of patios and patricide, leading ultimately to her disposal through death in custody. In a similar way, gay characters often have marginal or marginalised roles, aspects of their sexuality providing issues for the straight characters to contend with, rather than deserving attention in their own right. To give an example, the medical drama *Casualty*, notorious for producing the most unlikely happy couples from among its regular cast, failed to exploit the dramatic potential of a relationship between its two gay male characters in the late 1990s. Instead Adam's sexuality was largely reduced to his HIV status, and in particular the threat or otherwise which this might pose to 'straight' patients and staff, and Sam fell over a balcony never to return. Just as Adam was relegated to the sidelines of the operating theatre in the somewhat awkward role of a note-taker, the sexuality of the series' gay characters has been kept out of the main frame (Sam's boyfriend appears at the end of the shift and suggests an 'other' life while never fully becoming integrated into the storyline), or at best become a narrative of concealment and revelation which leads to questions about how their straight colleagues will react.[11]

A 1998 episode of the French series *L'Instit*[12] illustrates just as clearly how 'homosexuality' achieves the respectability of representation in mainstream television only in so far as it remains a straight issue. The format of the series relies on the eponymous relief teacher, Viktor Novak, going into a school and single-handedly sorting out the social problems he finds around him. In the episode entitled 'Le bouc émissaire' (the scapegoat), the teacher comes upon two schoolboys who are obviously unhappy and underperforming. The initial assumption, which camera groupings and framings throughout the first ten minutes or so of the programme help to set up, is that they are obviously suffering due to the fact that they are looked after by their gay dad and his lover. However, their real trauma emerges as the fact that their clearly psychotic mother and her even less stable boyfriend want to take them away from a relatively secure 'family' unit, and go off to Martinique. In addition to the obvious ways in which this shift in the moral dilemma confronts, after initially inciting, viewer homophobia, only to legitimate a good dose of misogyny in the process, the programme clearly sets up a didactic approach on a number of levels. In order to resolve the boys' problems, Novak is obliged to tackle their schoolmates' homophobia. He allays the suspicions of the headmistress and others who doubt the quality of the father's parenting; he even brings the mother's boyfriend round to giving him a chance. The combined effect of the teacher's efforts is to foreground his tolerance, guile, intelligence and citizenship (including a range of forms of acceptable homosociality) – superhero or detective qualities writ small. The programme's closure is achieved when, owing not a little to Mark Twain, Novak starts to erase the unfinished graffiti on the school wall, reading 'ERIC FILS DE PED', only to be joined by throngs of happy newly homotolerant schoolchildren. This is entirely consistent with the numerous shots throughout the edition of Novak comforting, rescuing, understanding Eric or his brother Kelian. The clear message is not so much that it is alright for gays to be dads, but that it takes a straight man to really gets to grips with their problems.

Enacting Narratives of National Sexuality

While Rubin's 'outer limits' issue of whether or not homosexuals should have parenting rights continues to function according to the full panoply of criteria of connivance and banalisation which earn homosexuality the right to televisual space, the episodes of drama programmes analysed above, I would argue, are also indicative of a further agenda which, throughout the 1990s in France, legitimated the interest of straight communities in such representations. The AIDS crisis facing the country, belatedly recognised and badly managed at the outset,[13] had, by the late 1980s, developed into an issue which threatened to disrupt tried-and-tested structures, systems and ideologies on a national level. From the reorganisation of blood transfusion technologies (and ultimately the legal system on which this issue impacted), medical and pharmaceutical institutions and operational practices regarding funding for charitable enterprises, through to the mobilisation of gay communitarian groups, consumer lobbies, and political victories such as obtaining limited cohabitation rights under the PACS,[14] the epidemic can, in retrospect, be considered, as having brought to a head a form of 'social revolution' which perhaps even surpasses that of 1968, constituting 'nothing short of a dramatic reconceptualisation of French policy towards minorities, health and social welfare'(Frogier, 1997: 356). However, some, including Didier Lestrade, president of Act Up-Paris, are far from convinced that any real progress has been secured, despite the achievements of groups such as his own (Lestrade, 2000: 445). He points, for instance, to the discrepancy between the effectiveness of a 1999 campaign by the French government to encourage safety measures in viewing the solar eclipse, and the simultaneous reduction in official spending on AIDS. Result: 25 cases of damaged vision against 120,000 known cases of HIV (Lestrade, 2000: 439–40). For Larys Frogier, even throughout the 1990s the state response to HIV has been a form of airbrushing, erasing specificities around treatment and prevention by overwriting these urgent issues with an agenda of promoting 'universal ideologies of tolerance and assimilation' (Frogier, 1997: 355). Frogier's reading offers a vivid account of the ways in which dominant national interests attempted to manage and control the situation – as much the situation of social revolution as the medical emergency itself – by promoting a consensus of 'We're all in this together', 'a mantra', which, he explains 'speaks only to the silent – and largely uninfected – majority, which takes pity on "AIDS victims", but which is never outraged by the fact that AIDS primarily affects homosexuals and intravenous drug users and that nothing is being done to prevent this' (Frogier, 1997: 354).

While the direct contestation of the consensual discourse outlined by Frogier has, itself, become a televisual event of note,[15] equally pertinent is the extent to which the whitewash appeal to the general public for 'solidarité' is a factor in the shapes which visible homosexuality on French television has taken, notably in debate-type programmes such as those considered here. Moreover, the emphasis on the recuperation of homosexuality within the family, and in particular the persistence of representations of stable gay couples, in the context of the AIDS crisis in France, can be seen as an ideological bid directed, as much at controlling homosexual behaviour and directed at gay men in particular, as an exercise in offering a heteronormative tag to straight viewers. Programmes such as *Casualty*, *L'Instit* and *Mea culpa*, in this light, belong to a kind of public education campaign, cynically exploiting fears about HIV, and assumptions not only of heterosexuality but also homophobia, in order to further the agenda of state regulation of homosexuality within non-threatening structures such as the family, the couple and the consumer. As early as 1992, Rommel Mendès-Leite and Pierre-Olivier de Busscher recognised television's role in 'broadcasting the following reassuring message to all good French families: homosexuals are ordinary people, (almost) just like you' (Mendès-Leite and de Busscher, 1992: 2). To gays themselves, the message is one which neglects questions of prevention in favour of a hard sell of 'the "real" values of the traditional, middle-class heterosexual couple, monogamous and faithful "till death us do part"'(Mendès-Leite and de Busscher, 1992: 2). 'Gay Paris', a 1996 edition of *Le Droit de savoir*[16] which attempts a fuller documentary picture of contemporary homosexual life than previous debates, illustrates the paradoxical doubleness of address which inflects representations of homosexuality on French television throughout the 1990s.

An opening sequence, beginning with an establishing shot of a street corner in 'Le Marais', can be considered as emblematic of this doubleness. On one side the street sign reads 'Rue Vieille du Temple', designating the heart of Paris's commercial 'gay village'. The chosen intersection, however, is with the 'Rue des Rosiers', still very much a street which bears traces of the 'quartier's previous incarnation as a Jewish area. The effect is of framing the documentary within a rubric of questions about the integration of the new communitarian homosexual community. The programme goes on to bear this out, focusing on socially assimilated gay couples throughout. One such couple, Jean-Marc and Vincent, are filmed in the gym, at home, and framed by the Arc de Triomphe as they walk through Paris in matching track suit bottoms. Interviewed, they respond that they want to be 'just like any straight couple'. The broadcast puts in play the familiar dynamic of 'banalisation', offering gay life-style models with differing degrees of conformity to heteronormative social roles (often about conventional forms of masculinity), and in each case circling around the open question of whether sexual difference can be assimilated within national identity. A good example of how this question is played out is a sequence towards the end when one of the 'typical' gay men featured is shown maintaining their car, a Jaguar XJS-V12, with the voice-over commenting on how they like passers-by to comment, 'Oh those queers have got unbelievable cars!'. The ambiguity offered here is understandable with reference to a heteronormed audience – is he 'working' on his car, or 'tending' to it, but equally upfront given the previous clip's comments from a representative of the gay commercial interest group that gay men have a spending power 30 percent higher than straight couples, is a question about whether these groups are 'model consumers', or evading financial responsibilities to society.

Related to France's AIDS crisis, the national imperative concerning representations of homosexuality has been to take control of the 'cultural agenda' according to which both 'problems' and 'solutions' can become thinkable.

Representations of the AIDS crisis in the West, and representations stemming from this crisis, are indeed structured according to logics similar to those outlined by Bourdieu according to Daniel Selden (Selden, 1993: 221–6), in that they become part of the '"cultivation" of the media, the industry's ability to "mainstream" public values, expectations and beliefs'. However, for Selden, the very framing of the medical fact as 'crisis', with national institutions and practices, through trial and error, eventually coming up with 'solutions', be they medical, legal, or ideological, is an equally valid grid for understanding televisual depictions. As with the modern myth of *Jaws*, the 'motivating narratival scheme' can be characterised by an appeal to these institutions not only for answers, but for the necessary surveillance, value definition and prioritisation which identify and frame the questions in the first place.

This explains the persistence with which representations of homosexuality on French television situate themselves in the margins of straight-normed forms of social organisation (families, couples, more recently questions about whether 'PACSed' gay couples have any rights to child rearing). The social crisis, to which only the institutions (of the state, national ideologies, television itself) have the questions and answers, is the confirmation of the heteronormative values of those same institutions, faced with the social contestations which the epidemic brings about. To the straight viewing public, the hook is a kind of 'queer-curious' voyeurism, a *frisson* of deviance and disruption from the norms which are nonetheless firmly justified and defended throughout. To potential gay viewers, the imposed agenda of social respectability, in the midst of an epidemic of fatally negligent political responses to HIV, can be considered as, at best, a kind of public information broadcast, at worst, a deadly form of propaganda which effects on a psycho-social level an elimination of difference similar to the physical ravages of the virus.

By interrogating further the logics imposed by Bourdieu's dictatorship of the 'audimat', it could be said that to grasp fully the agenda of debates about homosexuality on French television, the intended audience of a straight viewing community must also be put in the context of programmes' more incidental gay viewers. In theoretical terms, this would imply that rather than simply pandering to mainstream political and moral values, televisual representations of socio-sexual difference operate in more subtle, although ultimately equally oppressive ways. The debates analysed offer illusions of impartiality, entertain the possibility of homosexuality as a valid life choice and leave room for doubt concerning dominant attitudes – for both straight and gay viewers – only to (re-)confirm the primacy of heteronormativity as the only valid viewing perspective. However, the process is, if anything, more insidious than the model proposed by Bourdieu, in that it operates a dynamic enactment of the erasure of difference, holding out and working through imagined social Othernesses only to bring each deviant possibility back within the terms of the straight community.

Straight as Folk?

Channel 4's drama *Queer as Folk*,[17] in many ways, seems to be a quite different animal from many of the programmes discussed so far. Given the channel's implicit minority broadcasting mission, and indeed the different pace of the politics of homosexuality in Britain, it is tempting to perceive this 1999 drama series as primarily targeting a gay audience. Following its kitschy billboard promotion of *Tales of the City* some years previously, a similar brightly coloured marketing strategy hooked *Queer as Folk* as a niche-marketed consumer product for the gay market (complete with top selling video follow-up). The series certainly delivers according to these expectations. The lives of Vince, Stuart and Nathan, the three main characters, revolve around Manchester's gay village, with Stuart in particular completely ensconced in the obligatory life-style choices of 4x4, loft apartment, and eighty pounds T-shirts, or 'tops' as boys too are now meant to call them. Hip cuts and fades to the sounds of Canal Street, including up-to-the-minute choices such as Air's 'Sexy Boy', a smooth chest and flat stomach casting policy, and a recurring narrative pattern of stories about 'picking up', all combine to create a product strong on gay viewer identification, whether through recognition or fantasy, or more often, the recognition of fantasy. Numerous web-based fan clubs devoted to the series and its stars testify to its success in modelling gay life-style choices and roles on an international scale. In this, *Queer as Folk* perhaps offers one of the most radically complex (and in many ways accurate) representations of everyday gay life seen on television anywhere. That New Britain should give rise to such a development bears eloquent testimony to just how out of touch (and counter-productive) the country's previous Thatcherite agenda of prohibiting the promotion of homosexuality with the advent of consumer tribalism has really been.

An obvious critique of the programme could be raised on the grounds of the politics of consumerism, echoing perhaps Sarah Schulman's argument (Schulman, 1997: 377) that 'the illusion of normality without the fact of normality is the sinister centrepiece of niche-marketing', and her comment that '[i]t is very seductive for gay people to confuse the presence of limited gay images in advertising with some kind of social equity, but it is entirely illusory'. However, in many ways *Queer as Folk* actually offers a more intelligent representation of homosexuality than the happy same-sex couples found in gay-friendly magazine ads. As the series progresses, it becomes increasingly clear, largely through the introduction of Vince's older Australian boyfriend and his cynicism about the gay scene, that Stuart's exemplary existence as a queer consumer is little more than a hollow carapace. Part of the series' charm is that it is able to do so without passing moral judgements, maintaining a balance between the characters' disillusionments with the imperative of living life on the scenes as flesh and blood positive representations and, at the same time, celebrating its very real thrills and spills. It could even be said that *Queer as Folk* hooks its gay viewers on a set of dilemmas around issues of superficiality and commitment, working within similar dynamics of identification and difference with which straight viewers are normally interpolated.

However, despite the interesting ways in which this series begins to question the main hypothesis of this chapter, (namely that representations of homosexuality serve the interests of enacting national heteronormativities), it is equally useful to situate its narrative development in terms of its appeal to a straight viewing community. The opening episode of *Queer as Folk* attracted considerable controversy for its depiction of underage sex. Nathan is eventually outed as fifteen, making his encounter with Stuart illegal even by straight standards. Moreover, the 'naturalness' within which it depicts aspects of gay scene life, such as casual sex, together with its explicitness about sexual practices, combined to create a sense of 'scandal' which got the series national coverage. It is difficult to say just how many offices across Britain were caught up in earnest discussion about the joys of rimming on the day following the broadcast of the first episode.

While there is probably some truth in imagining that *Queer as Folk* tapped into a latent form of homoeroticism, as well as offering up soft porn for straight female viewers, where the series really hooked into a wider audience was through a subtle appeal to heteronormative values remarkably similar to those on the agenda of French debate shows. From the first episode, where Stuart becomes a father through his arrangement with 'the lesbians', through to the more fully worked narrative issues of later instalments, the family structure and disruptions to it provide a good measure of the drama. The key stories affecting Nathan and Stuart are both propelled by questions of coming out to their family, with much of the escapism conveyed by shots of them showing a fresh set of heels or revving away at every opportunity. The baby becomes a burden with no stable home; Vince is plagued by the possibility of going straight (into a dead-end marriage) and eventually forms a monogamous partnership albeit with a man; Phil's death only really achieves poignancy by setting the gay characters' responses against those of his mother's true soap-opera values. Most worrying, however, is the extent to which the three main characters, despite their sexuality, pass as straight-identified. The camp queens of the series are all secondary characters, as much the butt of its jokes as Mr Humphreys ever was. By contrast, Vince is not out at work, Nathan is accompanied at regular intervals by a pseudo-girlfriend, and Stuart's yuppy machismo and choice of partners is largely predicated on straight values. Ultimately their life choices are understood and mediated through the effects they have on their families, the social legitimacy of full consumerdom, and, despite the series' brave attempt to look beyond the monogamous couple as its base unit, their potential for attaining normative stable relationships even as gay men. In other words, even the gay aspects of the series are largely straight, since, as with the scene when Vince rejects a potential partner when he removes his jacket to reveal a girdle and beneath that a distinctly non-standard body, the values underlying the sexual choices within the series are fully informed by the norms and prejudices through which straight society produces and regulates its homosexual Other. Even as gay viewers, the audience of *Queer as Folk* inevitably watches its tick-list of new positive representations through the filter of their potential shock to the straight system.

Conclusion

In Beatriz Preciado's rereading of Deleuze and Guattari, she shows how the concept of 'molecular homosexuality', by which they propose to define (their) homosexuality in terms of local desiring operations rather than identities, is actually imbued within a centrifugal logic of heterosexuality (Preciado, 2000). With Hocquenghem, for whom the opposing 'molar' level of social institutions is produced through societal sublimation of homosexual desire (Preciado, 2000: 58), Preciado proposes that normative heterosexuality is effected through the appropriation of sexual Othernesses within the dominant economy of the phallus. Molecular homosexuality, she argues, starts off straight, going on to denounce Deleuze and Guattari's transversality as a relation of convenience, a riff enabling them to avoid engagement in the field of identity politics (Preciado, 2000: 141), and more crucially for Preciado, never stray too far from the safe shore of the straight white male and human.

In addition to Bourdieu's general logics governing televisual representation, the range of programmes dealing with homosexuality on French and British television, from the French debate format, through to the roles of gay characters within mainstream programmes, and even the often more challenging *Queer as Folk*, need to be considered in this context. It would seem that, in many ways, there can be no homosexuality on television, without reference, and often perhaps a voyeuristic nod and wink, to the colonising structures of male heterosexuality through which socially and nationally legitimate desire is constructed. Or, to put it another way, irrespective of who's watching what, the box is still square.

Yet, if television, even in its depictions of sexual otherness, serves principally to replay a Todorovian narrative of stasis, crisis and new resolution, confirming the primacy of the normative as constitutive of any active viewing position, Preciado's counter-sexual manifesto also indicates the extent to which its 'technologics' could lend themselves to radical subversion. If, for Bourdieu, the effect of the televisual is to produce the real as fabrication, so too for Preciado might sexuality be seen in terms of a 'dildonics', or an artificially constructed field, as the phallic signifier wilts and fades to a sham in the shadow of its majestic, and artificial replica (Preciado, 2000: 69). Preciado's resulting reinterpretation of sexuality in non-phallocentric terms enables a move away from the tyranny of more genitally defined 'natural' practices into a world where the subversive reinscription and cheap parody of the dildo unleash a radical uncertainty which undoes the relations between 'the inside and the outside, passive and active, the natural organ and the machine', 'hetero or homo', while calling into question the idea that our bodies are congruous with the limits of flesh, and effectively demystifying the phallicised centrality of the love/sex dyad (Preciado, 2000: 71).

Television, in a sense, can do for reality what Preciado's dildo does for sex, producing a hypervirtuality which spirals us beyond the parameters of those realities which it (for her) could be seen to precede and (for Jean Baudrillard) replace. One interpretation of the straight lens through which, it has been argued, gays are obliged to pass in order to view their own televisual reflections, could be to see this as a liberatory process, one which effects a kind of reverse, or perhaps double, transversality and opens up the potential for enjoying the privileges of heteronormativy to all, perhaps even loosening the link between the 'hetero' and the 'normativity'. This is the world, after all, of the webcam, television for the 2000s, where the everyday of any other can be 'accessed' and appropriated in the screech of a modem, where we are our own (worst) zap-happy schedulers. The etymologically signalled remoteness, characteristic of television, has already cut the ties binding human experience to the tyrannies of place and time, and the remote has given us the control.

To the extent that contemporary viewing is structured through processes of escapism or avoidance, control, fetish, fragmentary experience, television as a manifesto for counter-life, then, might suggest ways of displacing the centrality of the heteronorm. While the 'programming' represented by the construction of social norms commissioned, produced, edited and ultimately projected by the industry remains more or less in line with the dominant straight script of the nation, the actualisation of television has in many ways detached itself from this agenda, thus becoming an activity which *de*-programs as much as it confirms the dominant. Generations emerging through the virtual no longer 'watch TV' but rather 'have it on', as one available universe habitable in a variety of modes, including forms of irony which make a mockery of television's pretension towards social and national glue. Light years beyond treating the authority of the announcer with awe, the senses of doubleness with which we have learned to respond to the televisual, invalidates the notion of 'passive' viewers, or even 'active' hunters or 'bricoleurs' (cobblers together) of sense. Instead, we are evolving towards occupying indeterminate zones of interpenetration and transversality between the televisual and other (or no) technologies which remap and fractalise social experience.

Consideration of gayed programmes then, those few scraps of gaytime television which brand homosexuality within acceptable niches and forms, and as we have seen, ultimately as heterosexuality with a twist, is already in many ways an exercise in yesterday's technology. Instead, the more interesting experiment is to focus on the subversions and misreadings effected through patterns of cyberviewing, to simply pick up those strategies which are always already in the process of displacing the national, and often global, heteroscript. What could be funnier, for instance, than the seriousness with which television insistently, religiously – and desperately – undertakes to heterosexualise the world? The agenda of the US import for instance, as relevant in terms of impact in France as in Britain (despite the cultural protectionism of the former) from *Friends* to *Saved by the Bell*, can be (and is everyday) seen through and transactualised as a quite hilarious attempt at policing boundaries between the homosocial and the homoerotic. The pseudo-couples which people television as straight, from the obligatory matching news presenters on almost all British and French bulletins, to the gutsiness of that private-yet-public, public-yet-private drama that is Richard and Judy, do nothing better than reveal the arbitrariness of couplism as the dominant form of social organisation. Equally, despite the lack of eroticised homosexuality on national television, which, according to one commentator, 'makes pornography on cassette an absolute necessity for a complex view of the world' (Speck, 1993), desire for male bodies from Leonardo di Caprio to Michael Owen occurs as a routine part of television viewing by gay men, while Christine Ockrent, for many years the figurehead of Antenne 2's nightly news programme, and voice of the nation, figures on an internet 'sondage' as one of France's most famous lesbians.[18]

Broadcasters themselves are in on the act: in Britain, BBC2's *The Fast Show* has modelled itself on the parodic displacement of television's sexual policing, through its exaggeratedly homosocial portrayals of male relationships, such as the lordship/ancient retainer couple which manages to take sideswipes at class, mateship and marriage all at the same time; while an infinite regression of Des Lynam parodies, and, in the process, irons out, the crinkle of mystery in his seducer's smile, transforms the twinkle in his eye to jaded lechery, disinvesting the privileged mystique of heterosexuality as television's 'non-dit'.

Viewer displacement, however, goes beyond the manufactured smirk of alternative comedy. The process of transvaluation inherent in miswatching television, its potential to disrupt putative national continuums of heteronormativity by simply seeing them for what they are, can function not just as virtual reconfiguration but as a form of empowerment which shatters the politics of identity and identification on which straight surveillance relies. While specific gay and gayed representations on French and British television work insomuch as they construct viewing positions through the privileged image of the heterosexual, it is rather the everyday straightness of the televisual, the endless rerun of the heteroscript, which like any repetition, provokes difference. How else to respond to the tireless and patently see-through performance of national straightness than by finding it ridiculous? It is this disregard for the primacy of message, which, in practice, characterises resistant viewing practices, defuses and marginalises this script and contextualises its insistent whine in a wider and fuller sense of life's possibilities. Television's promotion of compulsory heterosexuality, far from regulating viewer response, denaturalises the primacy of the straight viewing position it intends to promote, ironically offering forms of centrality and empowerment to gay viewers, together with possibilities for affirmation, the expression of desire and imagination, and forms of commonality quite other to those envisaged within the national consensus.

Notes

1. My thanks to Sigrid Baringhorst, Hervé Chevaux, Dharman Jeyasingham, Rommel Mendès-Leite and Paul Milford for their help in providing material discussed in this chapter, and/or for their ideas and suggestions during conversations. Thanks also to the 'Inathèque de France' in Paris for enabling me to view two of the programmes discussed.
2. Phrases in French from this text and other visual and written texts have been rendered in English by the author throughout.
3. As a North American comparison shows, Michael's 'coming out drama' in Armistead Maupin's *More Tales of the City* plays out against a backdrop of homophobic consensus, largely evoked through references to the televisual engineering of small town America in his mother's letters. What eventually produces Michael's 'coming out' to his family is his reaction to an accumulation of references to the moral majority, represented by Anita Bryant and her 'Save Our Children, Inc.' group which his parents ingest whole 'on our new color set'. Maupin, 1989, p.21.
4. The trope seems to be well established as a kind of right won in the march towards fuller representation, with 'Ellen' and 'Brookside' in particular attracting attention from the British and American media. Even into the twenty-first century, gay broadsheets such as the *Sydney Star Observer* are celebrating similar landmarks: '"This is a milestone we needed to get past" – GLAAD's Scott Seomins applauding the first-ever US prime-time network TV kiss between two men.
5. Details of these earlier programmes from *La Marche du siècle*, France 3, 15 May 1996.
6. *La Marche du siècle*, France 3, 10 October 1990.
7. In the process of doing some research for this article at the Paris centre of the 'Groupe de recherches et d'Etudes sur l'Homosocialité et les Sexualités' (GREH), the group's president Rommel Mendès-Leite received by mail what he described as one of many requests from a documentary programme seeking participants in the forthcoming France 2 'Jour après Jour' edition on coming out. According to Mendès-Leite, the vast majority of so-called ordinary lesbians and gay men on relevant French programmes are recruited via professional gay associations and organisations.
8. Scherer, R., 1995, pp. 19–36. Scherer's speech was originally given at the Sorbonne during a GREH conference.
9. *Bas les masques*, France 2, 29 September 1992.
10. Carried to its extreme, this logic produces programmes such as 'Eurotrash', the British Channel 4 show which pokes around in the sexual fetishes of otherwise 'normal' European people and dubs them with ludicrous exaggerated regional accents.
11. See Allen, 1995, for an account of the ways in which homosexuality figures within straight discourse as 'a narrative of disclosure' (610).
12. *Le bouc émissaire*, *L'Instit*, France 2, 7 October 1998.
13. For a discussion of the French mismanagement of the AIDS crisis see Murray Pratt, 'The defence of the straight state: heteronormativity, AIDS in France, and the space of the nation', 'AIDS in France', Special Issue of *French Cultural Studies*, eds Jean-Pierre Boulé and Murray Pratt, Vol 9, October 1998, pp. 263–80. Edmund White, 1997, p.339, offers

a pertinent summary of the extent of the crisis when he writes, 'Since the beginning of the epidemic, France has had three times more known cases of AIDS than Britain'.

14. PACS stands for *Pacte civile de solidarité*. This piece of social legislation, passed in late 1998, extended the fiscal and financial benefits to non-married but cohabiting couples, irrespective of their sexualities.
15. See David Caron, 1998, pp. 281–94.
16. 'Le gay Paris', 'Le droit de savoir', 17 november 1996.
17. *Queer as Folk*, Channel 4, First episode (of eight) broadcast 23 February 1999.
18. http://www.geocities.com/WestHollywood/Heights/1761/sondage.htm.

CHAPTER 11

TELEVISUAL IDENTITY IN THE TWENTY-FIRST CENTURY

CONSTRUCTING THE POST-MODERN GROUP

Michael Scriven and Emily Roberts

The chapters in this book have in various ways assessed the political, social and cultural significance of the representation of group identities on national television in France and Britain. Particular attention has been given to exploring how nations should perceive and represent themselves, confronted as they are at the beginning of the twenty-first century by new challenges, both within and without their boundaries.

One affront to the concept of national identity has been globalisation. The idea of the nation is necessarily predicated upon a sense of difference from other nations; yet globalisation presents the possibility of a culture common to all nations, at work within the national boundaries. The fear of globalisation, most notably of the insidious influences of the ubiquitous American culture, is well documented in the French instance. That symbol of colonising American culture, McDonalds, has invoked the spleen of two vanguards of Frenchness, the farmers and the trade unions, in recent years. National television is now rivalled by international satellite, cable and digital television networks. Audiovisual and film industry policies have a history of being geared to protect the French language and French cultural productions, although American produced sitcoms and dramas have infiltrated popular television viewing slots, particularly in the case of M6. In Britain, the audiovisual

145

industry has reacted by drawing upon the strong tradition of producing home-grown British television programmes, particularly in the field of drama, sitcoms and long-running fictional series. Both the BBC and ITV, for example, have established digital channels that draw upon its past productions, or respond to perceived special interest groups, such as women.

Another pressure particular to the geographical location of Britain and France is that of ceding a degree of sovereignty to the European Union. The increasing sphere of influence of the European Union also constitutes a challenge to the linchpin of the nation-state, its ability to make and institute policies that affect every aspect of the lives of its people. Although there are some European channels, Europe does not threaten the existence of national television directly, as much as it disrupts the traditional basis for the conception of the nation that underpins these channels. The attitude towards Europe in France and Britain is characterised by ambivalence; some recognise what they perceive to be the economic necessity of a united European economic front, whereas others resent the implications for national sovereignty that this could entail.

The process of localisation is perceived by some critics as a necessary adjunct to the globalising (and by extension Europeanising) drive (Herb, 1999). The 'localisation' of the national culture, both in terms of regionalisation and minority groups, has eroded the foundations of the symbolic representation of the nation-state as a monolithic, 'one and indivisible' edifice. The call for the representation of smaller 'ethnic' nations within Britain and France constitutes one challenge to the supremacy of an overarching, centralised nation-state that values cohesiveness and unity over decentralisation and diversity.

The Internal Challenges Facing Geopolitical Identity

Britain and France have been under pressure for some time to grant the regions and stateless nations increased autonomy or statehood. The resurgence of powerful stateless national identities in France and Britain (now granted the status of self-representing nations, in Britain's case) increasingly poses questions concerning the future of Britain and France as unified states with a cohesive national identity.

Britain has always been an amalgam of three nations: Scotland, Wales, and England. Until recently, Wales and Scotland were granted limited autonomy, with London representing the real seat of power. The conflation of Britishness with Englishness was so great that there were only limited calls for sub-English representation, although the demand for decentralisation has always been placed somewhere on the British political agenda. Given the creation of the Welsh Assembly in Cardiff and Holyrood Parliament in Edinburgh, Britain now seems to be heading towards a more truly federal structure. This structure nominally comprises an equal partnership of nations, rather than an umbrella structure with one London-based national government presiding over two other 'national regions'. Ironically, devolution has shaken the foundations of the 'national regional' group left out of the equation in Britain: the English.

In his BBC programme entitled *The Day Britain Died,* broadcast between 31 January and 2 February 2000, Andrew Marr concurs, finding that 'England does not have a confident sense of herself. She does not have her own democracy. How can this be a happy, self-confident part of Europe or anywhere else if the core of Great Britain feels marginalised? And there's a rising sense that they do.' This is reflected in the decision of the St. George foundation to offer lessons on Englishness, to counteract what it itself calls 'a crisis of identity' (*Today programme*, Radio 4, 18 April 2000). The perception of Britain and England as synonyms has led to the current confusion concerning what it means to be English. The crisis of English identity appears to reside in the fact that it is rooted in the memory of the British Empire and war effort, Britain's glory days.

As Sergeant demonstrates, France is less far along the route to devolution of the 'national regions'; it is still 'poised to rediscover its regional diversity'. In the past, ethnic identities rooted in a geographical area have been recognised as little more than regions with specific languages attached, rather than as nations or even subnations. This having been said, there is a drive for independence, through official channels as well as through direct action. In 2000, the French government sanctioned the discussion of a plan put forward by the members of the Corsican Assembly, that proposed the 'suppression of two *départements*, to be replaced by a single collectivity' (*Le Monde,* 27 July 2000). This would be accompanied by a decentralisation of control over such issues as the economy, education, professional training, sports, tourism, the environment, transport and so on. The Government added the proviso that 'the state will retain, in all cases, the right to exercise its national powers and to implement its "missions de contrôle". (*Le Monde,* 27 July 2000). The most controversial aspect of the proposed reform was the transfer of new powers. Legislative and regulatory reforms, it was proposed, should be adapted to Corsica's specificities. The Government required a transitional period to be implemented, the maintenance of peace and order, and the agreement of the representative structures already in place.

This proposal did not meet with resounding support from all corners of the establishment. The president of the RPR party in the National Assembly stated that 'the Republic, the state and France are at stake'; furthermore, 'national unity, the indivisibility of the Republic cannot be the object of the slightest negotiation, the least compromise'. (*Le Monde,* 22 July 2000). The Minister for the Interior, Jean-Pierre Chevènement, eventually resigned over the issue, seeing this measure as a threat to the very foundations of the 'one and indivisible' Republic. After the proposed reform was approved, the debate continued, with Jean-Pierre Chevène-ment branding it 'a shameful day for democracy' (*Le Monde,* 23 May 2001). The call for subnational representation is still, it appears, distrusted as conflicting ' with the requirement for all citizens to integrate into the [...] national state'. (Hutchinson and Smith, 1996: 11)

How should the new nations represent themselves? In the British instance, the representation of Scottish and Welsh identity on their national television is suffused with a mythologised past that prevents a new, more accurate representation of the nations in all their multiplicities being achieved.[1] This harking back to the past as the locus of geopolitical identity mimics the trappings of a traditional conception of national identity. The same forces are at play in the rhetoric surrounding the 'one and indivisible' Republic, which is similarly plagued by references to a perceived golden age of unity and solidarity, that, if it did ever exist, did so at the expense of freedom of expression and linguistic choice.

The practice of representing national or regional identity in terms of a mythologised past, bypassing the multi-ethnic, multicultural, localised present, is inherently problematic. This is amply demonstrated by Scriven and Roberts in their chapter centred on French and British regional televisual representations of the millennium celebrations. Regional television struggled to encourage an upsurge in regional pride and identity, through the celebration of the region's past, present and future on the eve of the millennium. Yet this artificial device only served to underline the artificiality of the institutionally denoted umbrella constructs of West of England and Aquitaine identities. Basque identity was only represented in Aquitaine regional news in terms of a violent threat to order. The image of regional identity painted by regional television, as with the representation of Welshness and Scottishness in Welsh and Scottish television respectively, was awkward and unengaging, only succeeding in the context of the extreme and freakish weather conditions that hit Aquitaine in December 2000.

The period of the millennium afforded a significant perspective in terms of the conceptualisation of geopolitical identity. It was characterised by a rise in the rhetoric of an imaginary unified past, where identity was firmly related to a single culture particular to the land or region. Rather than embracing the diversity engendered by multiple social identities, communities, nations, and continents have used the millennium as an excuse to reinforce their preconceptions concerning the 'true', rather archaic definition of identity.

This atavistic attitude prevents the nation (and at a micro level, the region) from engaging with the potential for a positive federal paradigm of national (and regional) identity. Multiculturalism has indicated that different cultures, societies and philosophies can literally exist side by side. The blossoming of multiculturalism has coincided with the call for representation of other minority or 'Othered' groups. National (as well as national regional and regional) television needs to acknowledge and embrace internal diversity, to see it as a rich resource to be exploited for the purposes of both factual and fictional television. At this juncture it is unclear whether the new audiovisual media and telecommunications will be used to represent the multiplicity of national and regional identity as befits a tool of democracy, whether they will merely shore up constructions of geopolitical identity under siege as a national institution, or whether they will continue to maintain their current ambivalent role.

Televisual Representations of Minority Group Identities

Another challenge to the favoured conception of the united, monolithic nation-state is the increasingly multicultural nature of France and Britain. Nationality is often linked to a sense of ethnicity which implies shared kinship structures as well as cultural, linguistic, and 'racial' affinities. This conflation of ethnicity and national identity has caused much consternation amongst immigrant origin ethnic minority groups; with good reason, as the *droit du sol/droit du sang* debate and the rise of the extreme right-wing groups in France in the 1980s has demonstrated. There is a tradition of requiring assimilation from its ethnic minority groups that has held sway in France since revolutionary times. It has been argued by some that 'While French nationhood is constituted by political unity, it is centrally expressed in the striving for cultural unity. Political inclusion has entailed cultural assimilation, for regional cultural minorities and immigrants alike.' (Brubaker, 1996: 168–9). British ethnic minorities fear that they will not be represented in the newly emergent 'older' conceptions of ethnically based nations, and reject the perceived ethnic connotations of the terms 'English', for example, preferring to describe themselves as 'British Asians.'[2] The ethnic dimension to these smaller nations is more closely aligned to an idealised past than to the multicultural present.

The diversity of a nation is not restricted to its ethnic groups. Both France and Britain are populated by a plethora of groups characterised by different cultural, social and political practices, positions and beliefs. These groups are considered to be minorities or embodiments of Otherness; their very existence is considered as an affront to the prescriptions of hegemony. Given the unquestionable representation of minorities on French and British television, witnessed in the second section of this book, is there a clear desire to get to grips with the real nature of French and British society today?

Three different approaches to the representation of minority groups can be identified in the second section of this book, in relation to both French and British television. Firstly, in the past, the televisual policy towards minority groups has been characterised by the practice of omission. The very existence of any challenges to the hegemonic norm of the white, male, solvent, urban conservative figure was systematically denied.

More recently, minority groups have been portrayed in one of two ways. On the one hand, Helcké, Wall and Pratt have commented on a process that they variously identify as the preaching of 'assimilation', 'deradicalisation' and 'banalisation' respectively. The minority figure in each case is stripped of what defines them as part of a minority group. Although ostensibly there is a semblance of tolerance and politically correct intentions – the minorities are not portrayed in a negative light – the minority figure is forced to adhere to a normative conception of what is presumed to be acceptable in the eyes of the national viewer. There is an insidious pressure on television producers and screen-writers to tone down the content of their programmes which could offend the 'normative' views of the audience. On the other hand, at the opposite extreme is the practice of sensationalisation. All that could shock or titillate the normative assumptions of the viewer, including extreme stereotypes, is emphasised. This serves to keep up the boundaries between hegemonic 'normality' – the 'us' in the equation – and Otherness, or 'them'.

One effect of these approaches is that the hegemonic boundaries are shored up, reaffirming normative views of what is 'decent' and 'right'. These representations are therefore prescriptive, advocating assimilation or demonising those who dare to be different, either because of what they are, or what they choose to be. However, exposure to the existence of groups who do not represent the hegemonic norm raises awareness of the social, cultural, sexual, ethnic and political diversity within the nation, disrupting the chimera of uniformity that stands in the place of solidarity. In terms of the status and lot of the minority groups in France and Britain, even bad representation is better than none at all.

The impact of these representations also extends to the viewing experience of the minority groups. These representations can often prompt subversive readings of the televisual script, drawing out positive aspects that reaffirm the processes of group identification. Overtly negative portrayals may also give rise to righteous indignation, which confirms the group's opposition to hegemony. This crystallises group identification around an axis of defiance and opposition. In this sense, group identity is therefore once more strengthened by their televisual portrayal.

One response to the heavily mediated representation of minority groups on national television has been the appropriation of the televisual medium by the groups themselves. They can thereby achieve unmediated self-representation. This may result in an increasing awareness of the diversity within these groups themselves (hinted at in Gillespie's assessment of *Goodness Gracious Me*). It will be interesting to see where the repercussions of the representation of internal diversity within minority groups will lead.

Constructing Post-modern Group Identity

Our post-modern, post-colonial era is one of shifting boundaries of meaning, identities and values, with sites of collective identity crossing a multitude of boundaries, with the points of 'intersections' or 'interrelations' being of particular interest to academics (Appiah and Gates, eds, 1995: 1). Group identities do not exist in isolation. They can intersect and inform one another. The expression of smaller, localised group identities does not necessarily preclude the sense of an overarching national identity. The problem resides in the understanding of precisely what constitutes national identity. At present, the terrestrial television of the regions and of the newly autonomous nations mimics dominant images of national identity in forging its own images. In all probability, however, the future will hold a different vision of the relationship between larger and smaller geopolitical identities. In the context of British geopolitical identities, the federal paradigm suggested by the example of the structure of the European Union seems to be the favoured vision of political commentators of liberal or left leanings. In the final instalment of his three part series, Andrew Marr spoke of his vision of a federal Britain, with a federal Parliament and a new constitution of rights, following the European example. In France on the other hand, it would be more difficult politically to implement the federal structure of national identity in the near future, given the enduring power of the republican ideal of the 'one and indivisible Republic'.

Minority or 'Othered' group identities are increasingly asserting their presence on the national small screen in France and Britain, albeit in a heavily mediated form. It is to be hoped that a reconfiguration of the national paradigm will embrace internal diversity, allowing for a revalorisation of the experiences and specificities of these groups. If national identity is to persevere beyond the twenty-first century, it appears that it must come to acknowledge the federation of identities – geopolitical, political, social, ethnic, cultural and sexual in nature – that exist within its national borders. If political federation is not a logistical possibility in the near future, then a more federal conception of the constitution of national identity is a necessity. The importance of the role of national television in the redefinition of the nation cannot be underestimated.

Notes

1. Although Scullion does note that the depiction of Scottishness has witnessed a process of Europeanisation and internationalisation in a select number of television programmes in recent years, an outdated conception of Scottishness still appears to prevail on contemporary Scottish television.
2. Yasmin Alibhai-Brown was interviewed by Andrew Marr as part of his programme, *The Day Britain Died*, BBC 2, 31 January–2 February 2000.

TAKING THE INITIATIVE

REPRESENTATIONS OF THE MAGHREBI POPULATION ON FRENCH TELEVISION

INTERVIEW WITH AKLI TADJER[1]

I began to work on French television in 1985, adapting my first novel, *Les A.N.I du Tassili*[2] (The Non-Identified Arabs of Tassili), for Antenne 2. The presidents of the public channels, TF1, Antenne 2, France 3, were at that stage named by the state. The programmes on the channels reflected the current state of mind of the population. This was especially true of talk-shows.

In 1983, there was an event that dominated the news for several days: 'la Marche des Beurs' (The march of the *Beurs*).[3] The marchers demanded equal rights. Rights that they felt were less defined than those of their fellow citizens of 'Gallic' origins.

For the directors of the channels, it was important to translate the lives of the second generation immigrants into fiction. But how? There was still no script-writer born of that generation who could describe the world that they encountered on the television news. So they adapted the few novels that told the story of the Maghrebi community, from the inside. This is how I began my career as a script-writer on French television.

The telefilm adapted from my novel was on television a year later and did not receive a large audience, although it received very favourable reviews in the press. It has to be said that it was shown in the middle of August.

In 1987, I wrote a telefilm entitled *Messieurs les Jurés* (Members of the jury), the story of a race-related attack in a city. This is a theme that is still frequently used; namely the rivalry that exists between two ethnic groups.

In 1989, I collaborated with Henri de Turenne, a renowned writer, to write a long series of fifty episodes called *Sixième Gauche* (Sixth on the left). This was the story of two families, one of French origin, the other of Maghrebi origins, living on the sixth floor of a building in poor suburbs. Our intention was to highlight the similarities and differences between the two families. I realised the limitations of this genre very quickly. Once the family had overcome their racial, cultural, and religious prejudices, we naturally began to write episodes centred on the Ben Amar son and the Villiers daughter, who loved each other, in spite of their different origins. A Romeo and Juliette, situation, in fact. The series was broadcast in the summer of 1990.

Later still, I wrote a short sitcom called *Fruits et Légumes* (Fruit and Vegetables), that followed the lives of a Maghrebi greengrocer and his family. I had read a survey which found that the Maghrebi grocer was the best respected member of a non-European ethnic minority. The fact that these shops close so late is surely related to this result.

The series was completely ignored by critics. It has to be said that it was shown in the middle of August at 13:30 as well; a slot that finds very few viewers in front of their televisions.

Generally, critics are not hostile to programmes that depict immigrants. This is due to the fact that often they are not judging the form and content of the programme. Rather, they are happy to laud the initiative taken by the television channel that commissioned the telefim or series. There are so few efforts that this initiative almost constitutes a heroic act! When you look at French television, it is obvious that the fictional content does not reflect the social or sociological realities of the country. The minorities are largely underrepresented (especially those of Maghrebi origin). In my opinion, this is due to the fact that script-writers of 'French' French origin can't be bothered to include minority characters in their stories. This is why it is important to have more script-writers from minority groups, so that black, Arab, and Asian characters are represented. As far as actors of Maghrebi origin are concerned, it is more difficult to showcase your talent if you only appear for five minutes in a film as a drug dealer or addict, than if you are a positive figure, the star of a film.

The pressures – if one can speak of pressures in terms of the writing process – often take the form of asking the author to write pure fictions, rather than to translate documentaries or sensational stories concerning the Magrhebi population into telefims. Apart from this, everything is permissible. Especially as far as adaptations of the most classical stories are concerned; Romeo and Juliette, for example.

In terms of my own writing, I need to turn the page and produce stories that address subjects other than the lives of families of Maghrebi origins.

To this end, I have turned my attention to creating truly fictional characters. I have written the story of a Beur cop, Karim Haddad, for TF 1 (which has since been privatised). This telefilm is broadcast at 20:30 and has been very successful in terms of viewing figures.

I put forward several other subjects for telefilms after this, but did not hear anything from the channels. I therefore decided to go back to my first love: the novel. In September 2000, my second novel, entitled *Courage et Patience*, was published and most recently in January 2002, my third novel, *Le Porteur de cartable*, was also published.

In conclusion, I would say my experiences as a television script-writer – a role that I hope has not come to an end – were rewarding in a number of ways. I learned to step back, and visually represent the story of my community in a dispassionate fashion. I found that aggressive dialogues and tense situations – even if they were justified from my point of view – ran counter to the interests of my community, that is perceived as being hostile to its environment. I saw that it is essential for this same community to exist on television, to be able to integrate into society. And I still ask myself today why certain of these series, which were very expensive to produce, were broadcast almost secretly... . Perhaps you have the answer.

Notes

1. The interview was conducted in April and May 2000.
2. The Non-Identified Arabs of Tassili, for Antenne 2.
3. The *Beurs* are the children of North African immigrants, most often born in France.

MAKING THINGS SWEETER

INTERVIEW WITH NINA WADIA¹

Racism and the Asian Actor:
The Inception and Growth of *Goodness Gracious Me*

Background of Goodness Gracious Me

Before we started doing *Goodness Gracious Me,* I was performing in a show called, *D'Yer Eat With Your Fingers?* at the Theatre Royal, Stratford East. Immediately after that show, Sanjeev and myself were performing at the Oval House, as part of *The Secret Asians*. Anil Gupta came up to us and said 'Look, we really like what you're doing, how would you like to be part of a team that does British Asian comedy on television?'

Meera (Syal) and Kulvinder (Gir) were already doing *The Real McCoy* on television, so they took those two out of there and brought us in as a new team. Now I was very new to the whole television scene because at that stage I'd just done about seven year's worth of theatre and a year and a half on radio drama. They made us put it on in the theatre first of all, knowing that what we have done so far has been successful. We did that, producers came to see it, liked it very much; 'Okay, why don't you try it on radio for a while before you move to television?' So now we have to do a radio series. After the first radio series they said 'Yes it is very good but it might be a bit of time before it gets on telly so why don't you do a second radio series?' Now we just went by the book and we did that. Finally they said yes we'll book you for telly and within three months we had to get the whole series out.

The Lot of Asian Actors

As British Asian actors, basically you work twice as hard. You have to not only audition like all other actors but on top of that you then have to create your own work. Because there are only so many parts. England is very cosmopolitan and (television) has to reflect this society more and more. Or else you're not doing work that's real.

I think if you're a good enough actor they should use you because you can create stuff and people then go past the colour. They don't see the colour any more. That's where I want to get to. It's happened a lot in the States and it's happened with black actors. (It) hasn't happened with Asian actors. There was this interview I was doing and I was trying to describe it... to me it's this pyramid and at the top of the pyramid you've got white actors you know you can play anything you want to do and that's fine. Then you've got the black actors who have struggled a lot and are now getting there. Then you've got the Asian actors and right at the bottom you've got the Oriental actors who are even behind us in the struggle. And I want to erase that step. ... . There's going to be British Asian footballers soon, there's going to be famous British Asian tennis players.

Do You Feel that You Only Get Offered Certain Sorts of Roles?

Doctor, lawyer, nurse, and victim is generally it for me. You'll see when things come out on 25 February (2000), I'm playing Indian yet again. But again that's something I'm definitely out to change. I definitely want to make sure that when new Asian actors come out they don't have to go through this struggle.

Is It Difficult for Asian Actors and Writers to Get into the Television Industry in General?

Yes it is. It's very very difficult. But it is getting easier for Asian writers. I still think we are way behind the States. Look at the director, producer and writer of *Sixth Sense*, he was Indian. I don't think that could ever happen here. So I'm waiting.

Significance of the Ali G. Debate

(This debate centres on the fact that Ali G., who is white, depicts an Asian character. Some comedians have suggested that he is making fun of Asians.)

You know the whole thing that's happened with Ali G., right? I was interviewed about that and they said to me why do you think this had happened. First of all they couldn't get comedians to talk about this because all the comedians were saying my agent doesn't want me to talk about it. And I realised there's a very fine line that Ali G. is walking. He's Sasha Baron Cohen playing, in my eyes, a white guy who's trying to be black. And I think he does it very well. He's a very good actor, he's very intelligent, he's very talented, everything. Black comedians were interviewed, most of them said fine, he's doing good work. There were one or two who said he's making fun of black people by doing that. I said they've missed the point. He's making fun of the establishment with his character. I think the last intention he has is to make fun of black people.

What it does bring out though, this whole issue, was exactly the struggle that Asian and black actors face in this country. Which is, once we get successful like in *Goodness Gracious Me*, we still don't get the thing that happens to other actors, which is they pick you out and they go let's give you a show. That's where the difference lies. What this whole Ali G. thing has shown is that the problem is not with a white person playing black or Indian, the problem is when they don't see the talent. If this was a black actor or an Asian actor who had created Ali G. we still wouldn't be getting our own show, which Ali G. has now got. The point is we struggle, we work really hard, and we still don't get it because they don't think a non-British – by their standards, British meaning completely British, not of any ethnic origin – that we cannot hold our own in the show.

The Role of Comedy

Would You Say that Comedy Gets Past People's Defences?

Yes. *Goodness Gracious Me* has been taken on by the Metropolitan Police in order to help police officers understand Indian people and to combat racism within the police force. So that was a big shock to me. I'm going to be doing something for the Royal Air Force very shortly where they're trying to recruit more Asians. There is no payment for this job but the payment is going up with the Red Arrows. It has its perks!

What is the Value of Comedy in Combating Racism?

Comedy is a universal language. As is anything emotional. The arts have always been used to get people to make decisions, to get people to move on things. Comedy does it in a way that doesn't actually make people feel bad.

Comedy is a very important medium for getting things across. (It is) very unthreatening. I don't know how to describe it. Affectionate parody is a good phrase. It makes people want to watch it.

An Example

We'd gone to do a charity thing up in Yorkshire, where Kul (Kulvinder Gir, a fellow actor in the show) is from. He asks me to come to this pub with him. It's three roads away from where he grew up and he was not allowed to go there when he was a kid because they said 'No Pakis in this area'; literally, those were the words. So we drove by and we go in and there's this buzzing pub – this was at lunch time – and there was lots of laughing. We come in and there's dead silence in the pub. Dead. And I just thought Kul I don't want to be here. Under my breath I just went let's go. He grabs my hand, we go in for a drink, and out of the blue this young white guy just bounces along and goes 'Oh my god, it's you two from *Goodness Gracious Me* isn't it?' And the pub buzz starts again and people keep coming up to me and going 'Can I have your autograph please' in this pub in the middle of Yorkshire, it's the most surreal thing that's ever happened to me. Because *Goodness Gracious Me* has done so much. It's broken down barriers. If we can't rescue the older generation what we've done is rescue the younger ones. Because it's actually the confidence that we've got from the younger white and black British people that has allowed us to make this programme. Because we know that they know what we're trying to do, (which is) to say 'look, have a laugh, this is what we're like'.

Goodness Gracious Me:
Political Commentary, Role Models and Cultural Identity

Does Goodness Gracious Me *Set Itself an Overt Agenda?*

With *Goodness Gracious Me* it's almost like we've found a niche, a point that has not been pressed. Maybe because of people wanting to be too PC (politically correct). I mean, we're not a PC show at the end of the day. We're outrageous. We make fun of ourselves, we make fun of other people, we're the most '-ist' programme that's out there. It has balanced itself, but it's happened anyway. And we've had to do it also because of the programming side of things. We've been told by BBC programmers, the head of BBC light ents and stuff, that we can't do certain things. There's loads of sketches we've recorded that have never been shown because when they've been seen by people at the top they've gone, no, it's too much.

Who Are They Worried about Offending?

I think either side. To be perfectly honest, there are people who are offended by our show. There are older Asians. I've been stopped once and whacked on the arm by a woman saying 'how dare you show the Kapoors!' Because they think there are Indians out there who are trying to be English and that that's a very shameful thing. Which it is, it's really crap if you want to be something you're not; and you do it badly especially. But that doesn't mean we hide it. We've got to find that side.

Inversion: Getting the Point Across

This third series we've got a couple of very clever inversions that we've done. One is the New York Delhi Police, NYDP. There's one white officer, and he comes over and says 'ok look, it's been two years now and we really need to get this case going.' And we go 'Oh here we go, another complaint from our white bloke. Now who got robbed or killed or mugged.' And he goes 'Look, there's a guy who got stabbed in the back'. And we go 'So?'. He says 'Well it's obviously not a suicide is it!' We go 'Well, you know, you English have dogs right? You teach your dogs tricks don't you? That's what could have happened. it was an accident and the dog stabbed him in the back!' All we're trying to do is say look, when you come with a case like Stephen Lawrence or you come in with a case like Ricky Reel, the Indian guy who was murdered and thrown into the Kingston river... I mean, they actually have footage of him and his friends being racially abused and then he disappears. And the next thing you know his shirt's torn and his body's found thrown in the Thames. It was obviously a racial attack. But something's gone wrong somewhere and basically they've said, 'oh we're not sure if it was a racially motivated attack'. They think that when something like the Stephen Lawrence case comes out or the Ricky Reel case comes out that we're out to cause trouble because we say it's a racial incident. But there are genuine racial incidents out there. And we have to get the police to look at these things. I did a concert for Ricky Reel. I MC'd the whole night trying to get people in to make them aware of the whole thing.

I have always been aware of these things but just never realised I'd be one of the people who would actually fight for it. And then you have to find that balance as an actor; you also have to be careful and think well, if I go into that full-time I'll be seen as shrill and that's not good for my career. You have to find that balance.

The Asian Actor as Role Model

I got a letter from Mo Mowlam the other day, who I met at the Asian Traders Awards ceremony that I was presenting where she was a guest speaker. And she actually said to me you're a role model now for British Asian people in this country and asked me how I felt about participating in Diversity in Britain Projects. And I said well – see this is the role left for Asian actors. There comes a point where people think 'Quick there's no-one else around let's use whoever's there'. And I don't want to go into politics.

Has Your Work Changed in Nature Following the Success of Goodness Gracious Me?

In terms of acting, one effect of the show is that I have been pigeon-holed as a comic. Aside from that, the biggest change has been that now I do a lot of community-based appearances to help out different causes. I went up to a group called 'Roshni' in Sheffield. It's an Asian women's mentoring group. They wanted me to make a speech and say look you can come up from nowhere. I mean if you think about it I was born in Bombay, lived there until I was about eleven. I was quite underprivileged actually, to put it mildly. Came out to Hong Kong when dad finally got a job out of the airlines (India Airlines) where he was managing a restaurant. And I've seen the 'real' Indian side, I've seen the cosmopolitan side in Hong Kong, then to come to Britain, I feel like I've covered the whole spectrum.

I went up there so I could talk to the kids about starting from scratch. I've told them the truth about what's happened; it's not a joke, it's very hard work, and sometimes you don't really realise what direction your career's going in. I went into this profession just to be an actress, but I've suddenly been thrown into this very different pool, where I have responsibilities whether I like it or not. There's an Asian women's day coming up and they want me to represent Asian women all over the world. And I said I just can't do that, I don't think I do, no-one can.

Do You Think the Show Has Helped You to Situate Yourself in Terms of Identity?

I go back home probably every year and a half. It's where I get a lot of my material! I'm proud to call myself British Asian when I'm here, but India is my home. Which is why when something positive happens here I think it has repercussions back home and that's why I feel very proud to be doing the kind of work I'm doing because it makes me feel more and more Indian at the end of the day.

Asianness and British Asianness

If you go into an area like Southall, it is predominantly Punjabi, but they do have some Muslims there. Now the Hindu Punjabis and the Muslims have their problems. But you take *Goodness Gracious Me* and you put that in there somewhere and all of the sudden the Muslims and the Punjabis have something in common. They see 'British Asian' and as far as they are concerned that is what they are. What's holding them together is the British. Whereas in Hong Kong – we were very different over there if we were Parsee (I'm Parsee, but because I was born and brought up in India I consider myself Indian), Hindu, Muslim or whatever. Over here, they go past that when they need to bond together, but, at the end of the day, there is still that difference. But I think that the quality that's here is a sense of Asianness. It's the luggage on top of your parent's cupboard. It's the plastic on the carpet in the posh room in your house. It's that kind of stuff. That will be in any Asian house. That's a general thing. But again it's a thing that bonds them together. I think if it came down to it they will stick together against white or black but at the end of the day they will fight amongst themselves because that's what Indians do.

Origins of Cover-all Term 'Asian'

It came about because it covered all of us. If you say Indian you mean people not from Pakistan. We stayed away from the Muslim community in series one and instead most of the people we had were Hindus because we thought we were safer we didn't want *fatwas* on our head. But then we got death threats from the Hindu fundamentalists. Saying if you make a second series we'll kill you or how dare you make fun of Hinduism. We thought it's going over your head! Whichever way you do it there is going to be some kind of discrepancy there… you can't please all of the people all of the time.

Popular Reception of the Show

Have You Had Any Feedback from South Asia about the Show?

There are pirate copies doing the whole of India. Apparently they have *Goodness Gracious Me* parties out there. The videos haven't even been released. The problems with releasing them in India is that we'd have to cut out a lot of the humour, it's too explicit.

What Are the Viewing Figures for the Show?

We went up from initially I think 2.5 million to something like almost the 4 million mark. Which is massive for BBC2. And we've been sold to several different countries and we've won awards in Holland, in Germany, in France, and we've won the British Comedy Awards. We've won the Sony radio awards. We've won an award from the CRE (the Commission for Racial Equality).

Who Do You Think Watches the Show?

A whole spectrum. Initially (we targeted) British Asians. Because the black community had *The Real McCoy* to watch; Asians didn't have any-thing so we thought that might be it. But when they put us on Radio 4 (the programme) was on Saturday afternoons and Friday nights, targeting their main listenership, 30–45–year-old white males. And they had people write in and say we love this.

My white British friends actually adore the show because of sketches like 'Going for an English' where what we're showing them is, look, this is our experience of going to an Indian restaurant with you. The great part is the British can laugh at themselves. This sketch has been compared to the par-rot sketch (ed: canonical sketch by *Monty Python*). We did it at the (End of the Third World) Debt Wish live thing and we did it at Comic Relief.

When I watched 'Going for an English' with my white friends I was actually quite embarrassed, because I thought they're going to know that we know that they do this. But what they feel – I have spoken to them about this – is 'no, we don't feel like that, that's brilliant. We're sorry, we didn't realise that's how bad it was'. But there is a kind of respect that comes back at you for showing them in a way that doesn't make them go 'oh my God, I feel really guilty and bad'. What we've done is say hey, this is what you do, it is very funny if you think about it, let's have a laugh about it. Because at the end of the day, if you don't laugh about things in life you have a very miserable existence.

So You Think it Has a Universal Appeal?

Definitely. There are pirate copies doing the rounds right now in Canada and the States. And the Asian community especially out there is loving it. And we're thinking how do you get it when we think it's a particularly British programme? *The Jewish Chronicle* wrote about us and said something like 'they are honorary Jews as far as we're concerned, because there's such similarity'.

Vision of the Future: Making it Sweeter

I think we've arrived at a different point, generally, in people's lives. Some people say it's our turn. I don't believe it's just that. That is a part of it, but I believe that we're saying there is an area where we all believe the same things and this is the area where it happens. This is the area where we can make you laugh with characters that we've created that have nothing to do with being specifically Indian or not. Look at the Mr India character, the guy who thinks everything is Indian. It's this character who's a bit loopy, who could be any nationality. The idea is that we have created characters who are believable, but not racist. But ten years down the line I'd be interested to see what people thought of *Goodness Gracious Me* at this time. Because people might look back at it and go oh I don't believe they said that about us!

Do You Think It Is a Question of Time before Asians Achieve Equality?

Yes it is. What I'm worried about is the backlash. There is going to be a backlash at some stage. As you get the black community growing, the Asian community growing, the Oriental community growing, you will also get a community that doesn't want them to grow as well. Why does it make some people angry? Are they angry because we're not trying hard enough to learn the language? Or we're trying too hard? Or we want to replace them is that what they think? I don't quite understand where that's going? There was a woman up in Liverpool, we were doing this show, we did *Goodness Gracious Me* and then we were interviewed afterwards, just by this general crowd (who) asked questions. This woman put her hand up and said 'Look, I don't mind you lot coming in and taking over our this and that and you living in our council flats when we should have first priority, but if you live in our country, shouldn't you dress like we dress, shouldn't you talk like we talk? Why do you have to cover yourselves up from head to toe? Why can't you dress like me?' I just don't understand it. You want us to come into your country but on the condition that we don't have any of our cultural side left. She brought up a valid point after that, funnily enough; 'Well,' she says, 'because my school is 90 percent Indian, they don't have Christmas any more. We don't celebrate Christmas. We now celebrate what is called "World Greeting" or something like that, where there is no particular religion that's celebrated. I feel that is unfair'. And I said 'Well actually I do as well'. I do think that you should be allowed to celebrate Christmas in your own country. There has to be a point where people reach a middle ground. If it carries on in the way it's carrying on you're asking for trouble. I can see that coming. I understand there are certain problem areas. There are areas that have got too populated and they are trying to change it completely. I have yet to go to a city where I don't see an Asian person in Britain and that makes me proud.

The Ideal: Making Things Sweeter

Our Persian ancestors were forced out of Iran because we weren't allowed to be Zoroastrian any more and we had to convert to Islam. A whole bunch of Zoroastrians escaped through to India. When we arrived in India, one of our high priests around 936AD wanted to say to the Indian area of Gujerat, 'Please can we live in your country? We want to carry on our traditions of Zoroastrianism, and you're a peaceful race. We don't want to convert to Islam'. Apparently the ruler took a cup and he poured in some milk to fill the cup completely. He said, 'This is our country. We're already full, there's nowhere for you to be.' And the Persian priest took a teaspoon of sugar, poured it slowly in, and mixed it, and it didn't spill. And he said, 'We will not only come into your society, we won't overflow it, and at the same time we will make it sweeter'. That is really what I would hope can happen with the British Asian, and the British black, and the British Oriental communities in England. That we somehow don't disperse things and that at the same time we make it sweeter, that we make people like what we like as well and share those experiences. That is where we want to head.

Notes

1. The interview was conducted by Emily Roberts on 27 January 2000.

SELECT BIBLIOGRAPHY

The following select bibliography is intended as a guide for further reading. It makes no claims to comprehensiveness, and is offered as an indication of the key texts used by the authors in the preparation of individual contributions. Texts are arranged according to chapter and section headings.

Chapter 1: Fragmentation of the Nation: National Identity and Television in France and Britain at the Turn of the Twentieth Century

Anderson, B., *Imagined Communities. Reflections on the Origin and Rise of Nationalism*. London, 1990.

Delanty, G., *Inventing Europe: Idea, Identity, Reality*. London, 1995.

Friedman, J., *Cultural Identity and Global Process*. London, 1996.

Hutchinson, J. and Smith A.D., eds, *Nationalism*. Oxford, 1994.

Kuhn, R., *The Media in France*. London, 1995.

Morley, D. and Robins K., *Spaces of Identity: Global Media, Electronic Landscapes and Cultural Boundaries*. London and New York, 1995.

Patterson, R., 'Introduction: Collective Identity, Television and Europe', in *National Identity and Europe: The Television Revolution*, eds Drummond, P., Patterson, R. and Willis, J. London, 1993: 1–8 (4).

Scriven, M. and Lecomte, M., eds, *Television Broadcasting in Contemporary France and Britain*, Oxford, 1999.

Urry, J., *Globalisation, Localisation and the Nation-State*. Lancaster, 1990.

Introduction: Section I: Geo-Political Group Identities

Wagstaff, P., ed., *Regionalism in the European Union*. Exeter, 1999.

Chapter 2: Adjusting to Diversity:
The Case of England and France

Bogdanor, V., *Devolution in the United Kingdom*. Oxford, 1999.

Braudel, F., *L'Identité de la France*. Paris, 1986.

Briggs, A., *The History of Broadcasting in the United Kingdom*. Oxford, 1995.

Colley, L., *Britons: Forging the Nation*. New Haven and London, 1992.

Heffer, S., *Nor Shall my Sword*. London, 1999.

Pailliart, I., *Les Territoires de la communication*. Grenoble, 1983.

Scriven, M. and Lecomte, M., eds, *Television Broadcasting in Contemporary France and Britain* Oxford, 1999.

Chapter 3: Constructing the National:
Television and Welsh Identity

Aitchison, J. and Carter, H., 'The Welsh Language Today' *in Wales Today*, eds Dunkerley, D. and Thompson, A. Cardiff, 1999.

Balsom, D. 'The Three Wales Model' in *The National Question Again*, ed. Osmond, J. Llandysul, 1985.

Bevan, D., 'The mobilization of cultural minorities: the case of Sianel Pedwar Cymru', *Media, Culture and Society*, 6, 1984.

Blanchard, S. and Morley, D., eds, *What's This Channel Fo(u)r?* London, 1982.

Blandford, S. and Upton, J., 'Courting the Network', *Planet*, 117 June/July 1996: 70–76.

Constitution Unit, *An Assembly for Wales*. London, 1996.

Davies, J., *Broadcasting and the BBC in Wales*. Cardiff, 1994.

Griffiths, A., 'National and cultural identity in a Welsh language soap opera' in *To Be Continued…Soap Operas around the World*, ed. Allen, R. London, 1995.

Howell, W.J., 'Minority-Language Broadcasting and the Continuation of Celtic Culture in Wales and Ireland' in *Ethnic Minority Media* ed. Riggins, S. H. London, 1992.

Howells, K., 'Give the Real Wales a TV voice', *South Wales Echo*, 1 February 1990.

Hume, I., 'Mass Media and Society in the 1980s', in *The Welsh and their Country*, eds. Hume, I. and Pryce, E. Llandysul, 1986.

Humphreys, E., *The Taliesin Tradition*. Bridgend, 1989.

Jones, H., Public Lecture, University of Aberystwyth, 5 October 1995.

Osmond, J. 'The Modernisation of Wales' in *National Identity in the British Isles*, eds. Evans, N. Harlech, 1989.

Osmond, J. 'Broadcasting TV figures', *Wales on Sunday*, 4 March 1990.

Paterson, L. and Wyn Jones, R. 'Does civil society drive constitutional change?' in *Scotland and Wales: Nations Again?* eds Taylor, B. and Thompson, K. Cardiff, 1999.

Scannell, P. and Cardiff, D., *A Social History of British Broadcasting*. London, 1991.

Smith, D., *Wales! Wales?* London, 1984.

Talfan Davies, G. 'Broadcasting in Wales in the Digital Age'. Address to the Celtic Film and Television Festival, Bangor, 28 March 1996.

Welsh Affairs Committee, *Broadcasting in Wales and the National Assembly*. London, 1999.

Williams, K., *Shadows and Substance: The Development of a Media Policy for Wales*. Llandysul, 1997.

Williams, L., 'National identity and the Nation State: Construction, Reconstruction and Contradiction' in *National Identity*, ed. Cameron, K. Exeter, England, 1999.

Chapter 4: Changing Expectations: Holyrood, Television and Scottish National Identity

Anderson, B., *Imagined Communities: Reflections on the Origin and Rise of Nationalism*. London, 1990.

Bauman, Z., 'From pilgrim to tourist – a short history of identity', *Questions of Cultural Identity*, eds, Hall and de Gay. London, 1996: 18–36.

Bechhofer, F., McCrone, D., Kiely, R., and Stewart, R., 'Constructing national identities: arts and landed elites in Scotland', *Sociology* Vol. 33, no. 3, 1999: 515–34.

Beveridge, C., and Turnbull, R., *Scotland After Enlightenment: Image and Tradition in Modern Scottish Culture*. Edinburgh, 1997.

Beveridge, C., and Turnbull, R., *The Eclipse of Scottish Culture: Inferiorism and the Intellectuals*. Edinburgh, 1989.

Bogdanor, V., *Devolution in the United Kingdom*. Oxford, 1999.

Brown, A., McCrone D., and Paterson, L., *Politics and Society in Scotland*, 2nd edn. Basingstoke, 1998.

Brown, A., McCrone, D., Paterson, L., and Surridge, P., *The Scottish Electorate: the 1997 General Election and Beyond*. Basingstoke, 1999.

Cairns C., 'Myths against history: tartanry and kailyard in nineteenth-century Scottish literature', in *Scotch Reels: Scotland in Cinema and Television*, ed. McArthur, C. London, 1982: 7–15.

Cohen, R., *Frontiers of Identity: the British and Others*. London, 1994.

Geertz, C., 'The integrative revolution: primordial sentiments and civil politics in the new states', in *Old Societies and New States: the Quest for Modernity in Asia and Africa*, ed. Geertz, C. New York, 1963: 107–13.

Gellner, E., *Nations and Nationalism*. Oxford, 1983.

Guibernau, M., *Nations Without States: Political Communities in a Global Age*. Cambridge, 1999.

Hall, S., 'Introduction: who needs 'identity'?, *Questions of Cultural Identity*, eds Hall, S. and de Gay, P. London, 1996: 1–17.

Hall, S. and de Gay, P., eds, *Questions of Cultural Identity*. London, 1996.

Herbert, H., '*Tutti Frutti* (John Byrne)', *British Television Drama in the 1980s*, ed. Brandt, G.W. Cambridge, 1993: 178–95.

Hutchinson, J. and Smith, A.D., eds, *Nationalism*. Oxford, 2000.

Kiberd, D., *Inventing Ireland: The Literature of the Modern Nation*. London, 1996.

McArthur, C., 'The Scottish discursive unconscious', in *Scottish Popular Theatre and Entertainment*, eds Cameron, A. and Scullion, A. Glasgow, 1996: 81–9.

McArthur, C., 'The cultural necessity of poor Irish cinema', in *Border Crossing: Film in Ireland, Britain and Europe*, eds Hill, J., McLoone, M. and Hainsworth, P. London, 1994: 112–25.

McArthur, C., ed., *Scotch Reels: Scotland in Cinema and Television*. London, 1982.

McCrone, D., *The Sociology of Nationalism*. London and New York, 1998.

McCrone, D., *Understanding Scotland: the Sociology of a Stateless Nation*. London and New York, 1992.

McCrone, D., Kendrick S., and Straw, P., eds, *The Making of Scotland: Nation, Culture and Social Change*. Edinburgh, 1989.

MacInnes, J., 'Rise and be a broadcaster again?', *Scottish Affairs* no. 7, 1994: 135–41.

MacInnes, J., 'The broadcast media in Scotland', *Scottish Affairs* no. 2, 1993: 83–98.

Marriot, S., 'Election night', *Media, Culture and Society* vol. 22 no. 2, 2000: 131–48.

Meech, P. and Kilborn, R., 'media and identity in a stateless nation: the case of Scotland', *Media, Culture and Society* vol. 14, no. 2, 1992: 245–59.

Nairn, T., *The Break-Up of Britain: Crisis and Neo-Nationalism* 2nd edn. London, 1981.

Pittock, M.G.H., *Celtic Identity and the British Image*. Manchester and New York, 1999.

Schlesinger, P. 'Scottish devolution and the media', *Politics and the Media: Harlots and Prerogatives at the Turn of the Millennium*, ed. Seaton, J. Oxford, 1998: 55–74.

Scullion, A., 'Feminine pleasures and masculine indignities: gender and community in Scottish drama', in *Gendering the Nation: Studies in Modern Scottish Literature*, ed. White, C. Edinburgh, 1995: 169–204.

Sillars, J., 'Drama, devolution and dominant representations', *The Media in Britain: Current Debates and Developments*, eds Stokes, J. and Reading, A. Basingstoke, 1999: 246–54.

Smith, A.D., *National Identity*. Harmondsworth, 1991.

Smith, A.D., 'The myth of the "modern nation" and the myth of nation', *Ethnic and Racial Studies* vol. 1, no. 1 (1988): 1–26.

Smith, N., 'Broadcasting and a Scottish parliament', *Scottish Affairs* no. 9, 1997: 29–41.

Whyte, C., ed., *Gendering the Nation: Studies in Modern Scottish Literature*. Edinburgh, 1995.

Chapter 5: Storm Clouds of the Millennium: Regional Television News in Aquitaine and the West of England

Dossiers de l'audiovisuel, 'La télévision de proximité', no. 57 (September/October 1994).

Les écrits de l'image : les saisons de la télévision, no. 25, December 1999.

Guichard, F., 'Introduction', in *L'Identité régionale : l'idée de région dans l'Europe du Sud-Ouest*. Paris, 1991: 5–8 (6).

Hobsbawm, E., and Ranger T., eds, *The Invention of Tradition*. Cambridge, 1992.

Morley, D., and Robins, K., *Spaces of Identity: Global Media, Electronic Landscapes and Cultural Boundaries*. London and New York, 1995.

Pucheu, R., 'L'entrée en l'An 2000', *France Forum*, no. 327, premier trimestre 2000: 22–29.

Roche, M., *L'Année 1999 dans Le Monde: les principaux événements en France et à l'étranger*. Paris, 2000.

Trelluyer, M., 'La télévision régionale en Europe', *Dossiers de l'audiovisuel*, no. 33, September/October 1990: 10–11.

Verdet, P., 'Regard sur la météorologie : la planète perd la boule', *Sud Ouest*, 31 December 1999: 6.

Introduction: Section II: Minority and 'Othered' Identities

Abdallah, M.H., 'Networking for migrant perspectives on television in France and Europe: The Im'Média Agency's experience' in *European Television: Immigrants and Ethnic Minorities*, eds Frachon, C. and Vargaftig, M., 1995: 45–59 (56).

Frachon, C. and Vargaftig, M., eds, *European Television: Immigrants and Ethnic Minorities*. London: John Libbey, 1995.

Husband, C., ed., 'General introduction: ethnicity and media democratization within the nation-state', in *A Richer Vision: the development of ethnic minority media in Western democracies*, ed. Charles Husband. London: UNESCO, 1994.

Chapter 6: The Representation of Maghrebis on French Television

Battegay, A., 'La Médiatisation de l'Immigration dans la France des Années 1980', *Les Annales de la Recherche Urbaine*, no. 57–8, December 1992 March 1993: 174–84.

Bonnafous, S., 'Le terme "intégration" dans le journal *Le Monde*: sens et non-sens', *Hommes et Migrations*, no. 1154, May 1992: 24–25

Gaspard, F. and Khosrokhavar, F. *Le foulard et la République*. Paris, 1995.

Hamès, C., 'La Construction de l'Islam en France: du Côté de la Presse', *Arch. Sc. soc. des Rel.*, 68/1, July-September 1989: 79–92.

Hargreaves, A.G., 'La Famille Ramdam: Un sit-com "pur beur"?', *Hommes et Migrations*, no. 1147, October 1991: 60–6.

Hargreaves, A.G., 'Ethnic Minorities and the Mass Media in France', in *Popular Culture and Mass Communication in Twentieth Century France*, eds R. Chapman and N. Hewitt. Lewiston, 1992a: 165–80.

Hargreaves, A.G., 'La Fiction Télévisée face aux immigrés: une vision schizophrène', *CinémAction TV*, no. 3, November 1992b: 99–106.

Hargreaves, A.G., 'Télévision et Intégration: La Politique Audiovisuelle du FAS', *Migrations Société*, vol.5, no. 30, November-December 1993: 7–22.

Hargreaves, A.G., 'Gatekeepers and Gateways: Post-Colonial Minorities and French Television', in *Post-colonial Cultures in France*, eds Hargreaves, A.G. and McKinney, M. London and New York, 1997: 84–98.

Hargreaves, A. G. and Helcké, J., '*Fruits et Légumes*: Une Recette Télévisuelle Mixte', *Hommes et Migrations*, no. 1182, December 1994: 51–7.

Hargreaves, A. G. and Perotti, A., 'The Representation on French Television of immigrants and ethnic minorities of Third World Origin', *New Community*, vol. 19, no. 2, January 1993: 251–61.

Hommes et Migrations, `Pour une éthique de l'intégration', special issue, no. 1182, December 1994.

Humblot, C., 'Les Emissions Spécifiques: De 'Mosaïque' à 'Rencontres', *Migrations Société*, vol. 1, no. 4, August 1989: 7–14.

Humblot, C., 'Comme Nous', *Le Monde*, 31 July 1994.

Ouali, N., 'Télévision et immigration: un enjeu pour l'intégration et la lutte contre le racisme?', *Migrations Société*, vol. 9, no. 54. November-December 1997: 21–30.

Prencipe, L., 'L'image Médiatique de l'Immigré': du Stéréotype à l'Intégration', *Migrations Société*, vol. 7, no.42, November-December 1995: 45–63.

Weil, P. and Crowley, J. 'Integration in Theory and Practice: a Comparison of France and Britain', *West European Politics*, vol.17, no.2, April 1994: 110–26

Revue Française des Affaires Sociales, 'Insertion, intégration: concepts et pratiques', special issue, vol. 51, no. 2, April-June 1997.

Chapter 7: From Comic Asians to Asian Comics: *Goodness Gracious Me*, British Television Comedy and Representations of Ethnicity

Bakhtin, M., *The Bakhtin Reader: Selected Writings of Bakhtin, Medvedev, and Voloshinov*, ed. Pam Morros. London, 1994.

Bergson, H., 'Laughter' in *Comedy,* ed. by W. Sypher. Baltimore, 1956.

Cohen, T., *Jokes: Philosophical Thoughts on Joking Matters*. Chicago, 2000.

Freud, S., *Jokes and their Relation to the Unconscious*. London, 1960.

Gillespie, M., 'TV Comedy and Joking Relations in a British Asian Peer Culture' in *TV Talk in a London Punjabi Peer Culture*. PhD thesis, Brunel University, 1992.

Gokturk, D., 'Strangers in Disguise: Performing Ethnicity in Transnational Film Comedy'. Paper presented at *Media in Multicultural and Multilingual Contexts Workshop*, University of Klagenfurt, 11–14 November 1999.

Hall, S. et al, eds, *Representation*. London, 1995.

Husband, C., 'Racist Humour and Racist Ideology in British Television or I Laughed Till You Cried' in *Humour in Society: Resistance and Control*, eds Powell, C. and Paton, G. London, 1988.

Medhurst, A., 'Laughing Matters' in *The Colour Black: Black Images on British Television*. London, 1989.

Musser, C., 'Ethnicity, Role Playing, and American Film Comedy' in *Unspeakable Images: Ethnicity in American Cinema*, ed. L.D.Friedman. Urbana and Chicago, 1991.

Naughton, J., 'Tandoori Nights' in *The Listener* 11 July 1985.

Runnymede Trust, *Islamophobia: A Challenge For Us All*. London, 1997.

Shohat, E., 'Ethnicities in Relation: Toward a Multicultural Reading of American Cinema' in *Unspeakable Images: Ethnicity in American Cinema*, ed. Friedman, L.D. Urbana and Chicago, 1991.

Chapter 8: Curiosity, Fear and Control: The Ambiguous Representation of Hip-Hop on French Television

Bazin, H., *La Culture hip-hop*. Paris, 1995.

Bocquet, J.-L. and Pierre-Adolphe, P., *Rap ta France*. Paris, 1997.

Bouamama, S., *Dix ans de marche des Beurs. Chronique d'un mouvement avorté*. Paris, 1994.

Boucher, M., *Rap, expression des lascars: signification et enjeu dans la société française*. Paris, 1999.

Boyer, H. and Lochard, G., *Scènes de télévision en banlieues 1950–1994*. Paris, 1998.

Buxton, D., 'Le lieu du fantasme: le commentaire sur les images dans les magazines de reportage à la télévision française 1960–1992', in Buxton, D. et al, *Télévisions. La Vérité à construire*, Paris, 1995: 61–88.

Calio, J., *Le Rap: une réponse des banlieues*. Lyon, 1998.

Madec, A., *Le Quartier c'est dans la tête. L'histoire vraie de Stéphane Meterfi*. Paris, 1998.

Negroni, A., 'De bande à gang: la presse fait le pas', in CFREPJJ, *L'Actualité des bandes*, 1–8. Vaucresson, 1991.

Vulbeau, A., *Du tag au tag*. Paris, 1992.

Television broadcasts

'Hip-Hop', various dates from 1984, TF1.

'Tag a RATP', 19 April 1990, A2 Envoyé Spécial, journalist: Agnes Poirier.

'Gangs Montfermeil', 14 August 1990, TF1 Journal du vingt heures, journalist: Allan Rothschild.

'Rap', 1 November 1990, TF1 Journal du vingt heures, journalist: Bernard Gely.

'Bandes organisées', 13 November 1990, TF1 Journal du vingt heures, journalist: Louis Carzeo.

Videos

Suprême NTM, *J'appuie sur la gachette* (Director: NTM, Paris: Epic, 1995).

Suprême NTM, *Ma Benz* (Director: Yannis Mangematin, Paris: Epic, 1998).

Chapter 9: Green Activist Identities on British Television

Brosnan, J., 'Survivors' in *The Encyclopedia of Science Fiction*, ed. Nicholls, P. London, 1981.

Doherty, B., 'Manufactured Vulnerability: Eco-activist tactics in Britain', Mobilization, 4(1), 1999: 75–89.

Fiske, J., 'Postmodernism and Television' in *Mass Media and Society*, eds Curran, J. and Gurevitch. London, 1997.

Hall, S., 'Encoding/Decoding' in Culture, Media, Language, eds Hall, S., Hobson, D., Lowe, A., and Willis, P. London, 1982.

Hannigan, J., *Environmental Sociology*. London, 1995.

Howe, D. Stammers, M. and Walker, J., *Dr Who – The Seventies*. London, 1994.

Kimber, R. and Richardson, J., *Campaigning for the Environment*. London, 1974.

Lipsitz, G., *Time Passages: Collective Memory and American Popular Culture*. Minneapolis, 1989.

Martin. T., *Edge of Darkness*. London, 1990.

McAdam, D., *Political Process and the Development of Black Insurgency, 1930–1970*. Chicago, 1982.

Melucci, A., *Challenging Codes*. Cambridge, 1996.

Rendell, R., *Road Rage*. London, 1997.

Roseneil, S. Disarming Patriarchy: Feminism and Political Action at Greenham. Milton Keynes, 1995.

Rothman, B., *The 1932 Kinder Trespass*. Altrincham, 1982.

Rudig, W. and Lowe, P. 'The withered 'greening' of British politics', *Political Studies*, 34, 1986: 262–84.

Ryder, R., *Animal Revolution*. Oxford, 1989.

Veldman, M., *Fantasy, the Bomb and the Greening of Britain*. London, 1994.

Wall, D., *Earth First! and the Anti-roads Movement*. London, 1999.

Chapter 10: Going out to the Straight Community: Televisual and Heteronormative Logics in Representations of Homosexuality

Allen, D., 'Homosexuality and Narrative', *Modern Fiction Studies*, vol. 41, 1995: 609–29.

Bourdieu, P., *Sur la télévision*. Paris, 1996.

Caron, D., 'Liberté, Egalité, Séropositivité: AIDS, the French Republic, and the question of community', *French Cultural Studies*, vol. 9, 1998: 281–94.

Frogier, L., 'Homosexuals and the AIDS crisis in France: assimilation, denial, activism', in *Acting on Aids*, eds Oppenheimer, J. and Reckitt, H. London, 1997: 346–59.

Hocquenghem, G., *Le Désir homosexuel*. Paris, 2000.

Lestrade, D., *Act Up : une histoire*. Paris, 2000.

Maupin, A., *More Tales of the City*. London, NSW and Auckland, 1989.

Mendès-Leite, R. and de Busscher, P-O., 'Les respectables homos et les "joies" du puritanisme', *Gai Pied hebdo*, 523, 4 June 1992: 2.

Pratt, M., 'The defence of the straight state: heteronormativity, AIDS in France, and the space of the nation', *French Cultural Studies*, vol. 9, 1998: 263–80.

Preciado, B., *Manifeste contra-sexuel*. Paris, 2000.

Rubin, G., 'Thinking Sex: Notes for a Radical Theory of the Politics of Sexuality', in *The Lesbian and Gay Studies Reader*, eds Abelove et al. London, 1993: 3–44.

Scherer, R., 'L'Homosexualité face à sa banalisation', in *Un sujet inclassable? Approches sociologiques, littéraires et juridiques des homosexualités*, ed. Mendès-Leite, R. Lille, 1995: 19–36.

Schulman, S., 'Niche-marketing people with AIDS', in *Acting on Aids*, eds Oppenheimer, J. and Reckitt, H. London, 1997: 371–8.

Selden, D., '"just when you thought it was safe to go back in the water..."', in *The Lesbian and Gay Studies Reader*, Abelove et al: 221–26.

Speck, W., `Porno ?', in Gever, M., Greyson, J. and Parma, P., *Queer Looks, Perspectives on Lesbian and Gay Film and Video*, New York and London, 1993: 348–54.

Stevens, J., *Reproducing the State*. New Jersey, 1999.

White E., 'AIDS awareness and gay culture in France', in *Acting on AIDS: Sex, Drugs and Politics*, eds Oppenheimer, J. and Reckitt, H . London and New York: 339–45.

Chapter 11: Televisual Identity in the Twenty-first Century: Constructing the Post-modern Group

Appiah, K.A. and Henry Louis Gates, Jr., eds, *Identities*. Chicago and London, 1995.

Brubaker, R., 'Civic and Ethnic nation in France and Germany', in *Ethnicity*, eds Hutchinson, J. and Smith, A.D. Oxford, 1996: 168–9.

Herb, G. H., 'National Identity and Territory', in *Nested Identities: Nationalism, Territory, and Scale*, eds Herb, G.H. and David H. Kaplan, D.H. Maryland, USA, 1999: 9–30.

Hutchinson, J. and Smith, A.D., eds., *Ethnicity*. Oxford, 1996.

NOTES ON CONTRIBUTORS

Marie Gillespie is Senior Lecturer in Sociology at the Open University. She specialises in South Asian diaspora culture, media, politics and society and has spent ten years living, working and researching in Southall, west London (a predominantly Punjabi suburb); she has published numerous articles on media, ethnicity and national identities, and an ethnography entitled *Television, Ethnicity and Cultural Change* (Routledge, 1995).

Joanna Helcké is Visiting Fellow in European Studies at the University of Loughborough. She has published several articles focusing on France's Maghrebi population and the media, and is currently working on a new project on ethnicity and popular culture in contemporary France.

Murray Pratt is Head of European Studies, and Senior Lecturer in French Studies in the Institute for International Studies, University of Technology Sydney, Australia. His current research fields include masculinity, queer studies and AIDS studies, and his publications include work on contemporary writing, film, society and culture. He co-edited the October 1998 special issue of *French Cultural Studies* on 'AIDS in France'.

Emily Roberts was formerly Research Associate at the University of the West of England Bristol. Her doctoral thesis is on cultural identity and the colonial encounter in the twentieth-century French Indochinese novel. Following the completion of her PhD, she has published a number of articles on the contemporary French Vietnamese novel, and has recently co-authored with Michael Scriven an article on local specificity, regional identity and French television broadcasting in *Media, Culture and Society*. She is currently resident in Adelaide, Australia.

Michael Scriven is Professor of European Studies and Academic Director of the European Business School, Regent's College, London. He was formerly Professor of European Studies and Director of the Centre for European Studies at the University of the West of England Bristol, and Professor of French Studies at the University of Bath. He has published extensively in the field of French and European intellectual history, culture and politics. His most recent publications include *Jean-Paul Sartre: Politics and Culture in Postwar France* (Macmillan, 1999) and *Television Broadcasting in Contemporary France and Britain* (Berghahn, 1999).

Adrienne Scullion is Lecturer in the Department of Theatre, Film and Television Studies at the University of Glasgow. Her publications on Scottish cultural issues include articles in the journals *Theatre Research International* and *Comparative Drama* and essays in the collections *The Cambridge Companion to Modern British Women Playwrights* (Cambridge University Press, 2000), *A History of Scottish Women's Writing* (Edinburgh University Press, 1997), *Gendering the Nation: Studies in Modern Scottish Literature* (Edinburgh University Press, 1995) and in *Contemporary Dramatists* (St James Press, 1993 and 1999).

Jean-Claude Sergeant is Professor of English Civilisation at Paris III-Sorbonne Nouvelle University. He is currently Director of the Maison Française in Oxford. He has published numerous books, articles and book chapters on British politics, foreign policy and media issues. His most recent publications include chapters on public broadcasting and cable television in *Television Broadcasting in Contemporary France and Britain* (Berghahn, 1999) *and Les Médias en Grande Bretagne* (Ophrys [forthcoming]).

Akli Tadjer is a script writer and novelist. He has written two series focusing on families of Maghrebi origins, *Sixième Gauche* and *Fruits et Légumes*. His second novel, *Courage et Patience*, was published in September 2000; his third novel, *Le Porteur de cartable*, was published in January 2002.

Nina Wadia is an Indian born, British Asian writer/actress/choreographer, best known as one quarter of BBC 2's 'Goodness Gracious Me'. She started acting in 1990 and has appeared on stage in 'Macbeth', and spent a year working on the BBC Radio Drama Company. She starred in the BBC2 sitcom 'Perfect World', and has also appeared in the films 'Sixth Happiness', 'Flight' and 'Such a Long Journey'. She has taken part in a number of British Asian productions such as 'Women of the Dust' and 'House of the Sun', during a year on the BBC Radio Drama Company. She was the first ever female Asian stand-up comic in the UK.

Derek Wall is Researcher in the School of Politics, International Relations and the Environment, Keele University. His research is informed by a critical realist focus upon social movement mobilisation, green politics and anti-capitalism. His published works include *Earth First! The Anti-roads Movement* (1999) and *Green History* (1994).

Chris Warne is Lecturer in the School of European Studies, University of Sussex. His research interests are concerned with popular cultures and social change in contemporary Europe. Forthcoming publications include *Youth and Society in Postwar France* (Cassell), and an edited volume on stardom and modernisation in France (Routledge).

Kevin Williams is Professor of Media and Communication Studies at Swansea University. His most recent publications include *Get Me a Murder a Day! A History of Mass Communication* (Arnold, 1997) and the co-authored book *The Circuit of Mass Communication* (Sage, 1998).

INDEX

❦